Kid | Rex

Kid *Rex*

Laura Moisin

The inspiring true account of a life salvaged from
anorexia, despair and dark days in New York City

ECW Press

Published by ECW Press, 2120 Queen Street East, Suite 200, Toronto, Ontario,
Canada M4E 1E2 416.694.3348

To the best of her ability, the author has recreated experiences, places, people
and organizations from her memories of them. In order to protect the privacy
of others she has, in some instances, changed the names of certain people and
details of events and places.

LIBRARY AND ARCHIVES CANADA CATALOGUING IN PUBLICATION

Moisin, Laura
Kid rex : the inspiring true account of a life salvaged from anorexia,
despair and dark days in New York City / Laura Moisin.

ISBN 978-1-55022-838-0

1. Moisin, Laura — Health. 2. Anorexia nervosa — Patients — New York
(State)—New York — Biography. 3. Anorexia nervosa — Patients — New York
(State) — New York — Family relationships.
I. Title.

RC552.A5M632008   362.196'852620092   C2008-902381-1

Editor: Jennifer Hale
Cover Design: David Gee
Text Design: Tania Craan
Typesetting: Mary Bowness
Production: Rachel Ironstone
Cover Image: iStock
Printing: Transcontinental

This book is set in Bembo and Century

PRINTED AND BOUND IN CANADA

ECW PRESS
ecwpress.com

This book is dedicated to my fierce, fragile grandmother Elena.
As I walk alone I am still holding your hand.

Table of Contents

Ghost World

There is a space, somewhere in the universe — at least in mine.

It exists somewhere I haven't found yet, in a different dimension where words can create other entire lives, other entire universes where all good intentions and complicated thoughts are kept track of in some kind of cosmic logbook.

I think that I would fit into this world that I try to find now but always, somehow fail.

And if there isn't a heaven, if there isn't some rest at the end of this struggle, I still know that these spaces, like individual purgatories, exist.

I know it, but my words do not know, so they do not comply. They find their own pockets instead . . .

> they dissolve
> they disappear
> they fail to matter
> they leave no fossil evidence
> they are raw . . . raw flesh . . . raw fear . . .

What am I supposed to tell people when they ask me what I do for a living? Am I really supposed to say, "Well, actually, I am in the process of recovering from anorexia"? If I go that far I might as well delve fully into the discussion. Why not give people a more complete view of what my life has been like these past two years, trying to recover from an illness I've had for over five years? I may as well tell them every day is like an eternity, full of fear and trepidation about being left alone in a cold, shadowy world where winter is always approaching, without my greatest source of solace: my anorexia. I may as well tell them I have seen over twenty psychiatrists, therapists, doctors, and nutritionists in the past couple of years, and have often been left feeling more stranded, frustrated, and secluded. I may as well say that some mornings I wake up and think that without my anorexia I am at risk of vanishing into a sea of faceless, anonymous people, as though I never even existed.

How are you supposed to describe what you do for a living when what you actually do is struggle to live? Many years of my life have consisted of attending doctor's and therapy appointments in a maddening attempt to unscramble my mind and ease the disquiet in my soul. Any "accomplished" individual would think I'm crazy, pathetic, or simply disposable. I know how they would feel, because I used to be competent. I looked down on anyone who didn't excel according to society's standards. I used to be someone who made fun of anorexics and bulimics, meanly sniping, "Why doesn't she just eat?"

At my small, private high school in Newton, Massachusetts, I was always at the top of my class. I took the most advanced science, math, literature, and language courses, and always earned excellent grades. At the end of each school day I had only a few minutes to relax before starting a long night of homework. My moments of peace were spent every afternoon when my mom picked me up from school and brought along my brown-and-white cocker spaniel Caramel. The three of us would wander languidly through the vast school grounds that had once belonged to a wealthy New England family. The property was old and the land itself exuded a kind of sensual antiquity. It was a nuanced proof of stability, and a statement that not everything had to change.

My favorite time to walk was autumn, when the New England colors were unlike anything I had ever seen. My mom would take Caramel off her leash and we would stroll behind her as she stopped to sniff every tree root, leaf pile, and patch of browning grass. This was my time of meditation and control. I would look over the fields of the school towards the sprawling campus and realize that I had a place, an identity.

During our walks I would tell my mom about my convictions. In retrospect, it's as though I aged in reverse. When I was a teenager I had a firmer grasp on the way I viewed the world and what I believed my role in the universal schema would be. Accomplishment was what preoccupied me, not boys, drugs, or parties. I cared about my convictions and how they would shape the adult I would become. The older I got, however, I became inexorably disillusioned and increasingly doubtful about ever finding another place where I could explore my individuality, or ever finding another space for myself.

I had spent my childhood moving from Romania to Canada, Chicago, Boston, and New York; and in Boston, for one rare moment in my life, I felt like I had found a home in my secure school environment and in the friendship I developed with my mom. Later, when I moved to New York, I was torn down by a city far more vast than I ever could have imagined—I was unprepared.

During more innocent times, however, I had been baffled by

anyone who allowed their problems to disable them. I was dissatisfied by people I labeled as unproductive, vain, shallow, and weak. Because I was successful, I assumed that any ambitious person could likewise be. I was especially disgusted by girls with eating disorders. I took no pity on them because I didn't understand how, when life seemed so gratifying and stimulating, any girl could so blithely ruin her life.

When my best friend Caroline became bulimic I not only misunderstood her, I also judged her. Eating disorders seemed silly, and they certainly weren't openly discussed in my high school. All I knew was that Caroline stopped eating in front of me, began compulsively exercising, and became increasingly slender and frail. Her family was especially distressed by Caroline's emotional deterioration. She wasn't getting any kind of professional help. Nobody, including me, would talk to her about her condition, and she began to slip away from her own life.

By the end of my senior year, I saw Caroline much less often; I was more concerned about graduating and going to college. My greatest preoccupations at the time were academic, and I lived and breathed my scholarly responsibilities. I read about wars, human suffering, cruelty, and disease, but never personalized any of it. I never realized how much suffering was being endured by my supposed best friend. Ultimately, I cared more about my grades because I believed that Caroline was being dramatic and would eventually revert back to her regular self.

My life consisted almost entirely of writing papers, studying, reading, and doing endless calculus and chemistry problems. It was easy for me to obsess about one thing because if that one, controllable aspect was going well I believed everything else would too. I didn't realize that my obsession and Caroline's were very similar. Caroline was the last thing on my mind. To me she wasn't really sick, simply "stressed." Out of curiosity and concern I read about the symptoms and possible treatments of bulimia, but was still unable to genuinely comprehend them.

During my senior year I began to also reflect on my former

best friend in Chicago. Annabelle had also developed strange eating habits. She'd slowly started to consume less while neurotically tallying up each calorie. Annabelle and I had been best friends from third to ninth grade and when she began to act out in this alarming fashion I was neither impressed, nor jealous, nor concerned. I thought she was just trying to get healthy, be a better athlete, or that perhaps she was a little bit "stressed."

After I moved away, she visited me in Boston and I discovered that she'd become extremely slim and even more compulsive. That visit didn't make me feel compassion or concern—I was simply disgusted and annoyed. Why wouldn't she just eat so that we could go explore all the new cafés and restaurants? Why didn't she care enough about me to sit down and relax over a decent meal? The visit ended, Annabelle went home, and I never spoke to her again. Something in me was so repulsed and uncomfortable with what I had witnessed that I didn't want to ponder it for another second.

My mom, on the other hand, was terrified during Annabelle's entire visit. She'd hated to see what Annabelle was doing to herself and resented Annabelle's mother for "allowing" her to act so self-destructively. Most of all, she later informed me, the experience had given her a horrific premonition of what my family's life would be like if the same thing ever happened to me. She could see herself as Annabelle's mother, watching her own daughter disintegrate, as though nothing on this earth could hold her to it.

To assuage her fears my mother looked at me, her own daughter, and was reassured by my accomplishments and confidence. These reassurances mollified her. I could never turn out like Annabelle, or Caroline, for that matter. It simply wasn't possible. With that heartening but naive thought firm in both of our minds, life went on peacefully, but only for a little while.

I have only recently fully comprehended the grave mistake I made when I discarded my sick friends. At the time, I couldn't have seen how foolish and inhumane it was to judge Annabelle the way I did; and when my second chance came with Caroline I obtusely repeated my error. When Caroline got sick, she became unable to take her senior exams. I would find her wandering the hallways of the school. This place was like my second home, while she looked like a ghost haunting a place she had once been a part of, but from which she'd been swiftly wrenched. She was living in her own world and none of us understood it. From my perspective she lived in an absurd universe. Why couldn't she just take her exams, force herself to finish school, enjoy the summer off, and be safely on her way to college? The living can never understand why someone on the brink might choose a ghost world.

And I, who had once been the best friend of the girl drowning in her sickness, acted so as to put my own mind at ease. I graduated from high school at the top of my class and stopped talking to Caroline. The last time I saw her was at graduation, and I remember feeling justified in my choice to leave her, like it was something I'd done in order to preserve my own sense of the sane world.

The last time I spoke to Caroline, however, was different. She was desperately sinking in her illness and despair, and she called to ask me why I was avoiding her. I don't remember what I said, but I may as well have remained silent. I was just like the hundreds of people I would eventually encounter, who didn't care or want to understand the inner workings of this nightmarish disease. To know about it can forever skew someone's sense of what is right and normal in the world. If I didn't believe in karma before, I certainly have proof of it in my own life now.

Now I'm living in Manhattan. I live in a small apartment with an expansively broad mental view of the world. I find myself now walking the streets of a city that has been my home these past six years. There were years when I felt like I owned no part of the life or the activity taking place all around me.

On some days I walk to my old college campus of New York University. There I am reminded of the fact that nobody in this school or city really knows the person who once strolled with her mom and dog through an autumn garden at Newton Country Day School, who was on top of the world for the simplest of reasons. Nobody at NYU—a school I was expelled from during my junior year—knows the girl who felt like, no matter what happened, she was invincible.

It is autumn in New York again, but I have neither my mother nor my dog to walk with. I cross the same streets I have for years. I know almost every deli, clothing boutique, grocery store, bookseller, city corner, building, and tree probably better than any of my fellow pedestrians.

I remember leaving my freshman biology lab late at night after carelessly dissecting a diseased fetal pig and nearly ingesting a tapeworm, and walking to the neighborhood deli to buy apples as though nothing had happened. I remember my roommate, Miranda, and how during sophomore year we decorated our room for Christmas with as much cheap Santa and reindeer paraphernalia as we could find. I remember walking to class through Washington Square Park late in the afternoon and thinking, "This is where I live!" I remember going to the NYU chapel on Sunday and sobbing all through mass, because I missed my boyfriend in Virginia. And I remember all of my friends. They knew what it was like to leave your family and move to New York, young and stupid and full of crazy ideas, hoping to find companions who could fill a lonely void. These people I recall with love and regret. They were the ones I left, and who left me, after I became ill.

Now I walk through the NYU campus and see kids who are nearly my age, yet somehow centuries younger and worlds away. I see a girl buying flowers at the deli I used to buy the sweetest Fuji apples from, and I laugh. I see a group of girls walk into the funky West Village store where I bought my kidney-shaped, furry, leopard night table, and I know that despite all the conversation and jokes I made with the cool storeowner years ago, she would not remember me now. With each walk I become much heavier. I have not yet found a way to make peace with all my troubling memories. I must relive them, over and over, until I can build some sort of life for myself again.

That is what I have begun to do. I am not malingering or giving in to my disease. Now I am fighting; but it is hard. There is a sense of pride that comes with battling my anorexia, which I know most people would scoff at or simply never comprehend. Even I, after fighting my disease these past many years, have still not become entirely accepting of my mission. Just the other day I met a bulimic girl at a group therapy meeting, and before I could remember all the people who had ever looked at me with hate or fear, I thought about how disgusting it is to throw up food. Yet I know, too, that some families and friends comprehend, and they are noble in their understanding.

So perhaps the next time someone asks me what I do, I should just boldly declare, "I am waging the war of my life!" After all, shouldn't that be considered an accomplishment on par with beating cancer or surviving a plane crash? Then maybe I could also tell them, if they cared to delve a little deeper, that no one truly chooses to live in a ghost world. This is a burden that was placed upon me.

Chapter One

Two Blocks Below Canal

Lo and behold — what is the latest nutritional value of salvation?

Save the Rainforest, Reindeer, Rain Makers, on every back-boxed, industrialized carton of cereal.

Aisle for aisle, pound for pound, with each roaring, deafening, thundersmash pour of ultra-pasteurized, ultra-sanitized milk. Spoonful by spoonful.

How, then, should I save myself if this chomping existence is based solely on consumption and reduction?

Energy burner and calorie counter alike, one and all — it's the new price for simulated opportunity.

My life in Chinatown marked the early stages of my disori-enting anorexic existence. The summer I was set to return to NYU for my sophomore year I got a letter informing me I would be living with my freshman year roommate, Miranda, my best friend Stella, and a fourth person we didn't yet know. I also found out that my apartment was at Lafayette and White streets, in the heart of Chinatown. I had stayed in Chinatown only once with my mom, the summer of my freshman year orientation, and we'd both been a little frightened by our experience. We quickly switched our accommodations upon taking one good look at the dingy, narrow, winding streets. People navigated them so naturally compared to us. Going into my sophomore year and already somewhat accustomed to the eccentricities of New York City, I was decidedly less worried about my surroundings and more concerned about the number of people I could fit into my new apartment for parties.

On the first day of my Chinatown life, we packed the family SUV with my college belongings. I drove from Boston to New York with my parents, my sister Francesca, or Fran, and her boyfriend, Rick. My boyfriend Josh had just begun his senior year at JMU and was unable to accompany us. While Rick helped my dad with the heavy lifting and moving, my mom and Fran helped me put my clothes and books neatly away. We had to work around the wreckage Stella had wrought during a party she'd hosted the night before. The rest of the apartment was a perfect picture of college chaos, complete with overflowing garbage cans, discarded beer cups, an empty fridge, strangers passed out on the couch, and loud music blasting from the other bedrooms. This was a picture of the lifestyle I would live all year, and the rest of that day would prove to be similarly symbolic.

While eating lunch with my dad at a nearby restaurant Rick found a clump of hair in his garlic chicken that forever spoiled his taste for Chinatown. As I unpacked with my mom and Fran they munched on sandwiches that I refused to touch. I remember their puzzled looks about my attitude: skipping a meal because I was too busy was normal. Part of me knew, however, that this desire to refuse food was not born solely from my eagerness to get settled. But at that point, I didn't understand what was really happening.

Life in Chinatown was erratic. As soon as my family left, my friends from freshman year began to trickle in, and before long we were all camped out on the wood floor catching up and drinking. The people who'd been there a week were already living off of McDonald's takeout. Apparently McDonald's would deliver to residents of Chinatown, though, at the time, they did not deliver to any other part of Manhattan. None of us knew why exactly delivery was available exclusively to our neighborhood, but most of my friends agreed that it was a welcome convenience.

Those few days before the commencement of classes were spent in disarray. I liked to think that I was living a cool bohemian life. In fact, anytime I feared my lifestyle might be destructive, I excused it by calling it "boho," "hipster," or "indie." I liked the fact that my apartment was a mess, that there was never any food in the fridge, and that people were camped permanently on our sofa, loveseat, armchair, and floor. There was so little space and so many vagabonds. I liked the fact that I could go out and party as much as I wanted and still manage to wake up and accomplish daily tasks.

Freshman year had seemed so long and challenging, as I tried to figure things out, adapt to my surroundings, and make friends. But by sophomore year I had only one goal: party as much as possible and still do well in school. That year went by like a blurry dream. For a while my plan worked. I went out almost every night, had fun with my friends, and continued to perform well in my most difficult classes. I seemed to have a never-ending supply of energy, but in the rare moments when I paused and tried to look inward I knew something was seriously, dangerously amiss. I was afraid to admit that the real source of my boundless energy was my developing addiction to starvation. Infatuated with anorexia, it started to become my drug, and like most drugs will, it lit an artificial fire within me.

My addiction really began that year in Chinatown. The high my anorexia gave me, along with self-confidence, self-worth, and freedom I felt when not eating, made it seem like I was in control of everything. While everyone around me required food on a regular basis, I was strong enough to need none.

A few times, late at night, I remembered an intervention that had taken place at my old high school in Newton. I had been nearly dragged into the assistant head mistress's office and interrogated about my abstinence from eating. By then, my senior year of high school, I had built a very rigid lifestyle that was beginning to crack.

I realize now the problem was that I felt I had to be the best at everything I did: in high school it was academics; in college it was starvation. One problem bled into the other, because loading my high school schedule with the most difficult classes and indulging a need to get A's left me with little time for sleeping or eating. Eating, during my senior year of high school and for the first time in my life, had become an option and not a requirement. I began to do my homework on the treadmill, thinking that it would alleviate my constant anxiety.

My parents had been at a loss for what to do. My dad had begged me not to move to New York, failing to realize that my problem was internal and would manifest itself regardless of where I lived. After the intensity of my last semester at Newton, he wanted me close by where I could be monitored, but I didn't heed his requests. For several years he occasionally blamed my mom for "Letting Laura move to that stupid city!"

In Chinatown, in my bed, these thoughts sometimes crept into my head just as I was about to finally fall asleep. Sleep was my most dreaded time, when loud friends, alcohol, and even schoolwork didn't surround and distract me. I was completely alone with thoughts that were becoming steadily more aggressive. I didn't know why exactly, but food now felt like my biggest enemy and rejecting it felt like my greatest strength. But I knew there was a direct correlation between my fasting and the amount of time I spent obsessing over food. This had never happened to me before.

I had always prided myself on my ability to focus on important issues like schoolwork, my family, and topics that I was passionate about, things that make the people closest to me affectionately refer to me as a "big dork." People would make faces when I contemplated aloud the destruction of the Amazon, wondered who the true constructors of the pyramids were (my aunt Lia still maintains there was some alien influence involved), and whether Einstein's theories would all stand the test of time. I had never before committed my thoughts and actions to something as seemingly insignificant as my diet. Now it was nearly all I could think about, and I was disturbed by my helplessness in the face of this mania. The more I starved myself, the more I thought about it, and the more afraid I became.

I began to hate food. I hated the fact that food was such a large part of college life. Going out to dinner was often the only time to catch up with friends, and skipping this important ritual meant being left out of the loop. Missing meals also made people notice my behavior and increased their curiosity. I was grateful for my one saving grace: among my friends, it was considered very uncool to meddle with someone else's decisions. Advice was never offered unless it was asked for. This laissez-faire approach applied under even the most extreme circumstances, and the boundary wasn't crossed unless someone specifically demanded help. Anyone who didn't abide by the unspoken rule was immediately ousted from our group. At NYU nearly everyone acted irresponsibly at some time, in some way. So although my roommates picked up on my starvation trend, they held their tongues.

At the start of my second semester of sophomore year my odd eating habits, which had once been considered merely "quirky," now spiraled out of control. Attempting to fool myself and others into thinking I had eaten, I began to pick mercilessly at my food until it was almost unrecognizable. I knew my behavior was disgusting and turned my roommates off, yet I simply couldn't stop tearing apart my meals. A force compelled me to destroy nearly every food item I encountered, and this obsession would not cease until I had completed my task. Once in a while I could open the fridge, see something I wanted to pick apart, and find the strength to walk away, but I was then haunted by my inaction for the rest of the day. In class, conversing with friends, or lying in bed at night, I could think of nothing else. And I inevitably went back to demolish what I'd left intact, eat tiny portions of the resulting crumb mixture, then angrily tear at the rest until it no longer resembled anything edible.

Muffins became my favorite thing to break apart. I developed a routine that was comforting and almost loving, which involved purchasing a muffin at the downstairs deli, putting it in my fridge, and then returning hours later to gently open up its cellophane wrapper, place it slowly on the nearby counter, and, with nobody looking, tear it bit by bit into a crumbly mess. Sometimes I put a few crumbs in my mouth before balling the scraps back into their wrapper and sticking this mess in the fridge, thus finishing the job. I couldn't quite figure out whether I did this to the muffin because I hated or loved it. Now I know it was both. They had been one of my favorite foods, and I hated that about them.

Later when I went to Renfrew, which is a treatment center for women and girls who suffer from eating disorders, the doctors and staff prohibited us from giving in to our "rituals." That was the first time I heard of behavior similar to my own, and I timidly asked some of the girls at my table if they'd ever experienced anything like my "muffin syndrome." About half of them had, even though it wasn't their ritual of choice, while several others were just like me—they compulsively, obsessively picked apart all food. These were the rituals that made up our fanatical religion.

Thankfully, muffins were not part of the Renfrew diet, and I've had no contact with a muffin since my sophomore year of college. If I came across a muffin now, I'd like to think I could bite into it the way most people do, but I know it would probably light some of the old fires in me.

I was foolish enough in Chinatown to think my roommates either wouldn't notice the small packages I left behind, or wouldn't care. I even thought that maybe they would understand. But how could that be, since I, myself, could not begin to comprehend why I was doing it. Most of the time my friends said nothing, but I knew what their sideways looks meant. My roommate, Miranda, was the most vocal with her grievances. She usually didn't confront me directly, but would rather pull out a clump of muffin crumbs and state with a sigh to the room in general, "Gee, I wonder who did this." I can't say I blame her for being annoyed. To her, my contamination of the community fridge must have seemed like the epitome of strange, selfish behavior. I was even annoying myself.

My lack of control and comprehension kept me quiet, and I simply weathered all the indirect abuse my friends aimed at me. Soon the members of my wider circle of friends also grew suspicious of my emaciated body, and they began to inspect me circuitously. I always pretended not to notice, and still no one said anything to me directly. A few times acquaintances commented on how I looked too skinny, but I waved those worries off or deflected them with jokes.

Our fourth roommate, Thaana, moved out during the second part of second semester, and a new girl, Cindy, took her place. None of us knew why, exactly, Thaana had left, but we could only guess her conservative Indian upbringing clashed with our insane living habits. Most nights our apartment seemed like a safe house for drunken friends and strangers. I suppose it also didn't help that we regularly kidnapped Thaana's childhood Scooby-Doo stuffed animal, put a condom on his puffy tail, took pictures of him performing obscene acts, and left these on her pillow every so often as some kind of bizarre ransom. We thought it was hysterical that Thaana would choose to go to bed before midnight on a Tuesday. Her life simply didn't mesh with our sacred rules of partying, and none of us were entirely surprised when she finally decided to leave.

Cindy, my new suite mate, partied with us once in a while but mostly kept to herself. We did, however, have something else in common. We silently acknowledged it, but only mentioned it to each other once or twice in passing. Cindy was athletic, very thin, and had odd eating habits. After a month or so her food completely disappeared from the fridge and was replaced by a bottle of diet pills on her desk. One morning she asked to borrow my jeans, and when she put them on we realized we were the same size. That day, a barrier was broken.

One afternoon I ran into her on campus and she informed me that she'd stopped getting her period. I had recently stopped having menstrual cycles as well, and told her so. We both knew our lifestyles were changing us biologically, but neither of us was alarmed. We sat there chatting about it as though discussing the weather. When I asked her about the diet pills, she told me they gave her energy, something she greatly needed to keep up with her athletic activities. They weren't addictive, she told me, or dangerous. They were simply useful and "necessary."

The next morning I bought my own bottle of diet pills, the same kind Cindy used. But unlike Cindy, I hid my pills in my drawer. Cindy and I became unlikely allies in a very dangerous game, but at the time I appreciated having somebody who could understand without judging, and who wasn't whispering along with the rest of my friends.

By the end of that school year, starvation was no longer a fun game I was playing; it was a full-blown obsession, and I was experimenting with different diet pills and exercise. I began running constantly, whenever I had the chance, even if it was three in the morning and I was exhausted. My building had a twenty-four-hour basement gym, which I used to my full disadvantage. I slowly detached myself from my family and my boyfriend Josh, which was even more unlike me. I'd always been close to my parents and sister and had never before neglected these most sacred relationships. But I was slowly learning and living by the new, harsh rules of my altered life.

As an anorexic—a label I had begun using silently to describe myself—I could not cheat on this new relationship by pursuing others at the same time. The anorexia manipulated my subconscious mind and constantly outwitted me. I realized I could stay safely trapped in my confusing vault so long as I surfaced from time to time and pretended to be a healthy person in order to reassure my family.

One night I sat in a dingy, overly crowded Times Square bar watching as everyone around me laughed hysterically at a story a casual friend had just told. He was talking about his little sister, a twelve-year-old girl who always lost interest in her food halfway through a meal. Her parents and brothers, thinking her behavior was odd but humorous, joked that she might be anorexic and had begun calling her "kid rex." I seemed to be the only person at the table who didn't find that nickname amusing. Nobody around me really knew the daily struggle I was having. And the name kid rex suddenly made me feel so terribly sad and alone that I felt the urge to hide or run out of that bar. I wanted to shout, "Some of us have problems we can't control!" or "Life isn't easy for all of us!"

Instead I just sat at the bar, no longer listening to any other conversations, but inanely nodding so as to casually blend into the carefree crowd. From that day forward, in my own mind, I became Kid Rex. For a long time I used only that name in the privacy of my own turbulent thinking. Eventually it escaped my lips and I began to whisper that name of disguised self-hatred to anyone who happened to be nearby. Soon I proclaimed it loudly; with a wink I would tell Josh, Fran, my parents, therapists, and eventually Renfrew staff that I was Kid Rex. "Kid Rex can't start eating," I would say dispassionately, "or else she won't be Kid Rex anymore, and then she won't be anything." Yes, I even began referring to myself, my alter ego, in the third person.

In my immature, withered mind, Kid Rex was a cool, strong creature who had taken over and become a superhero version of my former, weaker self. I didn't know then that true strength lies in the quest for self-knowledge, including the shameless acceptance of our greatest, most troubling flaws. Instead this name, born of surprising pain, began to embed itself so deeply into the fibers of my personality and thought that I felt I could no longer detach myself from it, even assuming I would ever want to. No matter what I did, I couldn't *not* be Kid Rex. Kid Rex would always find me, and using deceptive charm, make me once again the secret butt of jokes in bars across the nation.

Entrapped in this new personality, I began to panic at the thought of going home for the summer. I knew that my parents would immediately intervene in my new habits. I had not seen them for a few months, so I also knew that they would be frightened by my emaciated figure and try to thwart my new lifestyle. I decided I could not possibly allow anyone or anything to come between my anorexia and me. It simply wasn't an option. I couldn't go back to eating regularly in front of others, or stop picking through my food. I was also taking diet pills each day and working out all the time. In Boston my parents wouldn't let me exercise the way I did in New York.

I was addicted to the feeling I got from anorexia, and decided I could never abandon it. It made me feel so powerful, superior, and capable of accomplishing absolutely anything I wanted. I felt independent, strong, beautiful, and unique. I reasoned that if someone couldn't understand and accept my newfound identity, then they were being egotistical. I was becoming so absorbed in the lie of my sickness that I believed that my mom, my best friend, who meant everything to me, wished to harm me by forcing me to come home for the summer. In truth she missed me, wanted to spend time with me, and knew that something was very wrong.

With all the panic in my head, I decided to remain in Manhattan for the summer rather than risk losing my anorexia. I informed my parents about this decision. They reacted in different ways, but with the same pain. My dad got angry and once again blamed "the City," which to him had become a character in the increasingly sad story of my life. My mom, on the other hand, became quiet, overwhelmed by disappointment, confusion and fear for a daughter she was losing touch with. My mom and I had worked hard on developing our friendship and now it seemed we might be on the brink of losing it. Still, I felt I had no other choice, and when my parents received my second semester grades they allowed me to remain in New York. I had done well in very difficult courses. Surely someone who was truly sick couldn't have managed that, they reasoned.

But I wouldn't be able to cope for long. After the initial boost the anorexia gave me I would soon become weak and truly ill. School would become impossible to handle and even the most basic of activities would turn into an insurmountable challenge. But I didn't yet know any of this. That summer, I got a new room in the same Chinatown building and transferred my belongings by the armful from one floor to the next.

That new apartment became what I now consider my first, full-blown anorexia headquarters. It's where I finally stopped eating for days on end and hardly even noticed. It was easy for me to never think of food. The apartment had one single bedroom and one triple bedroom, along with two bathrooms and a living room. The living room contained a fridge. I didn't use it, choosing instead to store my beverages in the mini fridge I had in my bedroom. Once a food fridge was no longer part of my life, food itself easily followed suit. I no longer had to consider shopping for meals, cooking, or paying for groceries. When I got thirsty I grabbed a drink from my mini fridge and the problem was solved. No longer dealing with food or even seeing it helped to quiet my obsessive tearing ritual. For a month I had the entire apartment to myself and it remained food free, as did I, for the most part. My rigorous party schedule became even more intense, which also helped with fasting.

Most of my friends remained in New York that summer. At night, hungry from a full day of abstinence, I went drinking instead. In a drunken stupor—a state that became increasingly familiar—I could forget about any hunger pains that had plagued me earlier. And even though alcohol has calories, it was psychologically easier for me to drink my calories than to swallow them, let alone to chew food, a process that now seemed repulsive and unnecessary.

During those three months, isolated much of the time and left alone with my perplexing illness, I became quite weird. Instead of walking around my apartment I would hop around, kicking my legs up as high as they could go to simultaneously burn calories and prove to myself that I was still strong. I would go to sleep wearing tight clothing so that in the morning I could wake up with the renewed motivation to lose more weight and make all the clothing in the world too big for me. I wanted to reach the point where everything normal became unnecessary. Eating, dressing, and resting would be superfluous activities. I was convinced I'd never have to eat again. Instead, I could sleep just a few hours each night and eventually reach the level where even the tiniest clothes would be loose, thus finally granting me a feeling of liberation.

I'm not surprised, looking back, that my world eventually came crashing down, leaving me friendless, out of school, sick, and tormented. I'm just surprised it took so long to happen. After the climax of my anorexic bliss and the period when I lived alone two blocks below Canal Street, the repercussions of my actions would finally come to light. Some small part of me always knew they would.

I tried to detach myself from everyone who meant something to me, to become the "best"—that nonexistent, anorexia-fueled ideal. I yearned to be independent to the extreme, never requiring help or advice from anyone, as though only I was capable of understanding my own life. These ideas propelled me to attempt an irrevocable and gruesome self-destruction, and it lent power to a sickness that eventually brought me to my knees, humbled, though I had once been so blindly confident. I couldn't control a disease that had been gaining strength inside me for years. Having already separated myself from my family and the people I most cherished it seemed easy, at the time, to let go of everything, even life.

My life then, in Chinatown, became not all that important. Like me it was a wisp, a haze, vanishing slowly, steadily. So what if I disappeared? I was convinced that after a long enough period of starvation I would rise up again, above the earth, and float away from what tormented me. It seemed different from dying. My plan was simple—I would just get smaller and smaller until there was nothing left. I would vanish like a fog, and then be unceremoniously lifted from the ground to reveal a fresh clear day.

Chapter Two

Misfits

Oh rein my savage animal!
Nobody can control you!
Nobody can tell you what to do!
I fill myself on your cold, misty torment.
I spread my wings in the tent that you provide.
Is it right?
A rage of pounding frenzy.
A herd of chilling droplets
Charging through my mind . . .
Racing blindly through my Serengeti.

By the time I began my junior year at NYU and was living in my new Soho apartment with my sister I had lost all contact with my friends, except for Stella. She was living in Brooklyn, which was geographically close, but its emerging hipster culture made it feel like an entirely different state. I was becoming more entangled in the clever web my anorexic mind was incessantly spinning; I knew it, and it didn't really bother me anymore. As long as I had my disease I never really felt alone. My dark thoughts sustained my actions and left me too busy for friends anyway.

Keeping track of the food I avoided, and the calories I had to burn in order to make up for past moments of weakness when I *had* eaten, became all-consuming. There was still a small part of me that cared about other things—the people I loved, the friends I'd once known, the memories of my earlier life—but it was being quickly, brutally dismantled. I would only later attribute this subtle spark of remembrance, which I kept hidden from my anorexia, as a boost in my ability to fight my dark disease. But that battle was a long way off.

At the start of my junior year I wouldn't have considered seeking help for a disease I struggled with even admitting I had. My obsessive thoughts were plaguing me in an increasingly vicious way. They had started as merely annoying hindrances, but soon the exasperation turned into a form of slow, methodical torture that caused me to seek some relief. At times I considered seeing a psychiatrist, just so I could have one quiet moment of respite from my own troubled mind; but in my deep denial I constantly rejected this notion. Finally, I came up with a solution that I thought was brilliant but would end up working against me in the long run. I decided to visit a therapist and seek treatment for depression, an issue I felt much more comfortable discussing. That way I could get some help, and maybe even a little clarity, without having to admit my true problem and thus risk giving up my precious anorexia.

Looking back, I can see that my immature solution was clearly doomed to failure. Going "undercover" to speak with a professional meant I wasn't presenting myself honestly. It was exactly this type of behavior that had caused me to live a life based on secrets, nervousness, and falsehoods. My actions had transformed my personality, and consequently they defined my life—a life of which I was now deeply ashamed. My mind was riddled with dark hollows, and my body was similarly deteriorating under the control of a brain that hated me, hated Laura. It felt like I was rotting, starved of fresh food and bright thoughts. The only nourishment I fed on was the sinister vision of maintaining the rigors of my self-punishing anorexia. As difficult as starvation and self-deprivation was, it was much less challenging than struggling through all of the subtle, unpredictable complexities of life that I couldn't control.

Obviously my disease was greater than mild depression, but I chose to ignore the truth and lie to everyone around me once again. I thus began to experiment with sessions with various psychiatrists, therapists, counselors, and social workers. During the course of my junior year I visited over twenty professionals. I classified them into groups, including clinical psychiatrists (who, within minutes, wanted to put me on high-dosage antidepressants); well-meaning but inexperienced social workers; novice guidance counselors; and a handful of knowledgeable people who may have been able to help if only I'd been honest with them. I never stayed long enough for anyone to realize how much weight I was losing. And after a while I got used to the system. I became so good at regurgitating everything these professionals wanted to hear that I easily convinced them I was only mildly depressed and suffered no greater trouble.

The sessions went something like this: I would start by describing symptoms common to both depression and anorexia, such as "I find that I can no longer sleep." I would never admit this was because I had stopped eating and my mind was therefore keeping me awake in the hope that I might rise and scavenge for food. Instead I would describe only those symptoms that fit under the larger umbrella of depression, and since anorexia also leads to a laconic, despondent state, this wasn't hard to do. It was the perfect trick.

Therefore, the blame for all these disastrous therapy sessions lay mostly on me. I never found the true tranquility I craved, but I soon discovered a new reason to continue therapy. Members of my family were slightly mollified when they found out I was finally seeking "help" for my illness, and this provided me with extra starvation time before their intercession. Any peace I did acquire was of the wrong nature, the kind that allowed me to go on living my dark life with fewer questions asked. It felt good at the time, but I would pay for it later.

The people I met with were usually well intentioned but generally easy to trick. Most of the time I had neutral feelings towards my doctors and their bedside manners; but once in a while my experience with a new professional could best be described as coldly clinical. I may as well have been an animal sitting on a metal examination table during those sessions. When this happened, or when I got bored with my current therapist, I would immediately stop attending appointments and move on to the next person I could find.

One of my worst and most memorable experiences was with the third psychiatrist I saw. I remember sitting in the waiting room of a six-story building somewhere on the Upper East Side. This space was occupied mostly by psychiatric offices, but clearly none were designated specifically for eating disorders. To my right sat a man in his late sixties who was rocking himself continuously back and forth. I couldn't tear my eyes from his sad form huddled in a rough gray seat, clutching crossed arms tightly to his hollowed chest and staring at his torn brown loafers. I was filled with pity, yet also incredulous that he and I could be in the same place, waiting for the same kind of help. My only slight consolation was the fact that I was forty years younger than this poor man. Maybe I still had a chance.

The waiting room itself was both relaxing and stimulating in a basic, infantile sort of way. The walls were a muddled blue-gray, as though the decorators couldn't quite decide on a color that would soothe the crazy people and please the healthy doctors. The carpet was one shade darker than the walls, and the eight rough, gray chairs with blonde, wood trim and wide armrests were spaced evenly around the room. Across from me in a small bin there was a pile of toys, the bright plastic kind you might see children playing with in a pediatric office. I found the sight of these stuffed animals and Lego blocks absurd, and in the process of averting my eyes disgustedly I caught sight of the hanging jaw and bulging eyes of the man now fervently rocking back and forth. I quickly looked away and continued to scan the room until something unexpected on the center of one gray wall suddenly caught my full attention.

There, so completely out of place in this depressing office, was a small, square window overlooking a busy New York street on a beautiful mid-spring afternoon. The window did not belong in this patronizing building. It seemed so out of place. It was quaint, polite, and charming in its own quiet way and I imagined that upon looking through it I might find a red brick colonial house sheltering a family of New England Puritans seated at a sparse but cozy dinner table. The window had suddenly become *my* window, out of time and place, exposing a peaceful scene in the midst of so much chaotic despair. I wondered for a moment if anyone else could see the marvels I beheld, or if in fact this window was a porthole into my own hidden soul. For the next half hour, as time passed slowly of its own volition, I was content gazing through the mysterious pilgrim window. In that time machine I was able to lose myself; I grabbed in vain at thoughts that flew too fast for me to grasp.

The doctor with whom I'd made my appointment was over forty minutes late and just as I was beginning to not care, his door opened on the waiting gray universe. This psychiatrist's face was loyal to a single, dour expression.

I followed him into his office and wasn't surprised to find even more gray furniture and toys. It was both odd and ridiculous to see a wall lined with Harvard, Princeton, and NYU degrees above a carpet strewn with building blocks. For a moment I doubted the instinct that told me the only good that could come out of this experience was the small window that had set fire to my imagination. Still, I hoped that all of those fancy diplomas could make up for the coldness I now felt emanating from the nonchalant man seated behind a chrome desk. Even his eyes looked gray.

When I looked fully into them I saw immediately what he perceived, and it filled me with unfathomable dread. To this doctor the young woman sitting before him and man still rocking in the waiting room were the same person, no different from the millions of other people who'd sought him out for emotional or mental help. To this doctor, the world was divided into different sets of groups. He and his wealthy friends, who may have been unhappy or disappointed by life's shortcomings, were still far superior to those of us living with our problems in a raw, vulnerable, exposed state.

I didn't want to be so needy, but I was. And when I saw the expression of superiority on his face, followed by the condescending tone in his voice, I immediately bristled. Maybe I was starving but I wasn't at the point of rocking myself in public— not yet, anyway.

Without asking me what I did or who I was, probably before even learning my name, he immediately demanded to hear my self-diagnosis. When I told him I was depressed . . . no, very depressed . . . no, maybe even suicidal (the gray room had made me feel especially desperate), he hardly blinked. I'd wanted to see if I could provoke any sort of reaction from this robotic man, but he simply clicked his Pfizer pen (had it been in his hand the entire time?), took out his Pfizer notepad (where had that come from?), and immediately prescribed a high dosage of Prozac.

"And perhaps," he continued, "you'd like to make another appointment with me sometime next week." My one-hour appointment had consisted of forty-five minutes in the waiting room and fifteen minutes in his office. Still, he didn't hesitate to medicate me.

I didn't know about the side effects of Prozac, and I still don't. I never filled that prescription, but left his office tearing up the paper bearing his sloppy handwriting. I never saw the gray doctor again, though I thought of him often for a long while after. I began instead to prowl the streets of Manhattan, attempting to distract myself by shopping for shoes, but nothing seemed to work. I was suffering immensely, and now I felt like I deserved it. Every time my thoughts drifted back to the gray doctor I wondered, as I do still, if he would ever guess that the best part of his treatment lay in that tiny, magic window, nearly invisible on the steely walls of his lofty office.

For some time following that visit I decided not to share my thoughts with anybody, not even Josh or Fran, as the details of that appointment grew increasingly appalling to me. For a while I even believed Dr. Gray's cold assessment of me had been justified. There were so many of us damaged people in the world, maybe our specific disorders no longer mattered. We were simply part of a faceless, nameless crowd. For months I tortured myself remembering the disdain he'd conveyed in a single piercing look. Yes, it made sense that my life was worthless. But I was *still* unable to give my body over completely to the land of the chronically unstable. I was still not ready to add my name to the list of living dead—those whose souls had been completely taken over by anorexia. I still felt compelled to seek out anyone who might be able to provide a small quantity of relief.

A few weeks after my meeting with Dr. Gray I began seeking help again. I met with a new cast of characters, and most of them prescribed medication and long-term therapy for what they thought was serious melancholy. Some asked about my diet, but I attributed my slender physique to this "depression" that kept me from sleeping and had caused a loss of appetite. Depression became the code word for my anorexia, and I felt both defeated and superior every time I tricked another professional into believing that this was the only problem I had.

A definitive pattern emerged. Following several sessions with a new psychiatrist I would always wait for the inevitable moment when the clicky pen appeared, the Pfizer pad was drawn, and a prescription was scribbled in illegible text. The topic of medication always marked my last visit with that particular doctor, and without any warning or written notice I would immediately stop returning their calls and start seeing a new specialist.

It's not that I was ethically opposed to medication. In fact, I feel that in many situations it may be necessary. But I was being diagnosed incorrectly and feared taking drugs for the wrong reason. I also began to worry that I was getting too deeply involved in what had become a complex charade. I hadn't intended for things to go this far, and realized somewhere inside that it was probably time to stop lying. I knew I should come to terms with my disease, quit feeling ashamed, admit I was one of the emotionally crippled, and start talking to someone who could treat anorexia specifically. But instead of being brave I came up with another terrible solution. I decided the answer was to see someone who wasn't certified to prescribe medication.

The NYU counseling department seemed like an ideal place to go. This was a way for me to get free help. I also reasoned that it might be easier to open up to one of the young adults employed by the university, someone who worked on campus and understood a little about the pressures of college life.

I called to make an appointment with a man named Marvin, and at the end of the call I asked for directions to the office. The woman on the phone sounded bothered by my question and tersely informed me that the counseling department was in the main building on the ninth floor.

At first I thought I hadn't understood the woman properly. The ninth floor of the main building? The *main* building, as in the building on Washington Square East, across from the dorm where I'd lived freshman year and the place where most of my classes had been held for the past two years? The ninth floor, where I'd gone countless times to make appointments with various deans about courses and to meet with career advisors? The ninth floor, where I'd once paced the halls trying to figure out whether to take music appreciation or something like "color theory" to cover my liberal arts requirements?

"Yes, the ninth floor of the main building," the woman replied snottily. I searched my memory for a precise layout of this location. Where could the elusive counseling department be located? Did it magically appear and disappear depending on the time of day?

The next day I set out earlier than necessary, thinking if I had extra time in my meeting and the opportunity presented itself, I would perhaps bring up eating disorders in a very general way and see what Marvin had to say. After all, NYU is a tough Manhattan school attended by women who live in a city where the pressure to be thin is very real. There must be a high incidence of eating disorders here, I reasoned. Maybe these girls were speaking to Marvin all the time; perhaps, under a veil of anonymity, I too could tell him a small piece of what was truly plaguing me. Maybe I could let go of my dark secret just a little. I was hopeful and nervous, but not quite certain I'd find Marvin.

I stepped into the main building and waited for the large steel elevator to take me to the ninth floor. For a moment I was convinced that the massive doors would surely open to a sight I'd never seen before. I doubted myself once more, ignoring my instincts and the facts I knew as truth. But sure enough the ninth floor still looked the way it had when I'd last left it. I walked down the wide linoleum corridor and this time, just in case I'd somehow missed it over the years, peeked through every office door and hidden corner in the hopes of finding a well-established counseling department.

Suddenly I remembered the one area I'd never previously visited—the bathroom hallway. I'd never used the restroom on this level but knew there was an enclave to my right with a small ladies room. I veered right, then right again, and found myself outside the bathroom. Some construction had begun in the hallway, but apart from the mess there was nothing else to see. I turned back and from the corner of my eye spotted a closed, thickly painted beige door with a handwritten note taped to it. In sloppy cursive the sign read "NYU counseling services . . . please knock."

I knocked firmly but heard no reply. I waited a few seconds before I knocked again, but still heard nothing. Deeply annoyed I finally pushed open the door and found an empty waiting area and an abandoned desk stacked high with piles of paper. I sat down and waited. Finally, a small, young-looking man walked in and sat down behind the desk before asking what I needed. I told him I'd made an appointment with Marvin. He handed me a few forms attached to a clipboard, told me to fill them out, and disappeared behind the door he had just come from.

I was surprised that this tiny space could be the entire NYU counseling department, but I sat down as instructed and began to fill out papers. Aside from basic student information there were pages and pages of questions, such as "In the morning I feel —" The answer spaces did not leave room for me to respond in words. Instead, I had to circle one of the five crudely drawn faces that best represented my emotion. These expressions ranged from an extremely frightening happy face with a smile big as an upturned rainbow, to a head with a straight line for a mouth that I took to mean neutral (eventually I started calling this the "Swiss Face"), to a visage with a proper rainbow for a frown. Now I was finally having fun. Only in a Woody

Allen comedy would an adult with serious problems be expected to express emotion by circling an infantile image. I was gleeful upon starting this task, but two pages through the packet my eyes began to blur. I could no longer distinguish one face from the other, and the hugely smiling man looked more freakish than the one meant to symbolize unhappiness. That big smile had to be hiding something, like a mad desire to kill.

After the third page I turned all my men Swiss, assigning neutrality to the remaining emotions. At the very back of the packet there were questions that required writing, such as which NYU support group I'd be interested in attending, and what specific problems I'd like to discuss. Here was my chance to begin talking about real issues. The counseling department seemed impotent, but it was at least unthreatening enough to make me contemplate a sincere conversation about anorexia. I circled the NYU eating disorders group as one I'd possibly like to join and wrote in the comments area that I wasn't sure whether I needed this type of counseling, but I'd be interested in listening to, and perhaps participating in, some of those conversations.

Finally, the little man emerged from his secret room and introduced himself to me as Marvin. I'd specifically stated it was Marvin I had come to see. Wouldn't it have been courteous and normal for this man to introduce himself as Marvin in the first place? The situation that had gone from shocking to amusing had now become exasperating. Did Marvin think that just because he had come out of an office and was no longer playing secretary I would now take him seriously? Did he think I had forgotten him from mere moments ago? I agreed to follow him into his little office, but decided before stepping foot in the door that I definitely did not like Marvin.

His office was cramped and contained a small desk and two orange plastic chairs. I sat down across from him and waited while he quickly scanned the packet I'd completed. As he flipped through pages and noticed all of my Swiss men, his face took on a neutral mask as well. He finally got to the last page, the only one with actual commentary, and silently read it before putting down the stack of papers. For the next thirty minutes Marvin and I discussed the pressure of being a young woman at NYU and living in New York City. The conversation was real, but very general. Only in the last five minutes did Marvin make reference to what I'd been waiting to hear.

"I noticed you circled the eating disorder discussion group as one you'd be interested in attending," he said.

I nodded.

"Well, that group is more for people who are dealing directly with anorexia, bulimia, and other eating issues, and not so much for someone like yourself, who is suffering only from stress, anxiety, or mild depression."

"Right," I replied, "I was just sort of concerned with, you know, the eating patterns I've established lately, and was kind of . . . oh, I don't know, curious, or something about maybe some information I could get from going to one of those groups."

"No," Marvin replied firmly, in what must have been his no-nonsense voice. The attitude struck me as hilarious since he looked twelve years old and was roughly four inches shorter than me. "I don't suggest you attend those groups at all. You wouldn't get anything out of them, and you'd be taking valuable time away from people who actually need to be there."

I heard a weak and mortified "Oh" escape my mouth as I stood up, shook Marvin's hand, and floated from his room as though my body had slowly filled with helium.

I can't quite remember the final bit of advice that Marvin gave me. I think it had something to do with going on Prozac, and perhaps seeing a therapist to treat my depression. It didn't really matter what he said. My first shot at truly talking about my illness had been a disaster. I was alternately embarrassed that I didn't look skinny enough to qualify for having an eating disorder and disappointed in myself for not insisting that I wanted to join that particular support group. I suppose I can't really blame Marvin for not seeing through my deception, but I also despised his lack of finesse and inability to realize that a person with an eating disorder is frightened and nervous about putting the truth of her trouble into words. I had dropped him a clue but he, the supposed professional, had blatantly ignored it. We were both at fault, but only I would suffer for it.

In the end, I took Marvin's rejection of me as an anorexic to mean I should never again try to tell another person about what was truly bothering me. In my pain, I turned to my anorexia more fiercely than I had before. It was my secret and I vowed to protect it forever.

My mom recognized what was happening mostly because of the quiet, distracted way I would speak with her on the phone. I was so unlike the daughter she had raised, and she was no longer willing to accept my assertions that everything was fine. I thought my excuse about feeling depressed and anxious would placate her, but instead it only made her more suspicious. When I told her I was going to the NYU counseling department the news unraveled her. I had seen professionals whose names she didn't know and whose numbers she couldn't get a hold of. Now even NYU would know what was going on with her own daughter before she did! She couldn't stand being left in the dark anymore, so she called NYU and got transferred to some extension—we never quite figured out which one—where some woman told her that whatever I discussed with the counselor would be strictly confidential. Sobbing, my mom told the woman that her daughter, her baby, was anorexic. The woman's reply was heartfelt, true, and chilling all at once. Calmly, she replied, "Ma'am, I'm sorry, but that is quite an uphill battle." My mom hung up the phone and called me, crying. I couldn't exactly understand everything she was saying, but I was furious when I realized she'd called NYU.

My immediate reaction was to hide even deeper, keep my life more secret, and further detach myself from my family. I felt sorry for my mom and couldn't blame her, but I was also infuriated with her, and with myself. I hated her for having a daughter like me, a creation that I perceived as some kind of a monster. I was suffering, but I accepted it without even the slightest hope of redemption. The persona of perfect girl and loving daughter was turning into a nightmarish farce, and as the beast was revealed, I became horrified by what it looked like. Over and over the same words rang through my mind, through my mom, through my entire family: "uphill battle, uphill battle." These cruelly resonant words soon became our reluctant family motto.

My junior year crawled by. Every day I became increasingly obsessed with thoughts of losing weight and starving myself. My schoolwork suffered drastically. I could no longer focus in class because my brain seemed to have stopped working. I looked drawn and isolated. My hair began to fall out in clumps. None of this impressed me. From time to time I got a lucid glimpse of what my life was turning into, and for a few days I'd attempt to meet with teachers, make up for missed work, or attend a class I'd been skipping for weeks. But each time I spoke to a professor my plea for help with schoolwork was far from impassioned—it was more nonchalant and slightly bored. I was too busy destroying myself to really give serious thought to my future, life after college, a career path, or my relationship with those around me. I'd still found no relief from the persistent nagging in my brain. I felt itchy, uncomfortable in my own skin, and I wanted the all-consuming oblivion to do its work faster, take over completely, and wipe out any remaining moments of normalcy so that I could die in peace.

But anorexia has a way of dragging on. It has a leisurely way of torturing its host. And it can be elusive—at moments you are able to wonder, "What am I doing?!" before it sweeps you back into its possessive, chaotic arms. Those near-moments of comprehension may have been the worst part. If I could have just gone instantly stupid rather than slowly and partially dumb, or if I'd had the power to fight the disease with all my strength, it would have been easier than gradually giving in and waiting to deteriorate. The torturer took its time and I was impatient, anxious for the moment Laura would fully become Kid Rex.

Yet part of me could still never truly forget the name my mother gave me. She'd picked it before she'd even met me, as a tribute to her beloved poet, Petrarch, and his one true love, Laura, to whom he devoted hundreds of lines. I remembered other things too, like how I'd decided at the age of five to move to the Amazon and save the trees. I myself had scribbled pages of verse about the marvelous, terrifying creatures that lived in the jungles of Brazil—to my mom I was both Laura and Petrarch the poet. In my soul, I could never truly forget these things, but I was trying. I was drawing on all the dark strength I possessed, from places I'd never known existed.

By the second semester of my third year, I had completely lost my grip on school, friends, and reality. The only people I was still talking to were Fran, Josh, and my parents. I had systematically cut everybody and everything else out, and I felt lonely and desperate.

I'd never returned to the NYU counseling department, and had taken Marvin's sorry advice about avoiding the eating disorder support group. I had visions of walking into a room full of anorexics and being ridiculed because I was too fat. I imagined them saying, "Yeah, nice try; come back in a few years when you're a hundred pounds lighter." I saw a few more therapists after Marvin but always with the same result, and soon the game became too boring, routine, and disappointing to continue.

In March of 2001, however, Josh got the name of a therapist who'd helped his co-worker recover from an obsessive-compulsive disorder. Dr. Zluger was apparently very good at what he did, extremely helpful, and a generally nice man. I was intrigued. Maybe I wasn't depressed; maybe I was just obsessive-compulsive about not eating. I was willing to accept anything as long as it wasn't tagged with the anorexia label. I tentatively called Dr. Zluger to set up a consultation.

New York had gotten warm by the time my first appointment finally came. The city was changing from winter gray to lime-colored spring, and I took some delight in the location of Dr. Zluger's office, near the budding trees of my favorite New York space—Gramercy Park. The select residents who live around this small, gated garden are the only Manhattanites given a key to the private park. In the summer they sit on cool stone benches surrounded by Asian birdhouses and tufts of wild purple flowers that smell like warm honey. In the winter, when the ground is covered in icy patches, the brief bursts of color visible through the iron fence remind passersby that the snow will melt again, life can't stop simply because it's bleak.

My first session with Dr. Zluger passed quickly. It was almost enjoyable. He was one of the first professionals I'd ever liked. He was young, smart, funny, and kind. He specialized in addictions and had treated many alcoholics, but also had a wide roster of patients. I left his office that spring day feeling uplifted, and when I walked around Gramercy Park I allowed myself to look at the blooming flowers through the wide spaces between the iron bars.

It was like my answer lay beyond that barrier—I could almost get a clear view, could almost reach it, but it took a key I didn't have to open the gate and fully grasp it. Near that park is one of my favorite New York stores, the Gramercy Flower Shop, a place that during Christmas becomes a wonderland of colorful ornaments hung from the delicate branches of slender topiary trees. That day, following my first appointment with Dr. Zluger, I felt so grateful a stranger had been nice to me that I took particular pleasure in roaming around the park.

The slight bit of compassion he'd shown me paired with my willingness to talk to someone again felt like a big accomplishment. I continued to make appointments with Dr. Zluger, but for the next month our conversations never evolved past generic ruminations about addiction. I was still unwilling to face my real problem, so my therapy became anemic, once again. I barely spoke about my relationship with my parents, what was happening at school, or the fact that I was becoming increasingly out of touch with everyone who mattered to me.

Dr. Zluger decided that I was suffering from some anxiety and stress, but I never cooperated with him enough that he could uncover the real truth. I had regular appointments with him that spring and always looked forward to walking to and from his building, trying to extract joy from the details of my surroundings as much as possible.

Naturally, this kind of non-therapy was short-lived. I realized that eventually Dr. Zluger would want to dig deeper and demand to know much more. He was perceptive and clever enough to scare me, and as I'd expected, our conversations soon veered into frightening new territory. He began to ask about my weight and other addictions I might be hiding. He was getting too close, seeing too deeply. I liked him as a therapist, I didn't want to stop attending appointments, but I knew that eventually I would. To this day I still regret the way I ended our brief relationship. I just lied to him.

That summer, our Soho apartment became horribly infested with mice, cockroaches, water bugs, and huge rats that lived on the ground floor of our building. The exterminator made trips to our apartment every other day. He'd spray pesticide, clean out mousetraps and replace them with new ones, check the building's foundation, and fill holes in the walls and floor. He would shake his head, telling me that the entire building was a health violation and should be torn down. I got to know this exterminator, named Damien, and after a while he shared New York horror stories of the rich ladies who lived on Central Park West—otherwise known as Golden Row—and who woke up in the night to find giant rats on their antique dining room tables.

The first time I canceled an appointment with Dr. Zluger it was because Damien was running late, and I certainly couldn't cancel on *him*. He was both a source of hope and a good luck charm. Missing an appointment with Damien meant spending the night with unwanted company in my apartment. That day I told Dr. Zluger the truth: my downtown apartment was crawling with pests, and I had to wait for the exterminator or else my living space would no longer be livable. Dr. Zluger understood and responded very graciously, but that triggered a tempting little idea in my mind. It just seemed so simple! All I had to do was end it with Dr. Zluger for good, and I'd be safe again.

The morning of my next appointment with Dr. Zluger, several days later, I was debating whether or not to call and cancel. Josh was at my apartment and while making up my mind, I asked him to take out the garbage and dump it in the giant bins behind our building. This disposal area was located in a back alley and guarded by an enormous rat—most likely the product of a nuclear accident—who we'd named "Manhands," due to the size of his thick, clawed fingers.

Josh had originally come up with this moniker, just like he'd first named the giant roach I'd spotted in our living room and had sucked up with a vacuum cleaner, pushing his rock-hard abdomen through the nozzle after I'd realized that squashing him with a shoe would never work. "So, you think we'll see Lobster Roach around again?" Josh would ask. Other times he'd mention "Petie," which was his general name for all the normal-sized cockroaches we saw on a daily basis. But more often we discussed the behavioral patterns of Manhands. Sometimes Manhands was gracious—he'd obligingly hop off the garbage lids so that Josh could throw our trash inside. Other times he was in a bad mood and refused to budge. To anger Manhands meant you were stupid, new to the neighborhood, or simply had a death wish.

That morning as I dialed Dr. Zluger's office number Josh returned upstairs with trash bag still in tow. I understood immediately Manhands must have been having a very bad day, and it was that fateful action that prompted my next move, which just seemed random enough to work.

Dr. Zluger answered his phone and I informed him that I had to cancel once again because our pest control problems had gotten much worse—we now had rats! I've never been a decent liar, so in the course of my convoluted explanation I said things like, "I saw a huge rat in my kitchen. Yeah, a big one! Can you believe it? I mean, come on now, who can tolerate a rat in their own kitchen, for Pete's sake?"

I followed those ridiculous statements with further bravado.

"Fran can't handle this. She's very fainthearted. So I, for all intents and purposes, have become the man of the house. And, by God, I will not stand idly by and watch as the rats take over my apartment!"

Dr. Zluger was perplexed but granted me the dignity I'd deprived myself—he did not call me out on my lies, even though it was obvious he didn't believe a word of my badly scripted play. I confirmed I would most certainly show up next week and he hung up, allowing me to battle my illusory, monstrous rats.

Needless to say, I never returned to Dr. Zluger's office. I took the cowardly route, the anorexic way, and never explained why I was terminating our sessions. I probably would have found it difficult to even vocalize why I was suddenly ceasing our relationship, except that I knew it had something to do with the fact that he was a good therapist, not incompetent like most of the others, and I was therefore afraid of what he would find. He left worried messages on my cell phone for several weeks, then finally stopped calling. I'd given him no other contact numbers and no home phone number.

I continued to walk around Gramercy Park, but now with much less frequency. The garden housed a new shroud of mysteries, the plants grew ever thicker, and I felt further away from this spot than ever before. My former justification for peering through the gates had been minor and insignificant, but now I had absolutely no claim left to these grounds. Once again I was alone, without someone to talk to, and I no longer took comfort in even the smallest gestures. Peering through the space between the park's narrow iron bars had been a privilege. I no longer deserved that honor.

I finished my junior year but was unable to complete all my classes or take my final exams. My grades came in and the results were disastrous—a completely new experience for me. I wasn't used to being a failure or having such a dismal academic record. Teachers and administrators were supposed to look at me as a prize student, a gifted member of their school, not a troubled burden! School was one of the first things that had enabled me to feel like I had a defined place for myself. Now I had broken that bond. Everything was falling apart. Actually, I was tearing it apart for a disease I felt was more important than my scholastic accomplishments, more significant than the love of my family, more vital than life itself. I was destroying everything, all for my beloved, malevolent anorexia.

Something changed, however, when I realized that I missed talking with Dr. Zluger. I was too embarrassed to ever go back to him, but the void I felt made me weary of turning myself so entirely over to the anorexia. I tried to motivate myself from giving up entirely by drawing inspiration from a myriad of sources. One was Franklin D. Roosevelt, my favorite American president, who contracted adult polio during what should have been the prime of his life. Nonetheless, he'd always believed that he would one day walk again, and because of his conviction he could never admit to being among the outcast victims of his disease. He began to visit a rehabilitating spa in Georgia called Warm Springs, with waters famed for having healing powers, and only once, while fully submerged, he walked again. That was the last time he would rise unaided. In his incapacity, he was like a grown man who'd reverted back to infancy. Adult control over his motor functions was torn mercilessly away, but all the while he rebelled against it.

As other polio victims began to visit the springs, FDR withdrew. They saw him as an equal, a fellow sufferer struggling for new hope, but he did not want to be counted among the crippled. Who among us really does? He eventually bought the springs, before being inaugurated as the thirty-second President of the United States, but in the Roosevelt circle this seemed like the action of a crazy person, not a reliable leader.

He died at Warm Springs many years later, a changed man. When he passed away in 1945 he was not only a great president, but also disabled. He had been the most powerful man in the Western world, yet he'd also accepted a position among his other peers—those who were ill but had once been healthy, those who were weak but had once been strong. How very symbolic that before striking up the New Deal, FDR had to resolve a new deal of his own. He'd learned how to draw strength and illumination from the wretched burdens of his debilitating disease.

My acceptance of anorexia was similar, with one slight but important difference. In order to even start fighting I had to first accept it, along with the other women around me. The frighteningly bony girls had to become my people, a company of peers. And yet in some ways I was luckier than FDR, even though I didn't feel it at the time. While he fought what turned out to be a losing battle and was never able to walk unaided again, I knew it was still somewhere in my power to rebuild my body and become a whole woman.

At first it seemed much easier to give in completely to the sweet oblivion of my vacuum disease. I didn't want to be one of the crippled, either, and I reacted just as FDR had when initially faced with the sight of fellow polio victims. I was shocked and enraged by so many fragile bodies—this couldn't be an accurate mirror; I couldn't be like them. I wanted to submerge myself in a pool of warm water, but not so that I could rise and walk, just so I could sink alone.

By summer I knew I had to leave school, or at least take a break from it. More than anything I really wanted to spend some quality time alone with my anorexia, but I decided to test out one more therapist. Dr. Zluger had given me a certain boost, and for the first time in a long time I'd felt some relief from the inner voices of my disease. I began to fathom that there might be another person who could understand me. Surely not everyone was like Dr. Gray or Marvin.

With this hope in mind I next went to see a social worker whose office was close to Washington Square Park. My mom, who was so concerned for me, knew, without any confirmation from me, that I was anorexic. She insisted on using that label long before I could own it. She often spoke with my aunt Lia, a doctor, about my illness. A friend of my aunt, whose daughter had suffered from anorexia, had referred this social worker. I made an appointment and took Josh with me on my first day. We walked in and discovered that her "office" was little more than a tiny Manhattan apartment. The waiting room was a converted living room with old, cushy beige sofas and matching beige carpet. Even the walls, once white, had faded into a dusty shade of beige. The color scheme, or lack thereof, immediately soothed me. To me, it was the West Village through and through, and nothing could have felt more like home than this bohemian space. It was the antithesis of Dr. Gray's high-rise building.

It was also stiflingly hot in the waiting room. By then summer was at its peak, and true to West Village standards, the building didn't have a proper air conditioning unit. For me that was a blessing since I'd been cold for the past few years, shivering violently even in ninety-degree weather. I only later learned that anorexics are chronically cold due to their extremely low levels of body fat and a disconnection in the nerve endings that usually warn the body to warm itself. Those two factors unite to produce a person who wears hooded sweatshirts in the middle of the summer, one who can relax in such a small, hot space.

Josh and I were alone—there was no one there to look at me oddly, as strangers were apt to do those days. By the time the social worker came out Josh was sweating . . . and he was panting in an experiment to discover whether it worked for humans, as well as dogs. I gave him a bemused smile and made my way around the corridor into another tiny, hot room. I sat down on a cozy couch and shook hands with a woman in her seventies who immediately perched on a leather rolling chair across from me. She even looked beige, with her off-white hair and fawn-colored suit. I instantly found her endearing. Feeling her bony hand in mine made me wonder if she'd once suffered from anorexia, or if age had simply taken its toll and worn her down to a fragile creature.

Somehow the heat and calming surroundings had eroded my defenses, because immediately after sitting down I heard the words "So, I'm anorexic. What do you think?" explode from my mouth. I couldn't believe my boldness, and I wasn't exactly sure where it had come from, but maybe I was finally getting tired of feeling alone all the time.

The beige lady responded promptly, and started asking questions about my diet, weight, eating habits, thoughts, and actions. For once I answered everything honestly, and with each response a terribly concerned look crossed her face. "Oh dear!" she kept exclaiming, and "Oh my goodness, you poor thing!"

I really liked this woman, truly appreciated her compassion, and for the first time in a long time felt somewhat at ease. It was like visiting a grandmother's apartment, though my own grandmother's bold style and spunk was so unlike the beige lady's demeanor. But I knew I would never see the beige lady again. I couldn't imagine coming back to regale her with more gruesome details of my unhappy life. My stories would surely wear her down, I told myself, and put undue stress on a frail old lady whose intentions were good, but to whom I'd probably have trouble relating.

I did know, however, that she could help me with my next step. I told her I'd soon be out of school and didn't know what to do next. Some conviction finally entered her voice and she informed me that no matter what I did, I had to take swift action.

"You should probably check in to an inpatient treatment facility, like the Remuda Ranch or Renfrew Center," she told me. She also told me about a psychiatrist named Suse Klab who worked exclusively with anorexic girls and women. Dr. Klab could assess me more thoroughly and suggest a treatment center that would best suit me.

My parents had done some research on Remuda and they pressured me to at least consider visiting, but the Renfrew Center was completely unfamiliar. The name itself rolled awkwardly off my tongue, and right away I couldn't picture going to a place I didn't even like pronouncing.

"So, how did you spend your summer months, Laura?" I could imagine someone asking.

"Well," I would reply, "I was at this place called the Ruff Ruff Center, or something like that—I don't really know how to pronounce it, but it was very helpful!"

My hour with the beige lady passed quickly. I poured my fears out to her, and felt a pang of guilt each time one of my emotionless statements prompted a dramatic "Oh my!" or a heartfelt "Goodness gracious, child!" from her kindly old face. By the time I got up to leave I felt much better, like I'd managed to shed a bit of my solitude and had come a fraction closer to finding the courage I needed to accept myself and unravel the complexities of my disease. I was at least convinced I had to do something. I wasn't quite sure what, but I knew it had to be real and drastic, and I was beginning to realize in order to be completely rid of my disease I would have to sever it with one sharp slice and mourn it later.

I thanked the beige social worker and told her I would not be making another appointment. I left the small beige office and walked back to the hot beige waiting room, but Josh was gone. The space was empty, as it probably was most of the time . . . as it probably preferred to be.

I knew Josh hadn't been able to handle the heat, and in truth, he'd really had no business being there in the first place. I was on a new journey, which had begun the moment I spoke the truth about who I was. I understood that on this trip I'd be traveling alone. Of course the people who loved me, the ones who'd never left, would engulf me in support. But the decision about whether to shed my illness or give in to its tempting lull and revert fully back was ultimately, exclusively up to me.

I sat down on the beige couch and for just a moment put my head in my hands. It was not a gesture of despair, but one born out of glum anticipation. Something told me the loss I'd already experienced because of my anorexia would be nothing compared to the bereavement I'd feel when I finally stepped away from it.

Slowly I turned on my cell phone, listened to my messages, and heard Josh's voice. "Hey Lars, it's me. I couldn't stand the heat in that room. I don't know how you survived through that entire appointment. It must have been hellish! Anyway, I'm at the bar across the street, grabbing a drink with Fran. I called her when I got out, about two minutes after you went in. Come meet us. Love you, bye."

Yes, that message said it all. Nobody could stand the heat but me. After all, the burden was mine to withstand.

Chapter *Three*

A Pillar of Salt

Somewhere along the way, across the space of my oddly segmented thoughts I began to live in a new old city. All of the streets were somehow familiar, like in a celebrated painting. All of the streets were you, but like in a sketch . . . a moving, breathing charcoal outline.

I remembered it all, every lucid detail that I wished to pray away. I remembered every corner and detail and nuance. I remembered every crease, line, expression, tone and spiked, second-day beard growth.

I remembered and got anxiously rebellious. I warned you of my uprising. I watched an old scene replay itself over and over again, like in a celebrated movie. "Classics" I think they're called. But in this scene there's an argument in Washington Square Park, and it unfolds before me as I sit quietly on a cold bench years later.

We were fighting—the old us—like hurried, harsh whispers. Only you were no longer there. And me—that me—is gone somewhere. Painfully, but gone.

But secretly, secretly, somewhere hidden on a bench in Central Park I sit and think—have I really changed at all?

And then a surge, a protest, an uprising . . . a grassroots rebellion.

There was a time in my life when Josh was afraid to walk into the apartment because he was unsure of what he'd find. When I ask him now what it was he feared he replies without pause, "I was scared you'd be dead, alone, on the couch, and that I would walk in and find you."

Or sometimes, when I ask, and he doesn't want to talk about it and would rather put the entire horrific experience behind him forever, he turns to me annoyed, and snaps, "I thought you'd be dead."

I have to ask Josh about those days because I've forgotten them, or at least they seem like one long, hazy day to me. I don't really remember waking up or how I spent my day. I do recall seeing Josh in my living room at around 5 p.m. every day, and him always asking how I was.

Now I can't believe I spent so much time sitting on the faded yellow futon of my Soho apartment, but there is no evidence to suggest any other activities were performed. I've searched my brain analogs for such data, but always return to the same vivid memory of Josh in his custom-made business suit and leather briefcase, standing close to me, his face betraying emotions that conflicted with the easy confidence of his attire. He would bend over, look me full in the face and in a barely audible whisper ask, "Are you okay, Lars?" My immediate reaction was always anger born of frustration. I was confused by what he was saying. Why was everyone always asking the same question? Couldn't they come up with a more creative repertoire?

I realize now that *was* the only question. No, I was not okay. I had recently left NYU, and in so doing lost my remaining sense of purpose. Almost immediately after walking from my school without turning back, I'd sunk into this laconic state of unawareness. I really had nothing left to hang on to, no function that could plug me into mainstream society and make me feel like one of the living. I hadn't wanted to leave NYU, but I knew there was no other option. I was physically and mentally unable to attend class or concentrate on schoolwork. If I didn't leave I was sure that I'd eventually be expelled. I was plagued by the image of a mighty dean taunting me with the diploma I so craved but now might never receive. So rather than make that frightening nightmare a reality, I decided to preserve my remaining shreds of dignity and obtain a medical leave of absence.

I'd been told my first step was to call the NYU administrator's office, set up an appointment with Christina, and explain my reasons for pursuing such a course of action. Where was I to find the all-powerful Christina? Why, in the NYU counseling department, of course! When I discovered I had to return to that sad place, where I'd been so badly humiliated by Marvin, I internally cringed. I seriously contemplated dropping out of school instead. It seemed easier to accept my failing grades and take an incomplete for the past semester, rather than hope that the counseling department might actually be useful this time and make it possible for me to return the following year. As the long days rolled by I knew I had to at least try to secure my future. If I could remain a member of the NYU community, even though inactive, I might be further motivated to work hard for my recovery. I still wanted to do well in school, graduate, and move forward with my career, which I was certain would involve science. I was eager for school and not afraid of the hard work, but I simply could not function any longer.

I finally resolved to brave the dark corridor of the counseling department's ninth floor, and made an appointment with Christina. A few months had passed since I'd been there to visit Marvin, and when I walked into the main building this time, everything seemed foreign. It was like I'd become small and insignificant, and this sparkling edifice was a reminder of all that I'd lost by no longer being among these privileged students. The kitten heels on my black pumps clacked loudly on the highly polished marble floor. Everything roared deafeningly around me in the nearly empty main building. I saw a few students wandering around, but most had already departed for the summer. The ones who remained certainly belonged, but I felt like an imposter.

The elevator, which took a long time to arrive, opened and puffed a distinctive rubbery breath. I had no choice but to step in. Maybe on the ride up I'd be swallowed whole and disappear, along with all of my complications. In this mammoth building, which had once felt so comfortable, I felt suddenly like Jonah living in the bowels of a whale, with only panic, fear, and loneliness for company.

When the doors finally opened I was struck by the buzz of drills and hammers, and bellows from burly workers. The construction I had seen in progress on my previous visit was now in full swing. I walked slowly past the immigrant workers, who seemed as out of place in this academic setting as I did, went into the bathroom, looked at myself in the mirror, and sighed. Perhaps I couldn't see how much thinner I was compared to the last time I'd been there, but I could see the hollowed-out features of my face and dark circles under my eyes.

My eyes have never drawn much attention, especially when I'm standing next to my sister. Fran has the most incredible eyes I've ever seen. They are a bright, startling aqua, ringed with black. Though Fran is very physically beautiful, people can't help but stare at her eyes. Strangers always ask, "You're wearing contacts, aren't you?" or "Do you know you have the most amazing eyes I've ever seen?" I know men who've fallen in love with my sister after just one quick glance in her direction. Luckily, I happen to like my own brown eyes as well. They aren't startling, like Fran's electric irises, but they convey a subtle seriousness I find quite pleasing. They are deer eyes, my sister says, and ever since I was born she has called me "Deer" or "Bambi," because of my large, dark eyes. They suit my personality. I wouldn't know who to be with bright blue eyes like Fran's.

But gazing at myself in the ninth-floor bathroom mirror made me realize that whatever fire had once burned behind my pupils had nearly been extinguished. I could still make out an ember—one national preserve left amid the clear-cutting—when I looked closely, but my eyes had lost most of their fierce energy. I wondered what it all meant, and what would be left if they burned out completely. Ash? In retrospect, the thing I find most frightening is that this thought was a mere bother. It was simply a question I pondered casually. I was simply curious about what lay at the end of this path. Though I've always hated the cliché "The eyes are the windows to the soul," I thought for the first time I actually understood it, whether I wanted to or not.

I spent at least ten minutes in the bathroom listening to deafening construction sounds. I was so reluctant to take what felt like the next fatal step, but knew I had to hurry up and get out of this colossal building before I lost myself completely. I was simply too small for it, too weak to keep up with its pace.

I pried my fingers off the edge of the sink and walked into the counseling department. Marvin was there, playing secretary at the reception desk. I knew he recognized me. For one satisfying moment I saw a wave of recollection cross his face; he turned slightly pink upon noticing my skeletal frame. But then Marvin pretended not to know me. He had not too long ago discouraged me from attending any anorexia support groups, and he couldn't now take responsibility for his destructive actions. He said hello and asked what I wanted, and his voice betrayed his discomfort, as it got squeakier with every syllable. I felt no sympathy for his awkward situation, and even if I'd been interested in playing along, I had no desire to match his falseness.

"Hello, Marvin," I said wearily. "I'm here to see Christina. Will you get her, please?"

Without another phony word Marvin hurried into the only other room. As I stood waiting I angrily picked up a packet of unmarked papers from his desk, identical to the ones I'd filled out a few months ago. I glanced at the questions and laughed out loud, just as Marvin walked anxiously back to his desk. I took a seat, but could see him from the corner of my left eye, staring at me from behind his desk. Still he remained silent. I kept reading through the questions and snickered aloud when I came upon a particularly inane one. I was being obnoxious in the vain attempt to get Marvin to say something, to at least ask me if everything was all right. After all, I was in the counseling department. Was it too much to expect a little counseling? Through all of this, Marvin remained amazingly quiet.

Finally the door to the corner office opened and a woman, presumably Christina, stepped out. I put the packet down, arranged my features into a pleasantly neutral expression, and attempted to appear normal, civil, and calm. Smoothing down the creases in my shirt I walked up to her, smiled and confidently shook her hand. Marvin appeared baffled by my sudden change in demeanor. Marvin, it seemed, was always baffled.

Christina asked me to follow her back into her office. Once inside I noticed a photograph on her tall bookshelf of Christina and presumably her husband happily hugging each other and smiling giddily at the camera. I couldn't stop staring at it, even as I sat down on the couch across from her desk. I couldn't stop thinking about the myriad lives people live. Some people get jobs, go to work each morning, fulfill their daily responsibilities, return home to their husbands every night, and are, for the most part, happy.

The woman captured in the picture, now breathing and moving beside me, was tall, with curly black hair and a serious expression. She could play the role of professional counselor one minute, then check out at 5 p.m. and turn into the happy, carefree girl, laughing cheek to cheek with her handsome husband. This duality astounded me, because I was no longer capable of it. Just by looking at me—the tiny body so out of proportion with my now huge head, the darkly circled, dull eyes, and deep unhappiness—anyone could plainly see there was something gravely wrong. When I stopped being able to put on a socially acceptable mask, I'd become naked to the world. I no longer had work or a life. I had no recent pictures of myself, posing so merrily for the camera. I now shied away from pictures, because I couldn't bear to look at the physical evidence they showed me. My life was a shambles. I neither wanted nor could I play the role of a regular, happy girl. My existence was irregular and extreme; every decision I now made threatened my survival.

Christina didn't make me feel at ease, but she didn't make me nervous, anxious, or self-conscious either. I no longer cared whether she gave me the anorexic nod of approval, like I had cared with Marvin. It didn't really matter whether she thought I was ill enough to be granted a medical leave of absence. Since I had no other option I was either leaving NYU with official approval, or I was walking out the door on my own. Either way I had to go. I listened and was able to reply to Christina's questions in a generic sort of way, but for me, this meeting held no real meaning, and I was more engaged with reading the titles of books on her shelf. Some of the volumes had to do with eating disorders, but I wasn't interested in them. I was *living* those books. I didn't need to be told about my life from a specialist or stranger.

Christina asked another question, and I perked up when realizing she was inquiring about the state of my electrolytes. In fact, I almost began to laugh. I had learned about electrolytes in my biology class, but until now, no one had asked me about my electrolytes. I knew they were important in measuring a body's level of hydration and balance of salts, but that was it. Of course, in the future I would become very intimately acquainted with them. In fact, I would become accustomed to people constantly monitoring my electrolytes to see if I needed prompt medical care. But at that moment it sounded like Christina was interviewing a robot. She may as well have asked how many gigabytes I had in my memory storage. It all sounded absurd.

"Who cares about my electrolytes?" I wanted to shout. "I've become incapacitated!"

I suppressed my laughter, already used to this type of sterilization when it came to discussing my very emotional disease. I put on my most pathetic-but-serious mask and told her a sad story of my electrolytes, how they were "very bad, indeed," and the doctors were "quite concerned." She looked at me and nodded earnestly. I could now go back to scanning her collection of pseudo-psychology tomes.

I sat in Christina's office for an hour and at the end she finally granted me my medical leave of absence. I told her I would probably soon be checking in to an inpatient facility, either Remuda Ranch or the Renfrew Center. She was unfamiliar with both, but said I should take as much time as I needed to get better. I asked her whether I had to call at any point and keep her informed of my progress, or set a date for when I might like to return to school. She said no, I didn't have to call, but when I did return I would need written proof of having spent time in a rehabilitation program under care of a psychiatrist. I would also need a letter from my psychiatrist, informing NYU that it was safe for me to be back in school. It all sounded fair and I felt grateful for the time I was being given to sort out my problems and gain control of my illness. Still, part of me couldn't quite believe I'd been given this break from NYU—it seemed slightly too good to be true.

I thanked Christina, truly astonished that she had managed to help in some way. As I walked through the empty ninth-floor hallway the terrible premonition came back. I was overwhelmed with the dreadful feeling I might not return here anytime soon—if ever. The elevator reached the lobby and binged. Slowly, I walked out to a midsummer afternoon knowing that I would, in fact, end up at one of those two inpatient facilities, even though I thought I'd been lying to Christina. I also realized I now belonged there more than I did at NYU.

I stepped onto the sidewalk. There were no smokers inhaling

one last drag before the start of class. There were no protestors in Washington Square Park. There were no honking taxis or purple NYU trolleys. I could, in fact, hear birds chirping loudly in the trees. Was this the Manhattan I knew? It felt like I'd walked into some weird play with the spotlight shining blindingly on me.

There was nothing left to do but walk away. I turned right and slowly headed away from the main building. For a while I could still see its shadow looming in my path. It was hugely engulfing, and for a moment I didn't want to be free of its force. For just an instant I knew that once I left its radius I would be alone again, away from the stifling yet protective tent NYU had offered. Before stepping from the shadow onto a sunlit sidewalk I paused. I wanted to start all over. I wanted to go back to freshman year when I'd been new and naive, when I'd thought the world was good and full of opportunity. I wanted to believe in the New York dream of excitement, youth, and possibility. I wanted to accept as truth the idealistic notion that help would somehow always arrive, miraculously, when I needed it most. I wanted to know I'd be okay outside the umbrella of this big building. I wanted a guarantee that God, my guardian angel, or Santa Claus would watch me always and never let me fall to ruin. For a moment I couldn't cross the line between shadow and frightening white light. I had to look back one last time.

I suddenly remembered the biblical story of Lot and his wife. They had been forced to leave the destruction of their home, and during their exodus God had assured them they would be protected. He would be with them and they would be spared, on one condition: no matter what they heard happening behind them, no matter what horrors they imagined or fright they experienced, regardless of how compelling the temptation might become, they could not under any circumstances turn back for one last look.

Lot obeyed the Lord. He walked forward without regret. But his wife, the weaker and more human of the two, could not restrain her curiosity. She took a single glance and was instantly transformed into a pillar of salt.

I'd heard the story of Lot and his wife countless times during the course of my twelve-year Catholic school education, and without fail I'd always related to the strong husband and been scornful of his weak wife. Why couldn't she just walk away? Why couldn't she let the past go and move forward with her life? I'd never felt pity because she had been clearly warned.

But now I suddenly understood Lot's wife. In that moment, the true enormity of her uncertainty and despair became brilliantly clear. I understood her humanity and for once I wondered at Lot. How could it have been so easy for him to walk away and not look back? What good were we as humans if we couldn't maintain attachment to the places and moments of our lives? What meaning did our actions truly have if they could so easily be abandoned and forgotten? Maybe Lot was a survivor, but his wife was a real human being. In the shadow of my own paralysis, remembering the life I'd left behind, I desperately wanted to turn back.

I didn't know the full depth of my own survival abilities, but that day I started to discover them. And so I crossed the line. I detached myself from the place that had meant so much to me. I wasn't turned into a pillar of salt, but I became a nomad instead, moving constantly, searching endlessly for answers and a true home. Something else broke, too. In my decision to keep going without reflection, a small piece of my humanity vanished. A little more fire from my eyes burnt out. I had cut myself off from the last remaining symbol of my life, and the person I'd once been, the one who was familiar, suddenly ceased to exist. I was now living in a stranger's body, controlled by an increasingly troubled mind. I made my way back to my apartment and promptly sat down on the faded yellow futon, staring straight ahead. I was in a new world now.

Chapter *Four*

Where's Renfrew?

I do not believe you that I am so weak. I do not believe that all of that pluck-plucking, fluttering flush in front of the mirror can ever, really weaken me.

Perhaps I am ruled by a system of underground physics and underground cars pulling my underground mind.

I noticed it, I even got on!

But I do not believe that I am so weak. Is what created you — you who I do not and will not ever really know — my own creator as well? It has created you, never to be held but always sought after. What a prevailing search! But I do not for one moment, by any principle of physics, believe you when —

by a sardonic look
when
by a flawless impediment
when
by a vehicle of escape, of underground
physics
you tell me that I am so weak.

A rmed with a referral from the beige lady's office I walked down
University Place to meet Dr. Suse Klab, the faceless decider of
my destiny. I had been granted my medical leave of absence by
Christina only a few days before. Motivated by the idea that I could
earn my way back to school and a regular life I decided that I would
accept any suggestions my new doctor had for me.

My first meeting with Dr. Klab consisted of her scanning my
body, making small talk for ten minutes, and telling me to go to
the Renfrew Center right away. I still had no idea what
Renfrew was. I knew more about Remuda Ranch, the other
place my parents were trying to push on me. According to
them, Remuda was like a spa for anorexics, where, if ill, one
went to "recuperate." When Dr. Klab told me about Renfrew I
asked her about any other treatment facilities that might exist.
She quickly informed me that she didn't really know any others
and that she had never heard of Remuda, but that Renfrew
would be a good place for me to spend a few weeks. The staff
was friendly, the facilities good, and the techniques exceptional.

I left Dr. Klab's office a bit confused. Although she was
brusque, Dr. Klab had a definitive, clear way of speaking that
made me inclined to believe her. No one had been able to give
me any clear-cut advice about what, specifically, to do about my
problems or where to go for help. Dr. Klab was the first to provide me with a blunt solution, even if it was given in an
apathetic, offhand manner. My mind was in a whirlwind and I
decided impulsively to not over-think the advice, but to readily
accept it. I had exhausted all of my resources and didn't know
where else to go.

There was another, slightly odd reason I accepted Dr. Klab's counsel. Her office was in another of my favorite Manhattan neighborhoods. University Place was where I'd spent so much time my freshman year walking to the gym in fall, through art-filled streets in the spring, sitting at my favorite coffee shop in the summer, and listening to vinyl records in the small, dusty music store that was so warm in the winter. I took the neighborhood itself as a good omen. Dr. Klab's office was also decorated in a quirky Navajo theme I found extremely funny. Anything that could make me laugh was good. With all these minute factors in mind, I decided to take her seriously. Even though I noticed how Dr. Klab treated me as a generic anorexic rather than interviewing me, I decided to ignore this more important consideration.

As promised to my parents I called Remuda that week, and as promised to Dr. Klab I called Renfrew a few days later. My parents, Fran, and Josh were optimistic for the first time in a while. I also decided that if Dr. Klab could offer any real help I would first have to take her advice by going to Renfrew. At that point I had no idea about what I'd inadvertently committed to, but both facilities called me ceaselessly until I made my decision.

The staff at Remuda called me three times a day and left me desperate messages. They called my mom and scared her by saying I had to get to their ranch immediately, before I dropped dead on the street. They insisted she call me and warn me about my upcoming doom. My mom, living in constant fear, heeded the warnings of all of these "specialists" and forwarded Remuda's messages to me. But rather than feeling convinced, I only felt increasingly frustrated, angry, confused, and annoyed.

I don't think it was a coincidence that Remuda, so desperate for my business, justified their exorbitant cost—literally one hundred times more than Renfrew for the same length of stay—by proclaiming to be a comfortable and functional "ranch," rather than a hospital. What could Remuda possibly offer that was so much better than Renfrew for the price they were asking? Both places would wake me up in the morning and weigh me. Both would make me share a room with two or three other patients. Both offered the same kind of meal services, community therapy, medication, and lack of free time and phone access. The only difference between the two was that Remuda had horses, which I couldn't ride anyway, since I was underweight and fragile. I was told I'd perhaps be allowed to pet or brush a horse, depending on my schedule. Somehow, through magic horse therapy, I was supposed to recover at Remuda. I love horses, but I immediately recognized idle promises in the form of ponies.

Due to my family's expectations, pressure from Klab, and annoyance with the preposterous Remuda claims, I chose to go to Renfrew instead, the public school of anorexic inpatient facilities. Having never been to an inpatient anorexic clinic before, or a public school for that matter, I had no idea what I was doing when I nonchalantly called Renfrew back and scheduled a phone assessment. I was told to have my cell phone by me on the first day of August 2002, a few days before my mom's birthday. I should be prepared to answer personal questions and remain on the phone for about four hours. My nervousness overwhelmed me.

On the morning of my Renfrew phone call I apologetically led Josh out of the apartment and set up a refreshment stand for myself, consisting of diet Lime Green Snapple, a very large cup of coffee, and a small glass of water. These drinks would also serve as my breakfast, lunch, and dinner, with perhaps a few crackers and another cup of coffee to finish the day. As I set everything in place so I wouldn't have to move for the next few hours I suddenly got a clear vision of my dismal self.

At twenty-one my life at that moment had whittled down to a very small world consisting of a chair, a table full of drinks and a cell phone. I could have remained in that spot for weeks and not needed anything, including food or human contact. In that moment of self-pity I realized the phone call I was about to receive might not be a joke after all. Maybe it was a chance for me to get my life back, or at the very least a view into the chaos of my illness. Perhaps it was an opportunity to find answers to the vital questions—what was I doing, and why?

The phone rang three minutes later than I'd expected. I'm always on time, and I was peeved. The woman on the other end apologized and told me she'd been late returning from lunch. Now I was furious. Why would she say such a tactless thing? Was she, in some mean or indirect way, trying to shame me for not being able to go out to lunch while she could eat, work, have a life, and do more than sit waiting in a chair? They should train these people better, I thought. But I didn't comment, thinking that if I was just being paranoid I should save myself from further embarrassment.

The trial lasted only three hours and the questions ranged from what I was eating and how often I was working out to how much I weighed, if I was sexually active, if I had ever been raped or molested, and if I felt suicidal.

Thus began the slow deterioration of rights I believe every anorexic faces. When people treat you like a disease or an outcast that is what you become. You learn to no longer expect fair treatment, privacy, respect, or even love. It is this acceptance I find most deadly. This is what every anorexic must first conquer in order to even begin recovery. It is acceptance that plays the most elusive character in the story of any anorexic.

A day later the decision was made. I was "invited" to join Renfrew's intensive inpatient program somewhere in Pennsylvania for an indefinite period of time. Since I had just poured my heart out to a complete stranger, and since I was living on a deserted island of Chair and Drink, somewhere in my Living Room Ocean, I accepted the kind invitation. But I still had no idea what I'd gotten into.

I spent the weekend before Renfrew celebrating my mom's birthday with the rest of my family, including my stressed grandmother, Elena, who didn't want to pretend to be happy. She had raised me for years when my sister and I were growing up in Canada. When my mom went with her architecture class to Rome for half a year I was not the worried five-year-old I could have been, because I knew my grandmother was a good replacement. In fact, Fran and I still talk about those happy childhood memories with great gusto.

I had not seen my grandmother in months, and I was deteriorating quickly, so, at first, she was unsure how to respond. Most Eastern European families, including some in my own extended family, hold the firm belief that anorexia is not a real illness. It is something spoiled children do out of boredom, want of attention, or lack of godliness. But my grandmother never fit into this group of judgmental people.

She is an incredible woman, the first female to become a doctor in her small Romanian town. While the rest of her family tended their farm, she went to medical school and met my Russian grandfather. Together they ran the hospital in the mountain village where my parents grew up. My grandmother has always been an open-minded feminist, whether she would embrace that label or not. She has never been an extremist, but quietly worked her way to the top using her gender as a source of empowerment.

Anorexia and other eating disorders are generally viewed as women's issues. An anorexic woman does everything in her power to shed her femininity: she loses her breasts, period, and hair. She slowly becomes gender-neutral or masculine, and in this silent way she is rebelling against her femininity. Thus, it makes sense that only another woman can truly understand and guide her to a less destructive path. This support is invaluable and was what I received from my grandmother the weekend before Renfrew. She lent me courage instead of pity. She told us all that anorexia is a disease and must be treated like one. Just as cancer patients are not looked down upon, so too must anorexics be afforded dignity and help. She made me realize I shouldn't be ashamed of my illness, only of myself if I gave up. And so I fully decided to give Renfrew a try. Maybe, as Bob Dylan once said, I could have my cake and eat it too.

The day before my trip I packed a huge suitcase with some of my nicest clothes, one pair of sweatpants, my favorite shampoo and lotions, and about fifteen packs of sugarless gum, because like most anorexics I was constantly chewing it in order to go through eating motions without actually consuming food.

I reluctantly got into the car, with my parents in front and Josh in the back seat next to me. We were going to spend the night in a hotel close to Renfrew, so that early the next morning I could go and check in. The car ride, for me at least, was tranquil. I enjoyed the constant change of scenery and the rapid motion, which helped me feel somehow freer than I had in months. My parents, however, were nervous and my dad tensely joked that we should all go out for a big steak dinner that night before my stay at Renfrew. I realized he was upset about where he was taking his daughter and that he wasn't thinking when he'd spoken so carelessly, but still his words stung me deeply. I felt he wasn't taking my life's greatest challenge seriously.

Looking back, I realize now how differently mothers and fathers react to their anorexic girls. In my case, as with most other anorexics I have come to know, my father became moody, angry, distant, and accusatory. He was brisk, unable to make eye contact. Mothers, on the other hand, tend to act depressed, frozen, hopeless, and full of guilty regret. My sister was desperate and helpless as well, but was somehow always accepting of me, no matter what I looked like or how antisocially I behaved. I realized she was probably the only person who didn't see the weight loss, emaciated body or slack spirit. She saw instead her little sister—someone she'd always see the same way, regardless of what I did, said, or looked like. I have no idea how she was able to treat me so fairly. I think, had the situation been reversed, I would have felt scared around her and been tempted to blame her for making my life so difficult.

I was ridiculously, annoyingly naive. I was innocent about

what I'd soon experience and about the gravity of my disease. I gave no thought to a future time when I might want to combat my anorexia, but was instead full of anger regarding my current situation, and those belligerent thoughts kept me up all night.

That night, in the hotel room, my mom was fidgeting and sighing in the bed next to mine—no one really left me alone anymore—and at about three in the morning we faced each other, eyes open, staring unblinkingly without uttering a word, until I finally severed the connection and turned around. I would think about that moment for years to come. When I was broken, alone, and tossing in the middle of the night she was the only one there with me, while the rest of the world slept. Everyone seemed to have turned their backs on us anorexics. We'd become outsiders, outcasts, the butt of jokes, objects of fascination.

The next morning I got up early, having not really slept, and I showered. Everyone was at breakfast and I waited quietly with my hands in my lap like an obedient child. The five-mile drive to Renfrew went by quickly, and we didn't get lost like I kept hoping we would. I wanted to stay safe in the bubble of my car, or remain seated forever on my chair in the Living Room Ocean, but before I knew it we had arrived at Renfrew.

We pulled into the parking lot, entered through a side door, and proceeded to the main hallway to check in. Next to us in the lobby there was another group—an anorexic girl, her uncomfortable father, and her quiet younger sister who had already seen and experienced things well beyond her years. I felt bad for the sister and scared of the anorexic girl. Here was a member of my own group, but I looked at her in horror and disgust. I thought to myself "I don't look like *that,*" and days later, when I finally had a real conversation with her, she said that she'd been thinking the same thing about me.

I checked into Renfrew in August 2002, at around 8 a.m. The four of us were then brought into a nice office where friendly people bombarded me with more personal questions, only this time I had to answer in front of my parents and Josh.

Then we sat and waited for nearly three hours while my insurance company decided whether to accept the charges for my first twenty-one days at Renfrew. The woman who finally informed me I had been approved also made it clear how fortunate it was I'd lost my period many months ago. "Numerous insurance companies," she said, "who don't normally consider anorexia a real disease, are often more inclined to accept menstrual cycle interruption as proper justification for seeking medical attention." When she saw a shocked look on my face— I was lucky?—she quickly laughed out a casual apology. Of course it wasn't *good* I was so sick, but at least the insurance company wasn't making a fuss.

I was finally taken to my room while my entourage waited outside. The room was small, about the size of my freshman year dorm in Washington Square Park, with two twin beds, one armoire, two tiny closets, and a bathroom that adjoined our room to another. There was one window, but the curtains were drawn and dusty. While I studied the room, a chirpy blonde ten years older than me plunked my suitcase on the bed, opened it, and immediately started searching through the contents. She removed my gum, razor, tweezers, and fashion magazines, and explained apologetically that these items were contraband. I could keep the tweezers and razor in a locked drawer, as long as I proved trustworthy and had the key on me at all times, but the gum and magazines were strictly forbidden because they were teaching me I didn't need food, and providing me with unhealthy and unrealistic body images. Finally, after all the other items had been deemed safe, I was sent to family therapy.

I reunited with my parents and Josh in front of my new therapist Amelia's office. After a few moments of waiting in reverent silence and overwhelming nervousness, we were allowed to enter her domain. Amelia was a middle-aged woman with short, tightly coiled Medusa hair, and a noticeably bitter demeanor. We sat down on the two small sofas surrounding her large desk; she mostly focused on a litany of grievances against my father. I had spoken only a few sentences, but I had mentioned my lingering bitterness regarding my dad's steak dinner comments from the previous evening. Amelia was able to feed off my emotion and seemed to enjoy the verbal beating she gave him for the next full hour. The moment would have been funny if it wasn't so uselessly pathetic. To make matters even worse, Josh, not even technically a member of the family, was occupying the seat that should have been filled by Fran. So we all sat there, my dad darkly mute, my mom crying quietly, while I did my own mental bashing of Amelia and Renfrew. Josh, it seemed, had spaced out long ago. Once Amelia's interpretation of my illness was over, she told me it was lunchtime and I was to go downstairs to the dining area and promptly join the rest of the women for my first real meal in years.

Amelia could have made herself useful and talked to me about the program and the fact that I was expected to eat. She did no explaining, however. Having already decided she was untrustworthy I simply ignored her, turned to my mom, and told her I couldn't eat. That was it. How was I supposed to *just eat?* I didn't know how! But before my mom could answer Amelia cut in once more, telling me the dining hall was painted a lively yellow and decorated with the drawings of all of the patients.

"Don't worry," she said, "it's a very uplifting, comforting room."

This did nothing to ease my concern, and two problems still remained. First, the idea that the dining room walls were decorated with the childlike art of full-grown women was quite disconcerting, especially since I'd grown up around my mom's incredible prints and paintings, which have been displayed in galleries. Second, I couldn't have cared less about the color of the dining room. Its bright yellow hue would do nothing to alleviate my anxiety. If eating had seemed impossible before, it was now beyond the properties of space and time. Yet there it was. Without further explanation, guidance, or any comfort save my mom's familiar hand on my shoulder, I was told I would be eating lunch.

I was given only a few minutes to say goodbye to my family. My dad, downtrodden after Amelia's tirade, was eager to go. As he rushed Josh and my mom outside into the blinding August sun, I trailed behind, trying to stall them. We passed the gazebo in Renfrew's yard, and then the little frog pond surrounded by white plastic garden chairs. When we finally reached the parking lot I felt my family was crossing a border into new territory, and I didn't have the proper passport.

I grew desperate, not wanting to be left in this new, strange place. I begged my parents to take me home. I asked Josh to help me convince them. I told them I would wait for them in the garden, in case they changed their minds on the road and wanted to turn around and retrieve me. But still they piled slowly into the car, and their silence spoke to the truth of my new reality. Josh rolled down his backseat window and waved, to the background noise of my mom's wracked sobs. My dad was stoic. The car peeled from its space, bumpily made its way down the gravelly parking lot, and was gone. Still, I waited. I was sure they'd realize their mistake and come back for me. I don't belong here, I thought, this place is too bizarre! I soon got tired of standing in the parking lot so I went to the gazebo and sat down on the hardwood bench. I waited for what seemed like days, and slowly fell asleep. When I awoke to Amelia's voice I was sure I'd slept there the entire night, but unfortunately lunch had not yet begun. I was chaperoned into the dining hall to meet my new peers, and more importantly, make my new acquaintance with food.

As promised, the yellow dining hall was decorated with infantile drawings and mottos like "Tomorrow will be a better day" and "The sun will shine in your life again." This made me feel even more disheartened than I had before. Without any formal introduction to the eating system everyone already understood, I was handed a covered tray and told to sit anywhere. I chose a place next to the woman who, I would soon find out, was my new roommate. Looking at everyone around that table—one of about seven in the dining hall—I also noticed a young girl with long, brown hair, an obese woman, a tall, beautiful girl, and a quiet, angry looking girl with curly, dark hair. I knew that, among these women, some were anorexic, some bulimic, and one was an overeater. I wondered how the staff at Renfrew could treat all these very different diseases en masse.

These women were all strangers to me, but by the time I left Renfrew several days later, I knew more about each patient than I've known about friends I've had for years. That's the nature of being ill; you drop your social barriers. Even though I was already taking mental notes on each woman, none of them was looking back at me. All of them were eating, slowly and methodically, while staring at the walls, the staff, their trays, the table, or at the inane posters hanging on the wall. At least this "art" served some purpose—it seemed to be distracting all attention away from the new girl.

When I finally lifted the cover off my tray I discovered oily rice with fried tofu drenched in a light brown sauce. Next to that were bread, butter, vegetables, a hefty slice of chocolate cake, and a large bottle of fluorescent blue Gatorade. The physical I'd gotten during my registration had shown that I was dehydrated and my electrolytes were off balance, so Gatorade became a part of my every meal. Now there was nothing left to do but eat. I picked up the fork, which I was no longer used to handling, and decided to tackle the tofu first—there was no way I could go for the cake or bread and butter. As soon as my fork stabbed the porous hunk of compressed soy product, all eyes suddenly turned to me. What would the new girl do? Here was a new person, a fresh study subject, someone who might give them some insight into themselves.

I placed the tofu gently on my tongue as though I was storing it for safekeeping rather than consuming it. A few moments passed before I finally chewed and swallowed it. Then I did the same thing with the rice and vegetables. I couldn't believe I remembered how to eat properly. I opened the bottle of Gatorade and started sipping. Soon I was desperately gulping it, Gatorade trickling down my chin like bright blue car antifreeze. I hadn't realized how thirsty I was, living off black coffee and one glass of water every day for the past few years. I finished the Gatorade and thought some congratulations were in order. After all, Gatorade has calories. What more could the Renfrew staff want? I had eaten *something*, which was good enough for me.

When the other girls saw me put my fork down, they all got the same look of knowing disappointment. I was just like them after all. We all felt the same at mealtime, and my actions had just confirmed it. I waited out the remaining thirty minutes of lunch in silence, looking around and watching people as much as I could without being noticed. Finally a staff member, a graduate student probably receiving college credit, informed me that since I'd finished only about thirty percent of my meal, I would have to be "supplemented" for it. I had no idea what she was talking about but I nodded my agreement enthusiastically. I couldn't believe skipping meals was so easy! If it was cash she wanted, she only had to follow me back to my room. Whatever amount she wanted me to supplement her with in exchange for not eating was perfectly fine. Instead, she went to the mini fridge, took out two large cans of vanilla Ensure, opened them with a sucking pop, poured the thick liquid into a large, clear glass, and clanked down the empty cans—nutritional information side towards me—while handing me the unwanted glass of toxic ooze.

I'd known what Ensure was before coming to Renfrew. The woman who had called my mom on a nearly daily basis from Remuda, telling her I would die unless I went to the ranch, had also suggested my mom purchase Ensure and somehow force it down my throat. Every time my mom mentioned Ensure at home I imagined myself as a big baby bird, being unhappily force-fed by its jittery mother. I'd never tried Ensure before, but in the pantry of my Boston house there were cases of it in various flavors and formulas, stacked one on top of the other. They are still there today, although by now they must be long ago expired. So being handed the Ensure at Renfrew, I could only feel a stab of irony. Ensure had gotten me at last! But even worse than having to be supplemented was the embarrassment I felt as the other girls who'd finished their meals looked at me with pity.

But soon all of our attention focused on the distracted grad student who had not only forgotten to discard the empty Ensure carcasses, but was now literally waving Ensure's caloric, fat, and carbohydrate content in our faces, causing all the women at my table to go into a momentary state of shock and fear. The crestfallen expressions multiplied as Ensure's secret nutritional information was whispered from person to person. When the clumsy student finally realized her error—the reason Renfrew put Ensure in glasses was to avoid discussion or obsession over calories—she became frazzled and frantic, but not apologetic. I hated her. She had just made my job that much harder, and I still had no choice but to take the glass full of more calories than I usually allowed myself to consume in a week. Somehow I managed it, and then I followed all the other girls to my first post-meal therapy session.

Post-meal therapy was held in the living room of Renfrew's hospice-style two-story building. The view was pleasant, overlooking hundreds of acres of forest and wildlife. I would have given anything to just be free and go hiking in those woods with my dad, like we'd done so long ago. Post-meal therapy was something I quickly added to my lifelong list of ideas that make good theoretical sense, but don't realistically work. I began this mental log years ago, as a child listening to my parents gripe about the reality of Communism and the way such an idealistic notion could turn so ugly.

During post-meal therapy we all sat on couches, chairs, and the floor. I could see groups starting to form. It was easy to distinguish the "cool" anorexics—the natural-born leaders, including the beautiful, tall, blonde girl, Mary—from the quiet loners. Like I had in high school, I somehow managed to fit into both categories, but never really belonged to either one completely.

After everyone was seated, one of the grad students asked

how we felt and how we'd done on each portion of the meal. What had we found easy to eat, what was difficult, and how did we feel now, a few minutes later? The answers to those post-meal therapy questions, and the responses given at each subsequent session, were pretty much the same: eating sucks, and now I feel lousy. Some of the girls would start by putting a pleasant spin on things, but eventually every comment boiled down to the miserable truth of the matter—no one was comfortable eating. It's true that some foods were psychologically easier to consume and physically easier to digest, but food was food, and food was scary.

This venting wasn't bad, however, because at least we could all discuss our feelings together. What I did hate about post-meal therapy was the feedback we got from the grad student who led our group. It always consisted of the same generic replies, such as, "Does anyone else feel that way?" or "Why do you think you feel that way?" and "What do you think you can do about that?" What made this ineptitude even more heartbreaking was the hope of every girl that perhaps this time she might be provided with a tiny piece of wisdom, some advice, or the slightest insight into how the destructive pattern could be broken. That never happened, and some of the girls had already been to Renfrew four, five, or six times. I was disappointed, and now I also felt angry at the staff.

We went to group therapy daily, and every other day we attended individual therapy sessions. But no one ever told me in advance when these appointments would be scheduled. We were simply left notes in our cubbyhole mailbox on the living room wall. It was this lack of order I found most infuriating. Renfrew should have been a place where a woman with an eating disorder could go to regain the self-respect she'd lost, but instead we were slipped messages like six-year-olds.

One of the most destructive Renfrew sessions was the nutrition class. The staff member who led the discussions—a woman in her thirties studying to become a nutritionist—would show us plastic models of what one correct food serving should look like. I attended this class on three separate occasions, and without fail each time, someone said, "Really? I thought a serving of cottage cheese was bigger than that!" or "Wow, when I thought I was having one serving of tuna, I was really having three!" We would then become discouraged, and frantic chaos would ensue. All the anorexics were horrified to learn they'd been eating more than they thought, but in response, the nutritionist would simply say, "Okay, well, let's just move on and I can show you the next food model." It was an hour of anxiety that I'm sure served many people ill, as it did me. If it hadn't been so harmful it would have been amusing, but after leaving Renfrew I became obsessed with measuring my food and then immediately throwing half out, remembering how small the plastic portions had looked in nutrition class. I wish I'd said something at the time, but instead I always sat there, laughing nervously, overcome with the sad irony of the situation and struck again by the incompetence of the Renfrew staff.

Despite all that, I still dreaded evenings at Renfrew the most. Dinner was served around six—a time at which I, having been raised by European parents, would usually be having lunch. After dinner came arts and crafts therapy, otherwise known as my own private form of torture. Everyone was forced to sit on the floor of the main room surrounded by boxes of paint, crayons, paper, plastic plates, and other crafty materials. An assignment would be given, like "Paint something on a plastic plate, and when you get home, you can hang it up and remind yourself of Renfrew!" All the girls would then clamor for the freshest paints, the prettiest plate, and the best seat. What was going on? I looked around and witnessed lawyers, chemists, writers, real estate agents, mothers, and beautiful, successful women sitting silently for hours, creating something sadly absurd. I know art is supposed to be therapeutic, but this seemed like an immense waste of time and grossly insulting.

How was this childish activity going to make us better? How

could this fail to be seen as the most degrading assignment in the world? Flashbacks of all the painted signs in the dining hall, on patients' doors, and around the Renfrew property flooded my mind, and I refused to pick up a brush. As a result, another nameless grad student gave me an ultimatum: complete each task or leave Renfrew. With each passing moment at Renfrew my animosity towards it grew. But what would my parents do if I called them after one night and told them I had failed yet again? I decided to obey, but challenge the rules as much as possible. Thus began my stint as the resident Renfrew troublemaker.

After my first night of art therapy I snuck to the downstairs pay phone and called my parents collect. As soon as my dad accepted the charges I broke into wracked sobs. My mom and Josh both got on the phone, but still I couldn't form a single, coherent sentence. Frustrated by my lack of emotional control I hung up and returned to my room. The living room had already been emptied and cleaned out.

My roommate was a tall British woman in her forties. She and her American husband had moved to the States where she'd been working as a chemical engineer. She had lost most of her hair due to severe malnutrition. I had lost only a few clumps, so I felt immediately bad for my nearly bald roommate. I introduced myself, gently shook her bony hand, and the first thing she said, before even asking my name was, "Why didn't you eat the bread?" At first I thought she was speaking in code, but then I remembered how intently she'd stared at my plate during lunch, all the while polishing off every morsel of her own food. In response I gave her the lamest answer, the truth: I just couldn't. She met my look of guilt with one of disdain and said, "Next time eat your bread; you might as well." So, next time, I ate my bread. I don't know why. Maybe, I thought, she was speaking symbolically and passing on a vital secret. The bread, after all, might not be just bread. It was life. In order to accept the life, you first had to eat the bread. The religious references weren't lost on me.

That was all my roommate and I said to each other before she turned off all the lights and climbed into her cot, leaving me standing in my day clothes, suitcases still fully packed, in a completely darkened room. This black was not like Manhattan darkness where orange and yellow lights still shine brightly regardless of the hour. This was wild darkness, deep, velvety, and hungry. It engulfed everything around it and left me standing there, alone and perplexed. But in that moment I decided I liked my new roommate. She was tough. No fondness for arts and crafts would be found in this room. I got out the mini book light my mom had packed for me and used it to find my pajamas and the blanket I'd brought from home. I found my soap, face wash, shampoo, Burberry flip-flops, and went to take a shower.

Four girls shared the bathroom, and it had the weirdest smell. After a while I attributed that to the vomit bucket near the edge of the toilet. If one of us got sick or induced vomiting, we had to leave it in the bucket as evidence. I padded my way into the shower, rinsed off in about a minute (I didn't want to be there any longer than necessary), and went back to my room. It was nearly 11:30. I was scheduled for my daily weighing and physical that morning at four. Everyone got a different time slot but they all ranged from about four to six a.m. I got into bed, pulled the covers over my head, and took out my favorite David Bowie CD, *Heathen*. I put "Everyone Says 'Hi'," a song I found eerily appropriate, on repeat, and shut my eyes. I've always had a passion for Bowie, but that night at Renfrew my real love affair with him began.

I slept like I was in a coma, for the first time in years. The only thing nagging me, even in my slumber, was my roommate's inability to get comfortable. She made continuous whiny noises like a sick dog and I didn't know how to help her, so I granted her some dignity and pretended to be oblivious. I knew she was in bad shape, probably worse than anybody else. Except perhaps the girl who had signed in with me that morning. That girl ended up in what we called the "fishbowl," a room in the entrance hall of Renfrew with three regular walls and one wall made of glass. This was designed specifically so the patient, or fish, could be monitored at all hours of the day and night. Any woman in the fishbowl was prohibited from getting out of bed, and if necessary, she was given emergency medical care.

That dawn I woke up, brushed my teeth, and dressed in the flimsy hospital gown we were all required to wear while weighing in. In the past some of the girls had tried to hide heavy objects under their gowns so as to appear to have gained weight, and thus be graduated to a less calorie-intense food program. Thus all gowns had to remain open in the back and we were allowed only underwear. I paired my new outfit with my Burberry flip-flops, which were still soggy from the shower I'd taken only four hours earlier.

When I opened the door to leave my dark, noiseless cave and walk into the hallway, there was already a flurry of activity taking place around me. Almost everyone I'd met the day before was awake, lined up to take her "meds." I too was supposed to accept the five different pills in the small plastic cup bearing my name. I had no idea what the pills were, or what, specifically, they were for, so I left them on the nurse's counter. As far as I knew, no cure for anorexia had yet been bottled in pill form. When I asked one of the nurses about the medication, she told me I would have to meet with the psychiatrist in order to get any answers, since she wasn't sure what he had prescribed for me.

That sounds simple enough, but there were two problems. The Renfrew psychiatrist, whom I referred to as Dr. Who, had met me for approximately five minutes the morning I'd checked in. He couldn't possibly know what drugs, if any, I needed to be taking. In addition, booking an appointment with him was harder than gaining a private audience with the Pope. At Renfrew this man, who never once made eye contact with me, was treated like a demigod. He somehow controlled all the other employees like puppets on a string, yet he was never anywhere in sight. Dr. Who was the only male employee at Renfrew, and I wondered how the rest of the staff expected to empower women when they themselves exhibited a kind of female subservience. So, in aggrieved rebellion I refused the medication, as I'd done with so many other psychiatrists, and sat on a bench outside the nurse's office waiting for my physical. All around me were fragile, ageless little girls in paper dresses, also waiting patiently to be weighed in and doped up. I was in hell. Dante would have found this scene a great source of inspiration.

At long last, I got called in to the nurse's station and was told to step up on the scale. The weighing was followed by a dehydration test, a measure of my blood pressure, and an EKG. The results of my previous morning's EKG test had been alarming; now the nurse was performing the exam over and over, and growing increasingly alarmed. She finally gave up, woodenly telling me not to move, and hurried out to fetch the head nurse. Another nurse informed me I would probably have to be rushed to the emergency room, because it seemed there was something wrong with my heart. I lay on the exam table, bare-chested and calm, observing the curious faces people make when they become frantic. I felt like an alien life-form, laid out on a cold medical table, watching all the other creatures act similarly discordant while I remained completely open and disconnected. I didn't really care if I did have a heart problem. At that point, I didn't really care much about anything.

Ten minutes later the head nurse walked in, a lovely, smart, blonde woman who checked all the EKG results, and immediately concluded that my readings were the product of a faulty machine, not a faulty heart. I laughed it off while they looked at me sheepishly, and said that since my heart was fine, the second biggest problem—besides my alarmingly low weight—was my advanced state of dehydration. I was placed on a twenty-four-hour Gatorade alert. At any moment of the day a staff member might come up to me, hand me a cup of unnaturally colored Gatorade, and watch me polish it off before sprinting off in a different direction. My first dawn physical was now over. I got back into my wet shoes and sloshed to my room where I crawled into my cold bed.

There's something very odd about the fact that Renfrew is kept so cold. Anorexics, known to be cold almost all the time, are like a new breed of human mixed with reptiles. During the day at Renfrew all the anorexics spent free moments outside, basking in the sun to soak up the heat and raise body temperatures. Before I got back into bed and shivered under my two blankets, I put on two pairs of pajama pants, a sweatshirt, three pairs of woolen socks, and spent the rest of the morning listening to my chattering teeth. I wondered if the staff kept it cold for their own comfort, or if they simply didn't notice so many shivering girls hugging themselves throughout the day. I finally fell asleep with these disturbing thoughts, only to be awoken three hours later by the jarring sound of a foreign alarm clock. It was almost time for breakfast, and at such an ungodly hour!

I was still trying to look presentable for the other people around me so I allowed myself twenty minutes to put on a nice outfit, do my makeup, and somehow fix what remained of my hair. Nothing was really working, though; I looked as miserable as I felt. Deciding not to wait for my roommate, who was in the bathroom, I went alone into the dining area. I was already becoming familiar with the routine, so I smoothly found my tray, got water, realized there was no way I'd be allowed coffee or tea—that was given only to the girls who ate their entire meal —and grabbed a Gatorade instead. I spotted some of the girls I had spoken to the day before and decided to sit with them.

At the table were the two Marys, both bulimic, one beautiful, bright, and outspoken, the other miserable and depressed but with a cynical sense of humor I found pleasing. I liked them both, and anyway, I'd had enough anorexia talk for a while. I was ready to discuss a new disease over breakfast, one I hardly knew anything about. We all ate as much as we could, and I made sure to finish my bread while my roommate watched from across the room, sitting at a table with the quiet, older women.

After breakfast I decided to figure out what specific meal plan the staff had put me on—all the plans were identified by a letter, starting with A—and what drugs they were attempting to stuff me with like an unwitting Thanksgiving turkey. In order to accomplish these tasks I first had to make appointments with a nutritionist, and, of course, with Dr. Who. I added my name to the long list of people waiting to meet both people, and was told I would be contacted at a later date, via cubbyhole mailbox. Having accomplished my most pressing task, I moved on to post-meal therapy, which took place every morning in an adjacent building. This after-breakfast group was always bigger than the groups after other meals, consisting of more staff and all the patients. I had been told this was my time to really bring up issues and have them examined by the entire group.

I entered the large room, feeling like I'd been at Renfrew for a full two years even though it had been twenty-four hours, and waited eagerly for the discussion to begin. Several staff members spoke, then came time for patient questions. During breakfast I had heard many girls complain about the treatment they were receiving from the staff, but during the question period no one spoke up and the room remained completely silent. Breakfast talk had made me so hopeful that we might all work together and start communicating with the nameless staff. Everyone seemed mute, until suddenly Mary, the bright, pretty girl I already admired, stood up and spoke.

She said disappointedly that she had tried to get an appointment with Dr. Who over a week ago, but still no one had contacted her about it. In fact, her therapist had left town without giving her any notice, and she'd been transferred to a new therapist who knew nothing about the specifics of her condition. She didn't want to take any drugs until she could first find out what the drugs were for, yet it seemed like none of the therapists cared. She felt that no one was taking any particular interest in her.

Mary listed all of these concerns calmly, but she was obviously distraught. She was a newlywed and a chemist. Her life had been stopped short and she, unlike me, had signed herself into Renfrew, believing it would finally help heal her. She went on with her suggestions and I mentally agreed with everything she said, but the staff became increasingly flustered. They informed her that they would talk to her in private later and asked if anyone else had a suggestion that they could address.

I observed Mary that entire day and began to really admire her. Unlike me, she'd been brave enough to speak the truth. I was too scared to do anything but act like an angry, spoiled child around the staff. Mary was someone who could make a difference, and I was acting like a girl who hid from life. I thought that if she was here, maybe it was acceptable for me to be here too. Maybe this place wasn't a graveyard for dreams, hopes, and opportunities. Maybe it wasn't a place where joy was sucked into the vacuum of despair.

That night, feeling Mary's helplessness, I snuck downstairs to call my parents. Next to me on the only other pay phone was Mary. She was talking to her husband, telling him the staff was warning her to be quiet, quit causing problems, and start following the rules, otherwise she'd be expelled.

I kept wondering what she'd do if she were asked to leave or was ostracized by the staff. As if in answer, Mary said something to her husband that I'll never forget. She told him that she could now eat a peanut butter and jelly sandwich without throwing up, and that it was a start. The fact that she could handle peanut butter and jelly meant she had some hope. She would build from there. She was so very brave! But there I was, poking through my food every day, bluffing my way through the program, getting supplemented after each meal. Sometimes I even refused to finish the Ensure. If I could be a bit more like Mary, I thought, I could create a better version of myself.

On the phone with my parents several minutes later, I sobbed until the world became a dizzying whirl. I became overwhelmed by all of the obstacles I could clearly envision ahead of me. I was frozen to the phone. I simply did not know what to do next. Here at Renfrew I had witnessed bravery in the face of disease, in the face of demons, but I had not yet discovered this bravery within myself. This great fearlessness was coming from inside some of the women, and all of them were in the fight of their lives. They were not drawing strength from the incapable staff, or from the walls of a building designed to harbor outcasts, but somehow from within their own strong souls and broken bodies. Many were failing, but some, like Mary, were beginning to succeed. All of them were beautiful, kind, wonderful women who deserved to live happy, fulfilled lives. They deserved some respect!

So why was I sobbing that night? The reasons are innumerable. Probably because I'd once thought, as most people still do, that it didn't matter what happened to these sick women since they were nothing more than useless waifs. Probably because until that night I hadn't considered myself a part of that group, but now I finally knew I was. And finally, because I realized that in order to get better I had to find the strength and resolve of someone like Mary, and I didn't know where it could possibly come from. I was still nothing more than a desperate, helpless, scared little girl.

The next morning I woke up for my weighing and physical as usual. I got behind the line of girls waiting for their meds, and suddenly the scene looked horrifying to me, like a new Holocaust vision. The girls I already knew so well were skeletal, surreal human apparitions. It was frightening and unreal, and I realized why, of course, the staff didn't treat us like people. We didn't look like people! How, I wondered, in the face of such despair, does the world not disobey the law of gravity and simply unhinge?

That morning at post-meal therapy Mary stood up and announced that she was leaving. Her demeanor was quiet and well behaved. As soon as she said this, however, I saw her give a sideways glance to a staff member standing at the edge of the large room. In that moment, as though it physically pained her to suppress the truth, Mary became revolutionary again. She told us she was being kicked out of Renfrew for failing to cooperate and asking too many questions. But she would have cooperated, she told us, if she'd gotten any answers. She told us that we should respect each other and stand up for ourselves, even if the staff didn't, and even if our diseases were fighting harder than we could. She then told us she'd be fine, that her husband was picking her up and that no matter how difficult it would be she'd somehow recover. Here she was, our general in combat, and she was leaving. After her outburst a staff member escorted her out of the room. She didn't return, and I never saw her again. But she sparked something inside me. She inspired me. I heard her battle cry. It resonated in my brittle bones. It resonates with me today, regardless of the challenges I face.

At the next group therapy meeting I decided the best help I could get from Renfrew, the best information I could gather, would come from the patients themselves. I started cutting "class" and going out to the gazebo to talk with as many women as possible. What was everyone's experience? How had they become anorexic? Did they really want to get better, or were they just going along with the pretense? What did they love? What did they despise? Everything I learned, not surprisingly, was everything I myself had experienced. Yes. I definitely belonged in this group, and that was fine with me now. I had never met a group of women who were as caring, considerate, smart, and beautiful as the women at Renfrew. We were all just visibly weaker.

The afternoon of my third day at Renfrew—what felt like my third year in prison—I realized I was finished with what Renfrew had to offer. I began frantically writing letters to my parents, Fran, Josh, my aunts and uncles, grandmother, and cousins. I wanted to tell them all that I loved them, and I wanted to talk about the hardships I had experienced. I wrote about how unfair, yet simultaneously beautiful, life can be. I wrote as though I had just been handed a death sentence, and of course, I was really writing to myself. I don't think anyone else could truly understand the level of emotional turmoil I was experiencing.

I had checked into Renfrew to appease my parents and Dr. Klab, but privately I'd thought I didn't belong in a treatment facility. And now, only three days later, I was a changed person. I saw how serious my disease was, how hungrily and completely it destroys lives. I realized that the only other people I could fully relate to at this time were those suffering the same illness. I had let myself become the disease, and now I needed to create a new identity.

Later that evening, I got a cubbyhole note saying Dr. Who could meet me the next day, only to get another note two hours later saying he had to cancel. No specific reason was offered, and no new appointment was made. I decided that until somebody started giving me straight answers, I would not cooperate.

That night, I met with my nutritionist, and she told me I had been placed on the most calorie-intense meal plan and would have to work my way down as my weight went up. But she refused to say a word when it came to discussing specific daily calories. I understood this policy but felt like Renfrew was being paternalistic. I was frustrated because I knew that once I got back to everyday life I would have to deal with calories constantly, and there'd be nobody to protect me from calorie-talk. I wasn't being given the proper tools I needed, but was instead becoming increasingly confused.

The rest of my third day passed quickly, though I often noticed Mary's absence. At dinnertime I looked around the room and realized that many of these women had already become true friends. I appreciated them and found them genuinely interesting. It was like I'd gotten past the superficial wall anorexia creates and glimpsed their true characters. Yet sadly, I also knew that upon leaving Renfrew the spell would be broken, and we would probably never see each other again.

I looked at Sarah, a tall, blonde, sixteen-year-old anorexic who always ate without looking at her food or at any of the other women. She simply stared straight ahead and finished everything on her tray, including dessert, in a manner of minutes.

It was like she couldn't bear witnessing her own actions; she just wanted it to be over. I knew she couldn't taste her food because she wasn't allowing herself the time.

I turned to Rachel, a thirteen-year-old, short, brunette know-it-all anorexic who was wise beyond her years, and so special; I hoped she would one day realize that for herself. She was finishing her dinner, and as time ran out she asked if she could eat the blueberries on her plate because they were so delicious. It was the first time I'd heard her speak positively about food. Nonetheless, her tray was yanked away—time was up, and blueberries didn't count as "points" anymore. She would have to be supplemented for them instead. Once again, the staff had entirely missed the point.

I gave Rachel a sympathetic smile, and I remembered meeting her mom earlier that day. I had gone to Rachel's room to lend her some shampoo and walked in on her poking at herself in front of the mirror and saying sadly, "Even when I get out of here I won't be cured of what I see in the mirror—my horrible body image." Instead of reassurance, her mom offered a snappy retort, "Well, you'll just have to get over it. Better yet, stop looking in the mirror!" I was so surprised by the mother's comment that my immediate shock didn't allow me time to politely excuse myself from the room. Instead I shot her a startled look. I towered over both of them by about six inches, and suddenly felt fully out of place in the room haunted by so many similar, past conversations of previous patients. Rachel's mom immediately noticed my grimace and looked away in shame, pretending to be arranging her daughter's bedspread. Yet her comments made an indelible impression on me. I knew that she was making the same mistake most parents make with their anorexic daughters—confusing the girl and the illness.

Rachel, like the rest of us, was living a tormented existence. As the youngest patient, however, she was also among the most eager to recover. Here in the dining room, her desire to finish her blueberries was just one example of a special kind of bravery that would be scoffed at in the outside world.

Shaking my head, I turned to smile at the remaining Mary, a twenty-six-year-old bulimic who possessed a simultaneous air of innocence and strength. Each of her disparaging remarks made me smile.

Finally, I looked across to the quiet table where my roommate was eating. She'd been having a hard time lately, consuming all her meals but failing to put on the weight she so desperately needed in order to stay alive.

I loved all these girls, but I didn't dare tell them what I'd already decided: I was leaving Renfrew. Later that night, I went out past bedtime to sneak a cigarette with one of the new girls who'd arrived that morning. She was blonde, from the South, and exactly my age. We shared similar stories, discussing mostly boyfriends and fathers, and what we wanted to do with our lives "once all of this was over." We could still afford to be hopeful. Our futures, unlike that of my roommate, seemed brighter.

Before bed that night I went through the same rituals, preparing my David Bowie CD, fluffing up my blankets, and chatting with my roommate. I had been rereading one of my favorite books, Milan Kundera's *The Unbearable Lightness of Being,* without much success as I had very little free time. My roommate, on the other hand, informed me she'd be doing lots of reading in the future, since she'd just been placed on temporary bed rest. This could mean only one thing. Her health was deteriorating and the staff didn't know what else to do. I told her to take my book, and then admitted I was thinking of leaving the very next day. She was upset, perhaps a little bit disappointed, and once again said something very poignant I knew I'd never forget. "Put on weight while you still can, before you know you're going to die but decide you want to live instead."

I looked at her, gave her a sad smile, and replied, "I know you're going to be okay, and when you get better, send me back this book. Then I'll know you're home again. In the meantime, I'll be checking for it every day."

When she agreed I opened the worn, dull-edged cover and wrote, "Dear Sara, isn't the title perfect for us? Here's my address . . ." I allowed a few months to pass after I left Renfrew and then began to check the mail each day for that book. More than three years have passed and I still haven't received it. I hope she just forgot. But in my heart I know she didn't.

That night, I was certain I had to leave Renfrew. I had learned so much about myself and had gotten to know and love these women who shared my disease. But I was also afraid Renfrew was causing me to lose hope. I knew that at least some of the girls would die, and that left me feeling broken. Filled with anguish, I called my mom to tell her about my decision. I knew she had been relieved I'd checked into Renfrew, where professionals could force me to cooperate, but as always she listened to my pleading, and my insistence that if I stayed in Renfrew my body might become stronger but my soul would be crushed.

Other parents might listen to these words and find them meaningless, but my mom still had faith in me, though I'm not sure where she got it. She also realized it was my own fragile faith I was trying to protect. So that night, we made a deal. My dad would bail me out the following afternoon as long as I left Renfrew armed with the names of a nutritionist and a physician in Boston, and the location of an outpatient program where I could attend regular group therapy meetings. In addition, Dr. Klab would treat me upon my return to Manhattan. I happily agreed. I was out.

I returned to my pitch-black room but didn't set my alarm for the morning weigh-in and physical. I was leaving, and so I slept until breakfast time, which felt like the greatest luxury. At breakfast I told everyone my decision, and was surprised by how sad they became. Sarah, the younger, blonde anorexic, began to cry. It struck me that, perhaps, I was her brave Mary. She had seen me take a stand with the staff ever since Mary had left. I had found my voice, and used it to try to protect the girls as much as possible, because that was one of the only things I still believed in.

I told them all how I felt closer to them than to people I'd known for years, even friends I'd made at NYU. Then we all fell quiet. There was nothing left to say, but much to think about.

After breakfast I left the dining room with five or six other girls and was abruptly stopped by Amelia, my therapist, who was coming towards me at full speed. While still twenty feet away she yelled, "Laura Moisin, you have a serious problem!"

"I know," I said. "I have a disease called anorexia that neither you nor your staff has helped me overcome. Only the girls around me have supported me."

My words further fed her fury and she continued in a louder voice. "You skipped your morning weigh-in, you haven't been taking your medication, and you never met with the psychiatrist!" That would be Dr. Who.

"Well," I responded calmly, "you finally caught on that I wasn't taking my medication. I won't because no one had ever explained to me what the medication is for, and the psychiatrist cancelled his appointment with me."

She was silent for a moment, clearly befuddled. Obviously she hadn't researched her case before attacking me. Amelia would have made a very poor lawyer. In the moment I gave her to think up a rebuttal, I looked around at my jury, a growing pool of nearly twenty women with eating disorders. It didn't matter that we were sick; we were all still human. And neither they nor I needed to endure the treatment I was at that moment being given. Amelia finally recovered from her stupor and shouted loudly enough to summon several nurses, "Laura Moisin, you have a serious problem!"

"Amelia," I told her, "I may be ill, but you're the one with the problem. And I'm getting out of here, and away from people like you!" Yes, I'd found my voice, and from the grins on all the other faces, I took hope that maybe I had helped them contemplate using their own authority as well.

After my tiff with Amelia—the most fun I had at Renfrew during my four-day stay—I went quickly to the nurse's station to fill out the last of my release forms. I still had time before my dad would arrive to pick me up, and the head nurse (who'd told me that the EKG machine was broken and not my heart) sent me to the nearby hospital to take a bone-density test. She had wanted me to know, for my own medical records, if I had developed osteoporosis during my years of waning health. She made that test happen, even though she knew I had checked out of Renfrew, because she genuinely cared. Sometimes, when you least expect it, people can surprise you. I was grateful to her and sorry that she didn't have more direct contact with the patients.

When I got back from the hospital I went to my room to pack, only to find one of the staff members, Florence, dumping my things into my suitcase and duffel bag. A small crowd of my friends had gathered. I walked in and watched with amusement as my possessions were carelessly tossed around. I no longer cared; I just wanted out. These actions only reinforced what I already thought of most of the Renfrew staff. But some of my friends—including Sarah, Rachel, Mary, and my roommate—stopped the nurse, took my clothes from her, and began to fold them nicely, placing them neatly in my bag.

My roommate Sara had been lying in bed with her husband, who had come to visit even though these weren't regular visiting hours. I was much more concerned about the purpose of his visit and the look of anguish on his face than about the state of my possessions. Sara had probably received more bad news about her health, though she wasn't burdening us with it. Yet there she was, so frail and strong, with the life almost palpably pouring out of her, fighting for me along with all the other girls whom I now completely understood.

When Florence saw our quiet rebellion, she became embarrassed. She noticed me standing in the doorway and made a comment about my nice clothes. Then she apologized and said she'd been instructed to evacuate me from the room, and that I should wait outside. I thanked her for her fine packing job and told her she could continue while I supervised. I then gave

Sarah some of my things, like the Body Shop banana shampoo, Brazil nut conditioner, and coconut body lotion she'd liked. She began to cry and told me how special she thought I was. I would have given her everything I owned, if only she could tell herself the same thing.

An hour later I was waiting on the steps outside and heard my dad's approaching footsteps. I was out of Renfrew. My father rounded a corner, dressed in his nice beige and off-white summer clothes, and I realized I had never been happier to see him. He was saving me, and I smiled to think that that morning, before leaving the house, my mom had dressed him in one of his nice outfits just for me.

Five hours later I was home and it was dark out. I walked up the front stairs to my house. My mom and Josh answered the door. I felt like I'd been gone for years. I was a changed person. I had a promise I'd made my mom to live up to—to get well on my own terms—but for the moment I was happy and carefree. That night I went to bed and slept soundly, finally warm. While drifting off in my own sheets I thought of the expression "You can never come home again." I had always agreed with that sentiment before that day. I now realized it's not that you can't come home, but that every time you do come home, you are a little different. At least I was. For one thing, I had finally eaten.

A few days later I got a phone call from the head nurse at Renfrew. I had lost almost twenty percent of my bone density. I had the bones of an eighty-year-old, but I was only twenty. But, she told me in that positive yet sympathetic way, the bone loss was not irreversible. I just had to take care of myself. I just had to eat . . . on my own terms.

Chapter *Five*

It Must Be September

The news guy himself just said "Good Lord, good Lord!" There are no words. Screaming on the street. Plumes of smoke and debris. Josh says, "You can't see anything downtown, everything's gone." This is the most awful, incredible thing I've ever seen and felt. Fran is downstairs buying water. Our water is brown. Look out the window, there's nothing! First the North Tower, plane, then the second. I'm on the phone with my mom, screaming, "Oh my God, oh my God!" Life is drowning. How can I breathe, how can I breathe in this city ever again? Can't watch news anymore. Every headline is bad news, bad news. Give me some hope to be able to live here, still. Fran is crying in the kitchen and I hug her, but she doesn't hold on. Josh's office is closed for a week. People are crying on the street — mass hysteria. Traffic is stopped, subways are stopped. People are slipping and literally trying to pick each other up off the streets.

— Journal entry, September 11, 2001

I was finally out of Renfrew after what seemed like years of intense, private struggle. It was the beginning of September 2002, and I was hoping to salvage the remainder of what had been a terrible summer. Instead I was sitting in my nutritionist Adelaide's Boston office. I knew she was possibly imparting some useful nuggets of wisdom, but I simply couldn't help but stare blankly out her fourth-floor window. Perhaps she was talking about nutrients, vitamins, minerals, and necessary daily caloric intake. I wasn't sure. I'd heard it all before.

I believe that anyone who has attended school in the United States has heard about the official food pyramid. There are foods we should feel bad eating and other foods we should constantly be eating, according to our government. The food pyramid is full of these "shoulds." With these thoughts swarming around my unfocused mind I began to wonder whether food has always been so universally tied to human emotion.

There is constant chatter about the American obesity crisis, caused in part by emotional eating. This is a disturbing notion. Are most of us really suffering from an eating disorder? How am I supposed to live in this society and gain weight when the public rhetoric so heavily focuses on new fad diets, low-calorie foods, low-carb secrets, and a populace so obsessed with losing weight? In a society that so values being thin and encourages weight loss, where do the anorexics fit in? More importantly, what place do the recovering anorexics have? Why do I only hear about anorexia in the media when some cruel, racy tabloid breaks the news about another celebrity who's seemingly fallen prey to this illness?

The realization that I'd already been in Adelaide's office for fifteen minutes without listening to a word she said made me force my gaze upon her. I focused on her expressive green eyes and those rapidly moving lips made more conspicuous by her layers of magenta lipstick. I liked her from the moment I stepped into her office, and, in truth, that's a rare sentiment for me. My experience with "experts" had been rocky before Renfrew, but after dealing with Amelia and Dr. Who I was especially doubtful about anyone who claimed to have any ability in treating anorexia. I wasn't thrilled at the prospect of someone telling me what I should eat, studying my food diaries, or weighing me, but I knew right away that Adelaide was somehow different.

Renfrew had also made it clear that anorexics are outcasts; they are underestimated and easily bullied. Most anorexics believe that they're essentially flawed and therefore should be persecuted—they *deserve* it. The relationship between professional and patient in such a setting can therefore turn slightly abusive. Naturally, much depends on the therapist, hospital, and treatment center in question, but most of what I'd learned up to that point was that I had been stripped of any personal power or rights. I toyed with the notion of simply letting go of my thoughts, opinions, and actions and handing my rights over to all those around me, including Josh, Fran, my parents, aunts and uncles living abroad, and anyone else, whether they wanted them or not—maybe life would be easier that way.

That first day, as I stepped into Adelaide's office, I experienced something refreshing. She was genuine, warm, and open. She didn't scan my body like I was so used to people doing. She looked me in the eye and welcomed me into her plant-filled space, asking my mom to sit in the waiting room. Then something even more radical happened—she told me right away that no progress I made could come from anyone who forced me to eat or forced me to think differently. No progress could come if I allowed myself to be ordered around and bullied.

"You are in the driver's seat," she said. "I'm only giving you directions to where you should be going."

That one sentence gave me a sense of inner peace I hadn't experienced in years. Nobody had been treating me like a *human being* anymore and I had forgotten I was even responsible for myself. That simple statement that most people would have taken for granted triggered a revolution in me, and reminded me of Mary's departing speech at Renfrew. Adelaide was a radical! Her words kindled the sparks of my personal inner fire. She had handed back to me something I hadn't consciously realized I'd lost in the first place. She reminded me of my own adulthood, and in doing so gave me the beginnings of a responsibility for and investment in my own life. Being an adult meant that I had to face a disease that had not only robbed me of dignity for so many years but that had left me with no *quality* of life. I had reverted back to childhood, but unlike a child I suddenly felt the heavy weight of my very existence.

I realized that help could come in as many forms as people themselves. I had to phase out all the people trying to tell me what was "good," what to eat, and what to do, because they compelled me to demonstrate just how completely I could rebel against them through my own self-destruction. I began learning how to distinguish useful forms of counsel; I sought out people who wanted to act as advisors rather than dictators.

The second tremendously important lesson I learned from Adelaide began as a theoretical concept of food's natural beauty. Even though I couldn't experience what Adelaide meant when she so respectfully, lovingly talked about food, her intriguing words tickled my palate. No one had been able to do that for me since I had started restricting my food.

On our second meeting Adelaide broke from what I thought would be a boring, scripted session by telling me a story. She told me about her nephew's upcoming wedding and the catering job she had been appointed with. In addition to being a nutritionist, Adelaide was also a food aficionado, especially passionate about the Slow Food movement.

She discussed her upcoming task while I secretly wondered

why she would describe all the foods I couldn't eat and all the events I couldn't enjoy. I was becoming increasingly vexed, but in my submissive anorexic haze I still couldn't vocalize those feelings. Instead I sat silently fuming.

Then Adelaide told me about a tomato—a striped purple-and-orange heirloom tomato—that she'd found at a farmer's market. This piqued my interest. First of all, tomato talk was much less offensive than talk of chocolate cake, or roasted suckling pig. Secondly, my love of the color purple borders on the obsessive. Finally, I found her use of the word "heirloom" very charming. I imagined my tomato taking a carriage ride through the nineteenth-century English countryside. It was as though this tomato, still fresh and whole, was from ages long past and therefore unique among all other present-day tomatoes.

I was transported to a magical farmer's market filled with all varieties of "zebra" vegetables and brightly colored fruit. They had all been in the earth longer than any living person and therefore all knew something we had perhaps forgotten. This food was a mystery, something I hadn't considered in my one-dimensional, paralyzing fear of all food.

Adelaide was creating a fantasy world where only a lucky few ever got a peek behind the dismal façade of everyday life. I could only imagine what an actual wedding feast composed of all this food would look like. For the first time in a long time I too wanted to attend a party that involved eating. Up until that point I had only considered joining social situations that involved coffee, not food or alcohol. What a magical wedding that would be, like a Tuscan picture at sunset, where everything is touched by the gold-and-orange light of a retiring sun, and the food glows with a sterling sparkle.

I knew I was creating an enchanted world of food in my head that didn't exist in reality. Even if I could attend the wedding banquet I still wouldn't be able to sample a single purple-and-orange zebra tomato. But for the first time in five years I was thinking a positive food thought. For a moment I could imagine a happy food experience and maybe even eating and liking it again one day—sometime in the hazy future.

On a practical note, Adelaide taught me something else that day. She helped me create a three-way food chart that increased in relevance over time. This chart consisted of three columns. On the left was the "yes" category, in the middle was the "maybe" section, and on the right side was the "no" group. The yes category consisted of all of the foods that were "safe" to eat. The maybe column contained everything I would consider trying, or had been curious about, but perhaps would not consume regularly. The no section had the foods that scared me most, though these foods could not stay in that section forever. The goal was to slowly, on a monthly or bimonthly basis, start moving maybe foods into the yes column and the no foods into the maybe column. Trying a maybe food was a victory, while a shift of an entire food group or item was a real triumph. Even if a food remained a maybe it was important to try it and slowly start expanding the yes catalog.

This system was useful because it acted as a kind of one-time pass. Trying a new food once seemed much less daunting than being expected to eat an entire tray of "well-balanced" food, as per the Renfrew method.

The problem at the time with the three-category scheme was that it had to be adopted and used in order to work. Though my chart didn't become active for weeks I eventually began experimenting with it. Every time I added a food I felt greater control without experiencing the daunting panic I had every day at Renfrew.

Adelaide's optimism was inspiring, but as we were finishing our surprisingly good session, she reminded me of something I had been desperately trying to ignore. "Next week is September 11th," she said, "and knowing what you went through in New York a year ago, I think it'll be good for you to have an appointment that day."

The thought was agonizing, so I tried to let the last traces of my magical farmer's market linger as long as possible. I left Adelaide's office and walked down to the street with my mom, and instead of telling her practical things, like the food chart system, I described my quixotic food musings. I told her all about the tomatoes that had taken on my favorite color . . . and you could actually eat them too! I told her about the heirloom apples, pears, peppers, and other types of ripe produce I was imagining. I told her how Adelaide was catering a wedding and using all these fruits and vegetables, and how any couple married under a banquet so natural, simple, and unique was bound to be blessed. I tried to envelop my mother with an image that would make her smile like I had. I wanted to give her a brief escape similar to the mini-holiday I had just experienced. My mom's reaction was the opposite of what I'd hoped for. It disappointed and angered me for a long time; but now, years later, I finally understand it.

She was so worried, confused, and furious; to her, fantasizing like that was irresponsible and negligent. She pelted me with hurtful questions: why wasn't I "doing something" to save myself, why had she let me leave Renfrew where at least I wouldn't be allowed to completely stop eating and die, and why was my nutritionist, who should have been devising a solid plan of action, telling me food fairy tales instead of making me eat. Rather than walking to the car, my mom took my hand and brusquely led me back to Adelaide's office for further interrogation. Suddenly I was a child again.

When Adelaide opened her door I became uncharacteristically impartial. I didn't know whose side to take. Should I choose my mom, who was going through so much personal torment and pain? She had stopped sleeping, having a life, knowing what it felt like to be happy and at peace for even a moment because of my illness. Or did I want to side with a woman who was able to relate to me even as I was hiding in my anorexic sinkhole? I liked them both, but knew that only one was acting out of commitment born of love. My mom, who couldn't control the pitch and volume of her voice, asked Adelaide if she couldn't see that I needed *immediate action*.

In contrast to my mom, Adelaide was superlatively calm and, patting my mom on the shoulder, told her, "She's doing great. She's going to be okay." My mom hadn't gotten the answers she was looking for, but Adelaide waved us goodbye and closed her office door in preparation for her next appointment. As we walked back into the bright September sun I thought to myself, "With all of this commotion and grief, it must be September again."

Things only got worse when we arrived home and my mom gave her rendition of my appointment to my dad; and he reacted almost identically. Nowadays, I can fully comprehend my parents' frustration and anger with Adelaide's passive tactics. I realize how desperate they were, but at the time I could only feel betrayed that they deprived me of my first good morning in years. Ironically, part of what had made that morning so special was my positive thoughts about food!

Adelaide's approach may have seemed irresponsible, but the truth is that any hospital and inpatient treatment center can force an anorexic to eat. They can even intubate her to ensure she will not die. For someone who is on the brink of death this is a necessary but temporary measure. It is no kind of lasting solution. Recovering from anorexia is a long, lonely process. It takes years of learning about the disease and how to master it. I was very weak and frail (I won't mention specific pounds), but I was not in imminent danger of death. If Adelaide had told her zebra tomato story to an anorexic on her deathbed I would have considered it irresponsible. But I was eating, albeit scantily, and I had been released from an inpatient hospital. I wasn't about to die at any moment.

The more my dad contemplated my ostensibly ineffective post-Renfrew treatment, the more he wanted to seize control. That's in his character. My dad is an engineer and a business-man. He's a man of math and science. He likes to think in terms of charts, graphs, and strict schedules. My mom is an artist, more flexible and open-minded. Naturally, my dad's solution was to create a "recovery schedule" that consisted of specific daily progress and a set future date by which I would be healthy again and fully recovered. This made no sense to me and I tried to explain how it was impossible for me to predict when I'd be able to go out for dinner with the family again. I explained that cancer patients have chemo schedules and post-operative patients have a predictable number of recovery days, but anorexia is atypical.

During my attempted explanation of how a mental illness is more complicated, both of my parents decided they disliked Adelaide and agreed she wasn't the right person to help me. I finally felt as though I'd found someone who understood me, but they believed she was sabotaging my recovery. In the weeks to come I continued to see Adelaide, but no longer told my parents the particulars of what we discussed other than my food diaries and weight.

That night, as my parents slept and I experienced a full night of anorexic insomnia, I allowed the thoughts I had been pushing out for almost a year to sneak back into my head. I was still angry my parents couldn't understand how important Adelaide's calm and optimistic mentality was for my troubled spirit. But soon Adelaide's foreboding words trickled in. That one sentence, "Next week is September 11th," and the realization that it was a good thing I'd be with a "professional" to talk about that day struck me like a physical blow.

As I began to meditate on the day's events, images of bright, autumnal fruits and vegetables transformed into apparitions of a smoldering gray city, like terrible slides from a film projector. Slide One . . . my Soho apartment becomes a barricaded trap. Slide Two . . . people prefer to jump off the Twin Towers rather than face what is happening behind them. Slide Three . . . suicide prevention posters now line the subway walls and buildings. Slide Four . . . I wake up every morning knowing that it is most certainly my last day. Slide Five . . . a thought . . . how should I live out this last day?

These overpowering, haunting images I was so frightened by had rediscovered me. They *were* me. They were not buried and gone. They were more present and clear to me than on that day when everything, literally, fell apart. That night, because of those few seemingly innocent words, I had a séance with the ghosts I'd hoped had vanished. Instead, they proved to be insomniacs as well. So I welcomed them. I started from the beginning, from the time before September 11th, 2001, when Fran and I decided to move to Soho.

When my sister and I decided to live together we agreed that what was most important was to embark on a bohemian lifestyle together, à la early Bob Dylan. We knew we had to stay downtown and yearned to live in Soho. I was living in Chinatown and preparing for my junior year while Fran was living in a gorgeous Chelsea studio. Any other apartment would have been an upgrade for me and a probable downgrade for her. For two weeks Fran and I searched for an apartment, walking the dusty, sweltering Manhattan streets, going up and down endless flights of stairs, flushing weak or broken toilets, running strangers' showers, and becoming increasingly disappointed by the lack of space and extremely high prices. One afternoon I got a call from Fran telling me that Gui, our cute, quirky Brazilian real estate agent (who had a tattoo of a troll playing a flute at the base of a giant mushroom on his hip), had found something really "swanky" for us in Soho.

I met Fran and an ice-cream-licking Gui at the corner of Thompson and Prince Street, mere steps from Dolce & Gabbana, Prada, DKNY, and our favorite coffee place. I couldn't believe that living in that neighborhood was even a possibility for us. We eagerly walked up six flights of narrow steps and entered what would become our apartment. It had two tiny bedrooms, a slightly larger "living room," and a kitchen that doubled as the hallway to the one bathroom apparently designed for little people, complete with miniature sink, half-bath, and a very low toilet. It was cute. But most of all, the view was incredible. The two large bay windows in the living room directly faced the World Trade Center . . . the Twins.

This view offered a strong form of symbolism for the two of us. Our entire lives we've joked that we're the "psycho twins," able to finish each other's sentences, read every minuscule expression on each other's faces, and even look strikingly alike, aside from some subtle differences. What better apartment for a pair of psycho twins? That day we signed the papers with Gui, called our parents/guarantors, and shook hands. The twins were in business.

On the morning of September 11th, 2001, Fran and I had been living in our Soho apartment for nearly two months. I had just begun my junior year at NYU and I was running late for a class I couldn't afford to get locked out of. As always, I rushed around the apartment getting ready while the *Today* show provided background noise in the living room. Fran's boyfriend, Xavier, and Josh were over early that morning to see us off before we went to school and work. A few minutes before I was about to leave, I heard a loud crash and felt the ground shake. I was convinced a car had smashed into the base of our apartment building. I opened the blinds to the large living room window and at first failed to notice the smoke coming from the first tower. I simply looked down to see what had happened on the street below.

It wasn't until Katie Couric began to frantically scream that a plane had flown into the building that I looked in that obvious direction. I called everyone else into the living room. At this point we were getting nervous, but I calmly explained that it was probably just a small plane. "It's definitely an accident," I heard myself repeating in a superficially reassuring tone. "Maybe the pilot was drunk, or had a heart attack. Either way, it was absolutely a Cessna carrying cargo."

During my soliloquy, as we all watched the plume of smoke

increase in size, we saw the second plane approach the other building. Nobody said a word. I was praying it was a fire plane coming to extinguish the flames, or a news plane investigating the accident, or Air Force One parachuting the President to the ground to assure everyone that it was no big deal, or a Martian plane making contact with New Yorkers . . . anything, *anything* but what we all feared most.

When the second plane hit the second tower, I felt as though my lungs had been deflated like a cheap balloon. Katie Couric emitted a noise halfway between a yelp and a scream. She wasn't the perky princess of daytime news anymore, and for me, she never will be again.

The four of us looked at each other for what could have been days, or weeks, or maybe even a couple of lifetimes. Whatever this was, it was unlike anything we had experienced before. Stories of Pearl Harbor came immediately to mind, and how I should have taken those survivors' tales more seriously. Maybe then I could have learned something and known what to do, rather than standing there paralyzed with fear. For a moment the world stopped, and everything was still and quiet.

After that, chaos erupted with a spiteful burst of energy. People on the street six floors below us began to run and scream in panic. They became primal and insane. Many of them simply stepped out of their shoes and kept running, or dropped their lightweight summer jackets, bags, purses, and fled at full speed. Where were they going? It simply didn't matter. People just went, just did, in order to somehow respond to what they had witnessed. The Twins, meanwhile, were hissing with flames and smoke, and the tiny Lilliputians the Twins had once calmly loomed over were responding in mass agitation. As Shakespeare so deftly phrased it, the world was "full of sound and fury, signifying nothing."

The first thing I did was tell everyone that we were going to be fine, as long as we didn't venture any farther downtown. The first thing Fran did was grab her camera and run up to our roof.

Many of our neighbors had already done this in order to gain a clearer perspective of what it was, and what it all meant. My sister is a photographer and has always been passionate about taking pictures and studying photography. At the time, she was working for a French news agency where she could submit her photos. Her mentality has always been one that's annoyed and worried me—she thinks that the harm a photographer puts herself in is secondary to the photo and the story being told. I have always tried to reason with her, asking, "Do photos matter more than people?" But my attempts have always failed. September 11th proved to be no different. As soon as Fran decided it wasn't enough to just stand on the roof of our building she hurried downstairs to tell me she was going to see the Twins so she could let her photos tell the story for others. I begged and pleaded with her, but none of it made a difference.

"I'll be with Xavier," she said. "It'll be fine. The police won't let anyone go where it isn't safe."

And there was only one thing I could respond with, one thing I knew for sure, and one thing I felt in my heart as though the fire in the buildings was burning through my body. This one thing I told Fran over and over again, repeating it almost obsessively as she collected her camera equipment and stepped out the apartment door.

"The buildings are gonna fall, Fran, I can just feel it, I just know it. The Twins are going to collapse!"

Nobody predicted that the Twins would crumble that day. Not the news agencies or media, not Josh or Xavier, not Fran, and certainly not my parents when I called and told them we were safe, and not to worry if the phone lines got cut. I neglected to tell my mom that Fran had gone downtown, and opted instead to tell her that her daughter was on the roof taking pictures. When my sister left I thought I'd never see her again. In fact, I believed we would all die that day, and that I would never again know a moment of peace or happiness. So I couldn't understand why Fran didn't want to be with me on our last day.

The twin apartment had failed me, the Twin buildings were on fire, and my twin had abandoned me altogether.

When I started to feel a deep, unhappy rumbling and shaking as though from the very core of the earth, I knew what was happening. I decided I would try to call my mom, my friend, who I knew was terrified because her only two babies were at the center of this hell. Somehow, miraculously, I patched through and told her what I knew was about to happen. It was something so scary and dreaded I knew the moment it occurred, I would be changed forever.

"Mama, one of the towers is about to fall," I said.

She consoled me, cooing into the phone, assuring me that could never occur. The Twins, she said, were built to last. One of them had been bombed in the early nineties, and still they stood. But I knew better.

Suddenly I heard a vacuum-like suction noise, followed by stillness upon eternal stillness. Nothing happened for a few long seconds. Then easily, like a child's game of blocks, the building caved in upon itself, fell straight down, and was flattened. All that was left were miles of dust and filthy debris. The air was thick with haze, muck, and misery. All I could say over the phone to my mom was, "Oh my God, oh my God," in an almost monotone, accepting voice. She knew what was happening. After all she was watching it, along with what seemed like the entire world. All I could think, through eyes shut painfully tight, was that my twin was on the ground, in that mass of prehistoric goop. I hated my sister at that moment. Why would she do that to me?

When the second tower went down I almost felt a sense of relief, like when a sick or elderly loved one dies after many months of suffering. I watched it fall with my head sticking out the window, and at that moment Fran walked through the door. She was covered in white ash. Even after she'd washed her face, it remained that pale non-color. I didn't hug her at first but stared at her as though I had seen a ghost (and her appearance certainly fit that image). I had assumed we would all die that day and that she'd been lost in the overpowering mushroom of gas and dirt.

Suddenly, I became truly frightened for the first time. My sister was here, in front of me, and we were still alive. We still had life to hold on to and to fight for. I was scared because I couldn't just sink into the haze around me. I had to struggle to make sense of all this and still keep calm enough to also plot out a survival strategy. After all, by this time Washington, D.C., had also been attacked. Planes were going down in Pennsylvania and there were rumors of many other attacks on every news channel.

In our neighborhood there would be bomb threats for the rest of the week. Often, we saw groups of people run and scream, for no other reason besides sheer terror. Crazed New Yorkers beat on the locked front doors of our building, begging for refuge from the devastation on the street and in the air. Our apartment became a safe haven that day for friends and acquaintances who had been downtown and now couldn't get home due to the lack of subway and taxi service.

As it turns out, in the confusion of the day there were no police barricades erected around the perimeter of the Twin Towers. People were free to go into either building as they pleased. Fran tells a story of how she and Xavier ran from the oncoming debris, while many others were swept into it. Fran took some haunting and remarkable photos that day and sold several images of the collapsing first tower to various newspapers and magazines.

As night fell on our neighborhood, every street below Houston—which included ours—was quarantined. Any individual who lived downtown had to show photo ID and proof of residence in order to gain access through the police barricades. Our neighborhood was under constant police surveillance, so Josh and Xavier, who had decided they wanted to stay with us, didn't leave our apartment all week for fear that they wouldn't be permitted back in.

The next few days, and especially the nights, have become lost time to me. I know that every morning I woke up to an inappropriately bright, sunny day, and couldn't believe that I was alive or that the universe hadn't simply stopped, or that the sun hadn't burnt out. That's what it felt like to us. Every morning I walked Fran to the subway she took to work, both of us in a haze, holding hands tightly, not needing to speak in order to know what the other was feeling. I would hug her goodbye and, since NYU was closed, proceeded with my daily errands. These consisted mostly of tracking down food, which for about four days was extremely difficult to find. But none of it was for me because I had stopped eating entirely. I didn't feel I deserved to eat, and walking around physically empty gave me an emotional release. I *felt* completely empty. It also wasn't difficult to fast since every grocery store, deli, and convenience store was either entirely out of food, or selling expired meats and dairy products.

One morning, on my single-minded quest for the milk the boys had specifically requested, I found myself walking over forty blocks and stopping in each store I could find. I walked up Broadway and was the only person on the street. I had never seen the city so wounded and abandoned. After six or seven minutes of walking the only other visible signs of life were three huge military tanks rolling slowly by. I stopped and watched the camouflage-clad soldiers as shivers raced down my spine. I was now living in a war-torn state, and all I wanted was a bottle of milk. If I could only find milk my problems would be solved. If I could only find milk everything would be fine and we would all be safe.

This kind of single-minded thinking is an innate part of my personality and has contributed greatly to my anorexia. It's a belief that if I focus on and fix one specific thing, all of life's troubles will consequently be solved. In high school the obsession centered on my grades, in college it was weight and sizes, and coming out of Renfrew, where I was monitored and forced to eat, I concentrated on shopping and collecting certain objects. For a time after September 11th the focus turned to the pursuit of food, particularly milk.

I finally did find milk, but I happened to wrap my eager fingers around the carton at the same time as a desperate father on speakerphone with his pregnant wife and little child. The man's family was hungry and frantic for milk, and he was attempting to calm them both down. Of course, I handed him the carton I had spent three hours and eighty blocks searching for.

I walked out of the "milk deli," and the memory of a story my mom once told me struck me hard. We had lived in Romania when Fran was three years old, my mom was pregnant with me, and Communist oppression was at its height. There were daily food lines and each person, depending on his age, social status, and health, was allowed a precise amount of food. My sister had a ticket for two slices of bread a day, while my grandfather, a prominent doctor, could get a whole round loaf of the good stuff. One morning after my father went to work, my very pregnant mother realized she had nothing to feed Fran for breakfast. She went downstairs and joined the long food queue but decided to expedite the process by having Fran wait for eggs while my mom procured the bread. When my infant sister got to the front of her line she was immediately laughed at and sent away. Little kids weren't really considered people and my mother, who had run to her rescue, violently chastised the woman who'd denied a small child just one egg.

That day my mother vowed she would get out of Romania and go to a land of freedom, where a person would never have to fight for such basic rights as food. Freedom for my mom meant the ability to live up to personal goals and not abide by the rules of a tyrannical government.

That day I couldn't find milk anywhere. Strangely, I felt more disappointed and worried for my mother than I did for myself. I couldn't believe that after my parents had risked their lives and spent years relocating to wherever an immigrant family from Eastern Europe might find the best life, this was happening again. I couldn't believe that in the place my mom had dreamed of living ever since she heard the word America, her only two children now existed in a state of fear and grief because of a terrorism similar to the one she'd sacrificed so much to leave behind. I knew that once I got home I would have nothing to show for my day, except for an internal revelation that has lived with me ever since.

Before entering the war-torn zone of my closed-off neighborhood I realized it was already close to 7 p.m. and my sister would be on her way home from work. I had left the house that morning at 10:30 and could not figure out how I'd spent the entire day, other than hunting for milk. I couldn't believe that task alone had occupied eight hours. During that entire time I'd been convinced that each moment would be my last. I was furious. Was this all my life consisted of? Mindless, fruitless, pointless errands that resulted in nothing, meant nothing, and eventually added up to nothing? I was starting to believe life was nothing more than a meaningless journey for milk you could never actually find.

That night I picked Fran up from work at the A train station, on the corner of 6th Avenue and West 4th Street. This was the subway I had taken to get home during freshman year when I lived in a dorm on Washington Square Park. Back then everything had still been innocent and fresh, though I was already beginning to self-destruct. The city had been full of wonderment, but now I could see my former playground with new eyes. Nothing was pure anymore. Things were evil and malicious. The vigilant mourners praying around the park's fountain were helpless. The young men screaming ethnic slurs at two guys who looked Middle Eastern were wicked. Who knows, maybe even the two men running were up to no good. The ominous shoes and jackets left on the street, which still hadn't been picked up, struck me with fresh pain. And my sister, despondently dragging her feet, was so vulnerable that the sight of her literally broke me apart. Just two days ago I had been sure I'd lost Fran in the debris of the falling Twins. Now, hours later, I was scared I'd lose her again, that her spirit was shattered. I was scared it was only a matter of time before we—the other set of twins—finally toppled.

When Fran and I saw each other we hugged silently. Then we walked home through the park, eyeing all the mourners with their signs, candles, and tears. We looked at each other wordlessly, as if to say, "Should we join them?" and then silently agreed not to, because what good would it do anyway? Near the police barricade two blocks north of our building, we pulled out our IDs and Fran produced a letter that had been addressed to both of us. The cops smiled, already familiar with the two sisters, and let us pass. As though there was a glass shield surrounding downtown Manhattan, a few short steps away the air became thick, gray, hot, and nearly impenetrable again. Without uttering a word we covered our faces with the bandanas we now wore permanently around our necks. I don't know how much protection they offered, but at least it was easier to breathe in the smell of my own perfume rather than the scent of burning bodies and asbestos. I rather like my scarf, I thought. It was purple, my favorite color, and the one my aunt Lia had bought for me in Egypt, a place I'd always wanted to visit but was now sure I'd never see.

Back at home there was more disappointing news. Our toilet no longer flushed and the water barely worked. It wasn't really bad, just annoying. Nothing was really bad news after 9/11. After all, we were alive. There was no way we could call a plumber since almost everyone had stopped working and the luxury of calling someone to fix a problem was no longer something we seriously considered doing. This wasn't a vital issue, so we just had to accept the poor plumbing, food shortage, brown water, dirty air, and constant feelings of terror and depression. When the toilet became unusable we went downstairs and asked the owner of Milady's—our neighborhood bar, which we'd frequented quite often—if we could borrow his bathroom. We were granted free access to functional plumbing. These were joyous moments.

A couple of days later my sister came back from work and told us she had opened an envelope full of white powder. I was still out of school and spent my days providing for the house-bound Josh and Xavier, meeting Fran at the subway, and trying to keep in touch with my parents. When Fran told me her story the anthrax scare was in full force, and news agencies like my sister's were all on high alert, along with governmental and post offices. Fran had heard about the symptoms associated with anthrax, and an old woman in our area had already died after touching an envelope that had been contaminated.

Unfortunately, my sister is a hypochondriac. She'd memorized all the symptoms—not difficult to do, since they were discussed constantly on all the news channels to the point where you almost wished you *could get* anthrax just so you wouldn't have to hear about it anymore. So Fran became convinced she had the disease and would soon die. But she put on a brave face, went back to work every day, and waited patiently for her illness to manifest itself. If I hadn't known my sister I would have thought she truly was on the brink of death. But having known her my whole life, I couldn't even be sure she'd come into contact with any powdery substance. Every time I asked her to recite the specifics of the incident they were slightly modified until the whole story had morphed into a new one.

Just to be safe, my mom had my aunt Lia and my uncle Andi, both doctors in Toronto, ship us the anthrax antibiotics that were impossible to find in New York at the time. Lia sent an order large enough to last all four of us several weeks. I was also given explicit instructions to keep the medication hidden from Fran and only give her antibiotics if she came down with any symptoms. Otherwise Fran would probably panic and medicate herself unnecessarily. Starting that night I surreptitiously examined Fran as much as possible without making her suspicious. I pretended to watch TV but actually inspected my sister as she vacuumed the living room or walked around the apartment. She never came down with anything. A few days later, she sold the first photograph she'd taken downtown on 9/11.

After the anthrax scare passed I had an overwhelming urge to get out of New York. I didn't care how—I just needed to be able to breathe again, if only for a few days. I booked tickets on Amtrak for Josh and me to leave that night. When he protested I slapped him full force across the face. He didn't protest anymore after that. In fact, he didn't speak to me for the next few hours. He left to go back to his apartment on the Upper West Side before meeting me at Penn Station, so Fran walked me to the subway station. We left our place, marched down six flights of stairs, opened the door, put on our scarf masks, and passed the police barricade where by now there was a constant influx of curious photographers and onlookers. Everyone wanted to see what the residents of the closed-off neighborhood looked like and what life was like for us. I'd never felt more like a *National Geographic* cover story. At that point, I had decided to wear only black for the rest of the year. I had on my favorite black Jackie O–style dress, the purple damask silk scarf around my head and nose, and oversized Armani sunglasses. A man with a wide-angle zoom lens camera snapped a picture in my face then quickly asked if he could publish it as he walked away. I hardly cared at that point.

We arrived at the subway stop and I looked into Fran's huge blue eyes and asked her if she would come with me. She said no in the way she does when she really means it and will put up a fight if you utter one more word. So I let it go, gave her a hug, wondered again if I would see her upon my return, or if in my absence something else would happen to wash away New York and my twin. Then I turned around and didn't look back. On the subway I was surrounded by people giving up their seats, smiling at each other, and showing kindness to their neighbors. Everybody's body language said, "We're in this together." I've never had a more pleasant and frightening subway ride in my life. Needless to say, New York is no longer like that, but I prefer New York rude. It means nothing bad has happened in a while.

It Must Be | September

I arrived at Penn Station and located Josh just as we were forced to evacuate the building. There had been yet another bomb threat in the city and the police were appropriately taking it seriously. I remember calmly picking up my bag—full of food I never intended to eat—and walking slowly out onto the street. Nothing really fazed me anymore, and I could no longer muster the energy to panic. I had prepared for an emergency by bringing two huge bags of potato chips and a gallon-sized Tupperware container full of stale pasta. Yet I continued to fast. When we were finally given permission to reenter the station, Josh and I sat down at T.G.I. Friday's to wait for our delayed train. He ordered a beer and I got a slice of chocolate cake, even though I knew I wouldn't even touch it. Instead, I sat staring at it in contempt as though it had perpetrated a crime against me.

An hour later we were on the train. I looked out my window to see the trees of New Jersey, Connecticut, and Massachusetts whiz by, and realized they had already started to change color. Life was going on outside of Manhattan, a site where everything had nearly stopped. I took comfort in nature, the scenery, and in the fact that I could finally breathe without consuming acrid, choking air. I was sorry Fran had stayed behind, but she'd said she needed to see the city rebuild itself around her. She had to *see* it happen.

When I got off the train, Josh's dad picked us up and cheerfully asked how our trip had been. I realized he was probably uncomfortable or at a loss for words, but I wished he could acknowledge what we'd just lived through. Watching him hug Josh, however, the relief he felt about his only son's safety was palpable. The three of us made awkward small talk while driving the rest of the way to my parents' Brookline house. Before I could even get out of the car my parents and grandmother Elena were outside waiting to envelop us in their open arms. I was home, everything around me was the same, but I had been changed forever. I realized September 11th would always evoke the same dreadful emotions.

In the land of 9/11, my anorexia was able to flourish. As days of fasting went by I felt as though physical incapacity would be my decision rather than the result of some random act of inhumanity. Anorexia is conniving. I was convinced that I was in control and that the only way I could continue to wake up every morning and merely exist was by neglecting to do that which bonds us all together—eating.

In one of my favorite Bob Dylan songs, *Lay Lady Lay,* he asks, "Why wait any longer for the world to begin when you can have your cake and eat it too?" Years after I stopped eating I couldn't bear to listen to Dylan's raspy inquisitions. Life, after all, was about suffering and deprivation, something I had learned a great deal about that September.

A year later, the night after my appointment with Adelaide, I lay in bed and opened the gates of my mind to the images of falling buildings and crashing lives. They had been loudly knocking around in my skull looking for release. A year had been too long to carry them around unshared. Maybe I could be more open with people and discuss my burdensome fears. Maybe I could enjoy life again. Maybe I *could* have my cake and eat it too. Maybe happiness was possible even though things had exploded all around and throughout me. Maybe if I could survive I could also, eventually, make sense of it all. Yes, maybe even in September.

Chapter Six

Mom's In Bed

"Ode to an Anorexic Mother"

My mother is a pilgrim with new-old shoes and leather bindings around
my heart,
and her legs. But I don't follow — my legs don't carry me that far.
My mother is teetering — it's what she's most afraid of. She's on the
edge and needs a home — a haven, cave, tent, nest, nook, leather
bindings, old-new fixtures, and dimmed bright lights . . . But she's a
nomad — a pilgrim — for always.
My mother is a nomad. What does that say about me?
My mother is a nomad. She gave away her home to me. She built
me a safe haven that is her. With soft, broken-in, new leather
straps, and old–new boots, which I will never use, or even try
exploring the outback with.
I have a safe place, and I sit . . . because it's her!
My mother is a nomad, and she carries me every day without tire.
She shows me the music of my place; not realizing it's herself. But I am
tired and I am safe and I have left her homeless.
My mother is a pilgrim with shells in her hat and beauty in her.
So much beauty that I am tired — and she never stops.
High ground, rough terrain, Mother, Mother Nomad, Mother Pilgrim,
Mother Earth. I am just a shell sitting in your hat, whispering in
your ear.

A few weeks after my September 11th meeting with Adelaide, just weeks after my return from Renfrew, I completely stopped eating again. The proper term for this is "lapse" and technically it can be overcome more easily than a long-term relapse. For me, there were no words to describe what I was feeling. Instead I just existed, waiting for the despair and panic that came at me in a rush, merciless and devastating. This would leave me limp and unfeeling, as though I simply could not take anything in anymore, including food. I was becoming one-dimensional again. I was devolving, again. I was left hopeless that I could ever exist in a world that equated function with success because I could not function.

Since my parents had taken me out of Renfrew in the hopes that I could start rebuilding my life, my mom became panicky when she noticed what was happening to me. She was the first one to sense that I was lapsing and slowly losing the belief that I could recover. She felt guilt. If I died now it would be her fault, she believed. She had agreed to let me leave Renfrew and come home.

The night of my Renfrew departure, my parents and I had worked out an agreement over the phone. I promised them I'd regularly see a nutritionist in Boston, create and follow a meal plan, and eat all of my meals in front of my family. Theoretically, my meal plan would slowly evolve and by the time I went back to New York I would be able to eat and function again. I agreed to this, although nobody outside of Renfrew had seen me eat in years. Somebody asking me to eat in public was the equivalent of showering in public—it seemed a highly voyeuristic act. It felt like an extreme intrusion on my privacy to have other people sit and watch me eat, but I was willing to take this extremely personal act into the public arena in exchange for my Renfrew release. I also knew that "normal" people enjoyed eating out. Maybe one day I could be normal, too.

That first night back from Renfrew I fixed my bowl of food—mostly cottage cheese, strawberries, and milk—and sat down with my mom, dad, and Josh. Everyone was overwhelmed at the sight of me consuming something solid, even though the mash I was now eating looked like something hospital patients eat. The three of them sat around the square, rustic table in the kitchen and stared at their hands, the wall, or straight ahead. Nobody dared look in my direction for fear of spooking me. A few comments were passed around about the weather or politics, but none of them were addressed to me. Even Caramel waited off to the side and didn't beg for food as she usually did.

The general mood was a mix of reverent silence and giddy, unbelieving happiness that I was eating (expressed by the goofy grins on my dad and Josh's faces) and a deeply entrenched fear that I would stop again. I felt this anxiety. It was palpable. It came from my mom. The whole time I ate my strawberries and milk dinner she had an artificial smile on her face and a furrowed brow.

When I finished my dinner forty-five minutes later, my dad and Josh cheered and went to celebrate dinner by playing a round of backgammon, but my mom stayed with me in the kitchen, quiet and somber. She wasn't pleased. We sat there and made small talk, interrupted once by Josh who came to get a glass of water in preparation for the big game with my dad. He approached my mom and said, "Aren't you happy, Mama? The baby ate!" My mom forced a smile and turned to him, saying, "Yeah, I know, Josh, it's great." Josh was placated but I felt deflated. If I ever needed support in my life, it was now. Instead of holding me up I could tell that she was being overtaken by her doubts and fears. I didn't know if I wanted to keep eating just to prove her wrong, or to give up, since if she suspected I couldn't do it then I probably couldn't.

Anorexics experience a sense of power, calm, and well-being when we deprive ourselves. By looking frightful and skeletal we are simultaneously pushing people away in a most destructive, passive-aggressive way, and challenging those we love to accept us and fight for us, regardless. It is a complete breakdown, mentally, emotionally, and physically. Food becomes symbolic of that which we can't control but must, that which we absolutely need but absolutely reject. Attempting to detangle oneself from this complicated interplay between pleasure and pain, destruction and creation, is in fact a metaphysical struggle for the very life and survival that become increasingly impossible to grasp. Anorexia comes from within; it is not an invention of the media or a disease owned by celebrities. Still, we live in an eating-disordered, dysfunctional society, where anorexia is glorified and adulated.

Anorexia is not a crash diet. You don't want to look thin; you want to scare people by how wasted you can become. You want to warn everyone to keep their distance. You want to look like death, a Halloween skeleton walking among the living. Because to you, every freakish day is Halloween, and your exterior appearance is a physical manifestation of the pain inside. Eventually you stop yelling, crying, or expressing emotion as the anorexia itself becomes a silent scream.

Despite all this, you are still a human being. You still have to finish daily chores and perform mundane activities, just like everybody else. You can't stop absolutely everything just to hurt. That's the way it works, and if the people who love you don't realize this, they will listen only to the anorexia and believe it's their daughter, sister, or wife talking. If the people closest to you, those who know you best, group you and the illness into a single category then you will do the same. The most dangerous aspect of anorexia is losing your identity and becoming the anorexia. As Steven Levenkron, author of *Best Little Girl in the*

World, says, "You want to meet the most boring person in the world? I'll show you a chronic anorexic." Why? Because it's no fun talking to a person who's morphed into a disease. The disease only wants to talk about itself. How interesting can that be in a world full of richness and complexity?

After a few weeks of meeting with my friend Adelaide, who had temporarily empowered me, I still lacked a fundamental understanding of what my anorexia was and how to begin disentangling myself from it. It became just too easy to revert, and so I did. I know that my mom was truly, sincerely betrayed by what had happened to me. What had gone wrong? Why had I let myself become like this? Of course I understood her sense of confusion and fear. I would have felt betrayed too. But I never consciously chose to become anorexic, and now my anorexia was using its voice in place of my own.

Other than meeting regularly with Adelaide, I spent most of my time in my house, watching TV, sleeping a lot during the day and not at all at night, lying in bed staring at my walls and ceiling, calling Josh and crying, writing in my journal, and reading. My dad was always working and I barely saw or spoke to him. My mom began to sink into a very deep state of depression and I began to lose contact with her and lose her as a friend. I knew she was going through a crisis of faith, questioning everything she had previously believed in. I knew my parents were fighting and barely communicating. I knew I wouldn't get any support from my father or sister if I pushed my mom to see a therapist. Just as I originally sought help for my illness after being encouraged by those who loved me, I now began to slip away because I was left alone to communicate solely with my anorexia. Every day I spent endless hours in my room. I spoke to my anorexia in my head, and it told me to once again stop eating, to make myself frail and helpless.

Worst of all, it said nobody loved me. It told me that the very person who had created me was tired of me, so tired she had stopped talking to me. It told me that I had a deep, unknowable flaw that doomed me to a lifetime of solitude. It told me that I was simply not made to be in this world, to prosper or be happy. I was malfunctioning and there was no way to fix me. If I left my anorexia, my only and most loyal friend, then I would *really* be alone. Then I would *really* know fear, darkness, and cold.

I swallowed everything the anorexic part of myself fed me— it was my only sustenance. I sank into a depression so great I lost track of hours and days, wallowing solely in my failure, misery, and impotence. The only relief came from talking to Adelaide.

Then I began shopping fanatically, uncontrollably. I wasn't just shopping for clothes, however. I bought dishes, glassware, towels—anything that could make me feel at home. I had never felt unwelcome in my own house, but now here I was, return-ing from the bleakest place I had ever known, only to find that my home had become even more hostile. I felt like I had nowhere to go, like I was destroying my mom, her marriage, and her ability to cope. I tried desperately to create a niche for myself, a place that had my stamp on it. So, in my embarrassing simplicity, I bought dishtowels and placed them all around the kitchen, only to have my parents get more annoyed by my apparent lack of effort in dealing with my illness.

Instead of dealing with my old problem I had found a new addiction. It wasn't just about purchasing an item. I was trying to distract myself from the world that was falling apart around me by focusing instead on easy, simple things, like plates. I was attempting to make a new nest for myself, a place where I could feel somewhat comfortable, surrounded by familiar objects. I was also using my parents' credit cards. They were getting billed for things they didn't need or want, while I tried to get a quick fix for the deep, throbbing hole in my heart. This feeling was ripping to shreds the lively, happy girl who'd once had a future.

I grew terrified of the time of month when I knew the credit card bills would arrive and land heavily in my father's hands. October was particularly fear-filled, because I knew what I had done that month. After the daily rigor of appointments and supervised meals, I always had a few free hours to walk around Boston, one of my favorite cities in the world, and do what I wanted. That October I purchased all sorts of things—things I can't even remember, and things I knew I didn't need. I just wanted to feel like they were mine. I remember going into Crate and Barrel and Pottery Barn, even though I didn't know what I would do with most of the objects I purchased. I fantasized about my family sitting around a beautifully decorated table, with new crystal dishes and perfect, matching outfits, enjoying one another's company. I didn't fantasize about the food or actual eating, just the sitting, like in a universe where animation has been suspended and a scene can be kept forever—smooth, simple, and pleasant.

My reality was the exact opposite of what I dreamed. For the first five weeks following my return from Renfrew, I was observed, analyzed, and discussed constantly by parents who were now attempting to take on the role of novice therapists. This was especially strange because the relationship I'd enjoyed with them had always been one of mutual respect and understanding. We had been mutual advisors and friends, and sometimes I'd even felt like the parent myself. I couldn't remember a time when I'd gotten in trouble with my parents, or been grounded or punished. If someone was disappointed with me, it was usually me.

When the October bill arrived, however, I knew I would be in serious trouble with the two people I'd worked my entire life to please. So I developed a plan. I would sort through the mail every day, aided by my accomplice Caramel, whose barking would alert me to the mailman's presence. Then I would find the credit card bills, separate them from the pile, and stash them in a secret spot. That was it. That was my entire plan! I didn't think of what would happen when the bills didn't get paid, or let myself worry about how my actions might ruin my father's credit—this in addition to the mountain of medical expenses I had left him with. I refused to think about the day that I would not only have to explain why I'd spent so much, but also why I'd hidden the bills and created bigger problems. I simply did not think about the consequences; I just went ahead with my lame scheme.

My plan was so much like my anorexia. I spent each day getting away with something I knew simply could not last a lifetime, while refusing to contemplate the fact that if I didn't die (or get caught), I would somehow, one day, have to crawl out of the enormous hole I'd dug for myself. This was a deep, dark void I could have avoided in the first place if I had found the courage to really examine myself.

Every anorexic has deep issues, and they aren't *really* the desire to be skinny, starve oneself, exercise maniacally, or lose weight. Those are just the symptoms we display when we ignore the true problem and choose, instead, to stop eating—and, in my case, to purchase every frivolous item I could find. The hard part, certainly, is identifying the real problem, and then, slowly, painstakingly, fixing it. I wasn't at a place in my life when I could even see the true nature of my disease, and the hidden credit card bills proved it.

A few days after I stole the statements I began to feel extremely nervous and guilty. My dad was wondering aloud what could have happened to the bill and whether or not he should call the credit card company. Ready to snap from all the pressure, I finally removed the crumpled invoice from my desk drawer and brought it downstairs to my father. I can't remember what I said, but I will never forget how embarrassed I felt. What made things horrible beyond belief was his look of unabashed shock at my pathetic scheme. Here I was, his daughter, stealing his mail, taking his money for things I didn't need, and worst of all, living at home after my early hospital release but making no progress. By all standards I was a failure. Recovering from the embarrassment of those weeks and trying to forgive myself for the heartbreak I had caused my parents is something that still makes me cringe.

Things got impossibly worse. That night my mom brought

me into the sunroom for a talk. She sat me down and told me how upset she was with me, how utterly disappointed that I wasn't, after all, the person she thought I was. She thought I was strong, but I had proven myself to be weak. She had hoped I understood the meaning and true value of life, but in fact I was shallow and vain, obsessed with material possessions, deceptive in my spending habits. She had prayed I would work hard to fight for my life and overcome my illness, but now she no longer saw any fight left in me. I sat there staring at the woman who had always been able to imbue me with strength by saying a few words or giving me a single look. She had meant more to me in my life than anyone, and now that little piece of strength was gone. I had lost—not just my battle with anorexia, but also the one relationship I desperately needed in order to continue fighting. I had always believed (and still strongly do) that a mother plays the most essential role in the life of an anorexic girl. In that moment my world was squeezed into a microscopic box. I felt there wasn't any trace left of me, and, therefore, no hope. I thought I might as well give up.

I don't blame my mom for what she said, and I never did. She was fearful. She saw me acting out in new, crazy ways, and she wanted to get a hold of me. Sometimes people simply can't find a way to communicate, and that wreaks disaster in their lives. Yet, when I ask my mom about that day, those twenty minutes, she simply does not remember what she said. She says she can't recall one sentence that was passed between us, and I believe that to be true. I know how traumatic that moment was, and often when we undergo a traumatic event our brain does us the favor of forgetting and erasing it. Maybe my mom does remember, but has decided to abandon that terrible memory for the sake of our relationship. Today, writing this down, I release it.

After that conversation my mom took to her bed. When I wanted to be around her I would tiptoe into her room and lie down on the floor next to her. She wouldn't open her eyes or move, but I knew she wasn't asleep. One afternoon, as I lay on the hard, wooden floor of the bedroom that smelled so much like her, I remembered being eight years old, sitting on my parents' bed and reading her my favorite book, *The Land That Time Forgot*. It was about a baby dinosaur and a mother dinosaur. When the mother, Big Foot, got trapped under a pile of fallen rocks, she urged her baby, Little Foot, to go on without her and never feel alone, because she would somehow always be with him. I would read this to my mom every night, and at the end we would both be sobbing next to each other, purging all our sadness and feelings of loss.

Lying on the floor next to my mom twelve years later I felt her grief but could no longer share it with her. I so much wanted to be little again, to climb onto her bed, give her a semi-toothless grin, and cry with her until we laughed at ourselves and each other. We'd been in the game together once, but now, twelve years later, we were not. We were sharing the same space, but inhabiting very different rooms in our lives. I felt as though my mom had shut off and abandoned me. I was helpless to do anything for myself, or her. I couldn't affect anything around me. It's as though I became a ghost haunting my mother's room, haunting her thoughts. It's as though I didn't exist at all.

When I wasn't lying down on my mom's floor, I would just walk into her room and check on her. The area that had once contained paint, brushes, ink, canvas, and all the other supplies she needed to do her work now seemed barren, suffocating, and always gray, heavy, and empty. Everything seemed to be on hold; but in fact, life was continuing without us. My mom and I didn't talk for days, maybe even weeks, after she got into bed. My home began to feel intimidating and foreign, and my mom's room was becoming a planet that looked creepily familiar but was now barren of warmth or love.

My mom and I hadn't always had an easy relationship. We had to build our friendship and work on it. We'd had to find each other and discover each other years before. I had always been a difficult, capricious child. I didn't accept my mom just because she was "mom" like my sister did. I looked at her as a fellow human being, someone who I had to learn about in order to connect with. The only person I never felt that way about was my sister, Fran. When I was growing up, my mom and I had a circuitous relationship where she would try to understand my personality while I would constantly, surreptitiously examine her. I always loved her and she was always completely devoted to me and Fran, but we weren't always the friends we are now.

I believe my suspicion of my mom began when I was six years old and she was a young architecture student at the University of Toronto. As a graduation requirement, she had to spend one mandatory semester in Rome, studying Old World art and architecture. But for a small child who relied on her mother, the requirements involved in fulfilling one's life dream were incomprehensible and mattered very little. I understood only my own anguish and knew the pain of missing her would be frightening and terrible.

On the night she left for Italy two strange men knocked on our Toronto apartment door, grabbed my mother's suitcases, and beckoned her to follow. My mom, with a broken expression that mirrored her aching grief and guilt, gave us each a hug, walked away, and didn't turn back. Fran and I stood in the doorway, watching her follow her two colleagues, and the entire time—thirty seconds that felt like years in my small life—I willed her to turn around just once more. I thought I would never see her again.

My mom, Michaela, had very little money while in Rome, but when she did manage to call I avoided speaking to her. My grandmother, Elena, and Fran replaced my mom for me, and when my dad went to Romania for several weeks things got even easier. A clean break from both parents helped me erase my past and start fresh at six years of age. I no longer wanted anything to do with them, especially my mother.

My mom finally came home six months later, but by that point I didn't care where she'd been, what she'd done, or where she'd purchased the gifts she tried to bribe me with. I now know my mom skipped countless lunches and dinners to afford all the presents she brought back.

Unlike me, my sister rejoiced in our mother's return and understood much better why she'd left in the first place. Fran had always known that our mother would come back. I'm not certain if this knowledge was born of age and comprehension (at ten years old, Fran seemed to know everything), or if it came about because Fran understood our mother better. Maybe it was a result of pure, blind faith. All I felt for certain was that my mom was virtually a stranger. I also decided that if she could leave once, she could easily do it again.

When she came into my room the night of her return I rejected her and almost all the gifts she offered. The crazy European clothing was stupid compared to the purple corduroy pants I wore to school almost every day, or the green-and-red velvet dress I donned on special occasions. The purple suede round-toe shoes she eagerly presented were returned with a shrug of the shoulders and a scoff. Although now I wish I had that same pair in a size 8½ they were so very cool. The only thing I accepted was a piece of candy bearing the image of a mustached man, and later, another sweet shaped like a strawberry, which, I was shocked to discover, even tasted like strawberry. Those Italians thought of everything!

The night my mom returned nobody cared what time I went to bed. The mood in our house was jubilant and charged. My dad was home, Fran could go back to being my sister and not my very young surrogate mother (although she never did relinquish that role), and my grandmother could get more time to herself. But for me nothing had changed. In the past six months I had grown distrustful. Where had my mother been? What had she done? What was Rome, this strange place where every piece of candy had its own distinct personality? Most importantly, what was to prevent her from leaving again, this time for good?

At the start of November, after two months in Boston with

my parents, I decided it was time to go back to New York. My mom and I still weren't speaking. I was older now, but still I felt very poignantly that childhood disconnect that had begun when she had gone to Italy. I was certain that because of my illness she would never see me the same way again and our friendship would be over. This thought nearly destroyed me, yet I knew there was nothing I could do to prove I was her same daughter. I could not convince her I was still the girl she'd raised, shared misery and happiness with, loved and supported through the good times—like walking in the leaves at Newton Country Day School—as well as the bad, like dropping me off at Renfrew and driving away. I could only go on with my life, and maybe she would give me another chance. Maybe someday we could be friends again.

I flew back to Manhattan and Josh picked me up at the airport. I was going back to live with him in his parents' Murray Hill apartment. Everyone agreed it wasn't a good idea for me to be on my own. I didn't want to feel isolated now that I wasn't returning to school, and my family was afraid that if left to my own devices I would be capable of any kind of self-destruction. Josh could at least provide some supervision and help with anything I needed, even if that was just companionship. That was the one thing I now missed very deeply.

The apartment was being renovated when I returned to New York. In fact, there really was no apartment. Everything had been demolished; a lone fridge stood in the center of what had once been the living room, and in the bedrooms and bathrooms there was nothing but a bed and a working shower. Josh hadn't told me the apartment was such a wreck, and he explained that since I'd been so miserable he hadn't wanted to further upset me by describing what our new home really looked like. Walking into the apartment made every hair stand up at the back of my neck. This was a nightmare. I had gone from being in a home I felt was no longer mine to living in a disheveled mess with a barely functional toilet, which we had to share with eight construction workers every day. I didn't have a place of my own where I could feel comfortable and safe. I didn't even have my mom to talk about it with.

Seeing the panic in my face, Josh put down my bag and took me to our neighborhood Starbucks. Since I'd stopped eating, I had developed a love affair with Starbucks. Josh and I sat and talked and I was grateful for his friendship, but I desperately missed my mom. My mom and I had exchanged a few words before I left, but it was polite, impersonal conversation. The pain and frustration of it was the only thing that filled me up those days. Along with everything else came the added stress of beginning regular appointments with Dr. Klab, who had sent me to Renfrew. That was the deal I'd made with my parents. My unhappiness was overwhelming.

That night I called home and my mom answered. This time we actually began to talk. I knew she had been thinking about the past two months I had spent at home and wanted to begin working on our relationship again. She began telling me about what had been going through her mind those endless days in bed, with me lying on the floor next to her. I began to understand, for the first time, the trauma and grief my mom was living with on a daily basis. I said nothing and for hours just sat on the phone and listened to her.

She told me, "Now I realize how wrong I was. I was interpreting your actions as though they were coming from you, but they weren't. It was your anorexia. I felt betrayed by you, like you were lying to me, deceiving me, but now I realize you were just letting your anorexia take control and do the deciding in your life. You can't let your anorexia run your life anymore. You can't let it do the talking, the deciding anymore. I'm sorry for confusing you with your disease. I feel terrible. I'm not going to listen to the illness anymore," she told me. And it made sense.

Then she said, "Let me talk to my baby. I want to talk to Laura." I knew she was right, that she could see through me. I realized that she still knew me, still loved me. I know that after

I left Boston that bleak November afternoon, my mom got the courage and strength to get out of bed and fight for her life, for mine, and for us. Suddenly the world was not so alien anymore, the apartment not so disheveled. Suddenly I had a place where I belonged, the same place I came from—my mother. I had always had it, we had just lost our way to each other in the dark, but we had also both been searching. I realized then that even out of the most hopeless situations we can rise again, like waking up to a sparkling new day after a long night's darkness and unrest. Even after a long night in bed.

Chapter Seven

The Klub

To you I may soon be gone, and that is speakable.
When we talk it is as though you are saying your farewells,
and when we smile it is only for a reference page in the
marked book of effects.
I am important, yes, but vanishing
. . . and then what am I but a thought?
Your thought, and only yours?
Let me be more eccentric, more memorable, more
compulsive! Surely, our humanness will betray us if I am
not! Surely, I'll be summed up to a point — a fleck.
Like the stars that I thought you purposely drowned to
effortlessly support me from sinking, then being engulfed.
Well, I am engulfed now.
You know.
Every moment is a goodbye. I am your goodbye . . . and then
what will I be?
Your thought? Your only thought?
Your destruction, devastation, damnation, carnal thought —
consumed?

Walking down University Place at seven in the morning I felt like the only person in downtown Manhattan. I could hear my three-inch heels clip-clopping. I was walking to my own beat. If I never had to go anywhere special or do anything specific, I could have gone on forever, just walking, not too fast and not too slow, in time with my thoughts. I didn't have to be anywhere until 9 a.m., two hours away. I had to meet my former Irish professor, Lynn Alma, to try to complete the work I'd missed during my leave of absence. I knew why there was no one else walking beside me. I was in my old NYU neighborhood and college kids didn't get up that early. Even when I'd had an 8 a.m. class I never actually left my apartment before 7:50. Having a morning class in college is like being reincarnated as a worm—you must have done something very bad or very stupid to deserve it.

But now, college seemed like a million years ago, although it hadn't been so long since I'd been a college kid. Still, it was worlds away. By now all of my classmates, friends, and the world in general had moved forward without me and left me behind. So I was alone on University Place. Clip-clop, clip-clop—it was the only other audible noise besides the birds. This was the first time I had heard birds in Manhattan making more noise than the traffic and people. Being on campus in the early morning had definite, Zen-like merits. I wasn't sure why I'd gotten up so early or why I was now walking around with nothing to do. There was still plenty of time before my meeting with my Irish professor.

A week before this meeting I had emailed all of my former professors, but I had heard back from only two—Professor Alma, and one of the professors who taught a liberal arts class called "Violence" (an odd requirement in my program). The email I'd sent had taken me three hours to write. I couldn't decide whether to "come out" and inform my professors that I had left school because of my struggle with anorexia, or if I should use vague language like "eating disorder" or "personal problems." Anorexia fit under the banner of those more general problems.

My hesitation was a result of my shame. I was deeply uncomfortable discussing my illness with anybody. Now, trying to reenter the world, to fit into a bustling, functioning city like New York, I feared that I had an innate, unfixable, unacceptable flaw. I was terrified that there was something *fundamentally* wrong with me. While other people could deal with their lives and not self-destruct I was perpetually teetering on the edge, just because of my urge to simultaneously punish and soothe myself by not eating.

The final emails that were sent out included the word anorexia because I wanted to release that word along with all that it meant to me. I no longer wanted to carry that burden by myself. I wanted to be free. I sent my emails and imagined the text, made heavy with the "a" word, slowly flying away from me and into cyberspace—I wanted it gone.

Professor Alma was the first person to write back to me, and I attributed this speed to her being a woman and a mother. She assured me with great understanding that of course I could make up my work. She proposed that we meet once or twice a week at NYU's Ireland House in Washington Mews to go through all of my unfinished material. I was surprised by the ease with which she gave her sympathy. Just the idea that someone had the emotional capacity to be so generous to one anonymous student astounded me. I couldn't afford or understand that kind of giving anymore. To me, life had become only about survival. Favors were impossible.

My Violence professor, an older man, was a bit more cynical but still polite in his response. He explained I should visit him during his office hours and "we would see." I didn't know what to make of this email, but I felt hopeful enough. Maybe this was all it would take to get my life back on track. More than anything I wanted to graduate from college and be able to move on. After all my hard work in high school, countless sleepless nights, so much writing and studying, I desperately wanted a degree. I didn't care about my GPA, or what field my degree would ultimately be in. A degree was a starting point and I could build from there, attend graduate school, eventually specialize in my field of choice, and perhaps no longer feel like a ghost haunting a life that I'd lost.

All of these thoughts preoccupied me as I continued my stroll. I reached Washington Mews and was so happy to once again enter my favorite little Manhattan nook. The Mews had once been a row of stables for the horses of the wealthy people who lived in the adjacent 5th Avenue town houses. NYU eventually bought the Mews without changing the structure or architectural details. They now serve as the school's language department. I appreciated this kind of historical perpetuity in a city defined by restlessness.

I decided to enter the Mews and walk through the enormous, wrought iron gate that led into the narrow, cobblestone path flanked by skinny, brightly colored town houses. I walked past the Deutsche House, the Maison Français, and on and on until at the very bottom of the Mews, on 5th Avenue, another fence opened to reveal the Ireland House. It was, of course, painted a dark kelly green. Walking this path always made me feel like I was trespassing on the property of an eighteenth-century gentleman who would surely challenge me to a duel at dawn, or like I was visiting a quaintly artificial "Euro Village" in Disney World. Even after all I had been through, the magic of the Mews was not lost on me. I felt briefly like I was out of the overpowering city, because for a moment I was transported— the exact location was unimportant compared to the peaceful feeling of being enveloped by the secure little street.

I often told my friends about the history of the Mews and the Ireland House. After a while, Josh became so familiar with my impassioned lecture that he often beat me to it, giving his own rendition before we'd even reached our destination. On any given day, if we happened to be walking in that neighborhood, he would stop me and say things like, "We are about to walk past the Washington Meows, the location of the bloody cat gang fights that occurred in the late seventeenth and early eighteenth centuries. The little houses that you see on each side of the street represent the nationalities of cats that were the strongest and won most skirmishes."

I walked through Washington Mews and realized that I still had more than an hour before my meeting with Professor Alma. I was alone on this journey and felt scared and excited, nervous but brave, and somehow new in a way that I hadn't felt since I had first moved to New York. Even though I had been living in this city for nearly four years, my brief absence had made me lose my grip on it somehow. I realized that without constant attention and devotion New York will cruelly cheat on you, turn its back and find another lover so you're left behind, walking her seemingly empty streets. The city is mercurial and unapologetic, and maintaining one's love for it requires a certain amount of masochism. But here I was, starting over with New York, NYU, my body, and myself. I hadn't believed in second chances before, but now I thought that maybe I could begin again. Either way, I was thrilled to be a schoolgirl even for just this one day, and no longer a hospital girl—one of the institutionalized anorexics.

I called my mom to tell her that I was in the Mews. We had walked this same cobblestone path together several years ago, discussing the history and design of our favorite buildings. At that moment I realized that maybe I loved Washington Mews because it felt like a haven in the center of a cold city that had become unfamiliar, and now represented the hope I had for myself in dealing with my anorexia. My mind and body were alien, even to me, but perhaps out of the chaos of this illness there could emerge a new being, full of light. Even on the foreign, lonely streets an anorexic must tread, there can be a spot of rest, and from that place, good things can grow . . . orange things, yellow things, and most of all, kelly green things.

I finished describing my outfit to my mom that morning on the phone. This is something she still asks us to do when she misses Fran and me most, so that she can picture how we look and pretend she is with us in that moment. Perhaps a lot of our lives are lived this way, in our minds. That day I fit the image of a schoolgirl completely, with a sleeveless black dress, white knee socks, and high-heeled Mary Jane pumps. It was like the cool version of what I wore in fifth grade, and my mom and I had a good laugh about it. But everything was steeped in a kind of accepted sadness, something we were all getting used to as we dealt with this disease. Talking to my mom made the time pass quickly, and as I spotted Professor Alma I quickly ran over to meet her at the door of Ireland House.

I said good morning to her, and received a look of uncertainty in return. "Laura?" she asked hesitantly. She had no idea who I was. "You're looking better," she said, but I was convinced she had no image of a previous Laura to compare this one to. She was being polite in an awkward way.

"Thanks," I replied nervously, "and thanks for agreeing to meet with me and help me make up this work."

"Well, when I found out *what* it was that prevented you from finishing the class, I thought of course I would help you make it up. You know . . ."

Suddenly I felt anxious. First of all, I could not believe she didn't remember who I was. The student and Irish history lover in me felt disappointed for not having been a better, more vocal student in her class. I began to recall the many times I had raised my hand and made comments I'd thought were astute. The heated class debates that I so fully launched myself into now seemed wasted, juvenile, and foolish. It *all* seemed so pointless. I began to recall every other Irish professor I'd had at NYU (there had been a multitude) and how I knew something specific about each one, due to all the after-class talks we'd had about Ireland's past and present. I remembered how I'd met famous Irish authors at Ireland House, and how I'd been so chummy with them and all of the other professors there. I thought back to all my solo field trips, attending any photo exhibit, museum opening, or lecture that could further my knowledge of the Irish history and culture that I so adored. How could Professor Alma not remember me? She had talked to me about the Bloody Sunday exhibit at a photo gallery in midtown just a few months ago, and we had spoken about it after class many times.

The anorexic in me also reacted this way, but became even more agitated. I had been at a very low weight while attending her class and it was before her lectures that I always examined my frail body in the bathroom mirror and consistently found it to be huge and hideous. How could this professor not remember having an anorexic girl in her class a few months ago? I began to panic. I thought maybe I hadn't been skinny enough at the time, and certainly not skinny enough to scare people. I hadn't been memorably thin, and not thin enough to resonate in this woman's mind or leave a lasting impression. How could I now try to overcome my anorexia and start gaining weight? That would be a terrible mistake! If I hadn't been skinny then, what would I become now? These thoughts sent me into a frightening tailspin. I felt cold, clammy, uncomfortable in my own skin, and no longer able to make eye contact with her. I had been pulled back into my old world, and I realized that I was not an NYU student but a full-time anorexic.

Professor Alma must have noticed the change in my demeanor, but probably thought that I was nervous to be back and doing schoolwork again. She smiled at me and reassured me that the work was "doable." I no longer cared about the work; I only cared about the size of my body. She smiled at me again, this time a little more apprehensively, and asked me if I was all right.

I didn't answer for a moment. When it finally registered that I was acting strangely I forced a tight-lipped smile and told her that I was "a little tired." I could see relief make its visible mark on her face. This girl isn't crazy after all, she must have thought, just a little sleepy. I sat across from her, nodded at everything she said without actually listening, and privately gave in to all of the menacing, devastating voices that had once again taken over.

Two hours passed that way as I sat across from Professor Alma in Ireland House, a place that now seemed cold and decrepit, with musty, dirty green carpets. I looked outside the window and saw all of the busy students walking around campus in droves. I felt jealous of them all, and realized just how bitter I had become. Once in a while Professor Alma cut into my thoughts by asking me a question, which I would then answer in a kind of flippant, uninterested way. I was basically proving that she was right to have forgotten me as a student, but I simply couldn't focus on anything but the malicious voice in my mind.

At that point, I realized that I was already fifteen minutes late for my first appointment with Dr. Klab since leaving Renfrew. I didn't want to be late, but I was helpless to leave, overcome by a fear that everyone was staring at me, judging me, deciding that I was mentally insufficient and physically too big. I couldn't get up or move or tell Professor Alma that I had another engagement. So I simply sat in fear and shame, disappointment and grief. It wasn't until Professor Alma checked her watch and realized she had other things to do that my spell was broken. She stood up, told me to email her my work, and wished me luck. I was alone, late, and miserable.

I ran quickly down the winding stairs covered in the dull green carpet that now made my stomach lurch. Nothing is as disappointing as converting a happy memory into one full of vehement angst. The symbolism of my hasty departure from Ireland House was poignant to me, even as I was doing it. I was fleeing what I had once considered my "home base" at NYU.

It was a five-minute journey to Dr. Klab's office if I ran, but

I felt too tired for that kind of physical strain. I decided to call and let her know that I would still be showing up. I took out my cell phone and scrolled through the numbers. Those days most of the names read something like "Cheri, from Renfrew," or "Susan, from Remuda," and of course, there was one that simply said "The Klub." I pressed the number, hit talk, and waited for Dr. Klab to answer.

After four rings I thought she had either left or was no longer accepting my calls. I was perplexed, but also a bit relieved. The last thing I wanted was another hour-long discussion with a stranger about my life. Finally she answered, sounding extremely exasperated. Caught off guard I fumbled with my words, telling her I was late due to an appointment with a professor that ran over time. It seemed like I had become perpetually awkward.

Her unhappy, obviously annoyed response was, "You're twenty minutes late. Are you going to be here at all?"

Assuring her I'd be there soon, I hung up the phone and ran the rest of the way to the narrow pink and aqua building that her office was in. This pink thing had just replaced my formerly beloved Ireland House. It was now my new base in New York City, the building I would be visiting most often outside of my apartment. My new job was not to attend classes along with all my friends; it was to go to constant therapy sessions where I could hopefully find some answers and start to somehow mend.

As I walked into the bowels of the rose-colored monster, I thought, "Maybe, just maybe, I can have my cake and eat it too." This idea was followed by an immediate, weighty sigh that was my way of saying, "Probably not." As I stepped inside the elevator I silently cursed Bob Dylan. What kind of a cliché was he selling? Have my cake and eat it too? It sounded like an ad for an all-inclusive vacation, and suddenly had nothing to do with the reality of my life.

The elevator doors opened to the general waiting area that was shared by many psychiatrists, doctors, and therapists on Dr.

Klab's floor. I sat down, told the receptionist I had arrived, and waited for the big explosion. After two more minutes, I heard footsteps and then my name. I turned around and found a slightly pissed off Suse Klab glaring and motioning for me to follow her. The hallways and rooms of the building were mostly dark gray, and I hoped she hadn't changed the décor of her own office since it was one of the reasons I had chosen her as my psychiatrist in the first place.

Moments later I sat down on her soft leather couch and was relieved to see nothing had been rearranged in her Navajo-inspired space. The décor was in poor taste, but it made me simultaneously cringe and laugh. Maybe it was the incongruous nature of the situation that amused me. It was hard to imagine a person like Dr. Klab—six feet tall, somewhat burly, with a deep, aggressive voice—choosing to decorate in a kitschy south-western theme. I tried to imagine her choosing paint samples, carpets, furniture, and posters, but simply couldn't match her up with her office. Her workplace clashed so badly with the metropolitan city surrounding it that I wondered whether she really wanted to be in New York at all.

I was also perplexed by her personality, which was tough, bordering on mean. I had thought that was exactly what I needed—someone to beat me into submission and pound the anorexia out of me. I didn't realize at the time that I was beating myself up enough; there was no need for me to hire other people to help me do it. In truth, I was afraid of Dr. Klab. Her apathy and the strictly scientific way she talked about my disease always left me anxious and upset, but she never sensed that.

Dr. Klab was clearly annoyed with me that afternoon. I got the strong impression that no one ever dared to show up late for an appointment with her. We had only half an hour left in our session, and this was the first time I'd seen her in three months. She took out a little notepad and asked me to tell her about my experiences at Renfrew. I began to talk, and the meeting went by very quickly. It's easy to chatter when you don't make eye contact with someone, and I found myself mindlessly droning on with the general clichés most people use when speaking of anorexia. I wasn't talking about myself in any way I was rambling impersonally, but she either didn't notice or didn't care. I could just as easily have been reading a pamphlet I'd found on her desk.

At the end of our time I got up and said goodbye. Waiting for a response, I turned around and saw that she was simply staring at me. There was no expression on her face, and she offered no farewell of any kind. I may as well have been a poster on her wall. I left the building feeling drained. I didn't know whether this doctor would ever change her attitude towards me, but I felt that I should stick it out. After all, I had been through so many therapists already.

I walked across the street to Dean & Deluca, where I had arranged to meet Fran for a cup of coffee. Fran had found time between jobs and working on a writing project to see me, and she was waiting for me at a table. I hadn't spent any time with her since I'd returned from Renfrew and I wanted to tell her at least some of what had been happening in my new world. I ordered my coffee and took a seat across from my sister.

"How's The Klub?" she asked, and I began to giggle uncontrollably. I can't remember how exactly we came up with Dr. Klab's nickname, but I'm pretty sure it was a simultaneous invention we created after I described how stern and harsh my new psychiatrist was. I had half-jokingly explained that she would "club me" if I didn't follow all her orders. From that moment, it was easy to immortalize Dr. Klab as "The Klub."

I looked at Fran and realized that even though we hadn't been together physically, she and I had been speaking the entire time. It must have been related to that psycho twin business I'm not too keen on mentioning in public. Now reunited we began to recount the turmoil of recent events, and for the first time that day I realized some things would never change. It wasn't true that my new Manhattan home base was a stomach-turning pink structure. My true home base was, in fact, my sister.

Fran asked me about school, therapy, and eating, to which I succinctly replied with a mere shrug of my shoulders. That small gesture was enough for Fran to understand that I didn't really feel like going into details, so she didn't further press the issue. My day, which early on had had all the promise of a fresh, clean beginning, had quickly turned into yet another disappointment. We decided, without actually talking, to change the subject and focus on something else. Fran was working as a freelance magazine writer, and she wanted to mention the pet lobster I had taken care of throughout high school in one of her upcoming articles.

Gilbert Sebastian Benjamin Simon Libster Theodore Trevor Café Brazil Moisin, to be exact, had been a rare animal. He'd been entrusted into my care as part of an endangered species program at my high school where vulnerable young creatures are raised in captivity for a number of years, and then, upon reaching maturity and strength, released back into their natural habitat. Gilbert should have one day returned home to Australia—we were planning a trip for the summer after my high school graduation—but he'd become sick and died while molting, only a year prior to his release.

It is often still hard to explain how attached I got to a lobster. I loved him, even though he was not the most cuddly, beautiful creature on earth. But maybe that's why I felt so protective towards him. My maternal instincts told me to love him for what he was; it was that simple. I wondered if that was how my mom now felt about me. Fran and I spoke about Gilbert until we finished our coffee, paid the bill, and went our separate ways again.

It was November and getting cold in New York City, but I took my time walking home. I knew that what awaited me was an apartment—a space really—filled with dust, cement, empty take-out containers, cans of soda, holes in the walls, a dirty bathroom that was barely functional, and strangers who stopped talking the second I stepped through the door. This situation was a slap in the face for a girl who so badly wanted a tiny corner she could call home.

Upon returning from Renfrew I had been convinced that I could break the hold my anorexia had on me. But it now began to seem pointless. Disappointed and disgusted by my current living situation and by my life in general, I lost hope again. As winter began to settle onto New York, like a vast, winged creature, so too my anorexia began to spread through every corner of my being once again. The feeling was so familiar, so comfortable, that I decided to bask in the temporary warmth it provided me.

I wasn't really motivated to pursue my other more elusive professors. I put minimal effort into completing Professor Alma's class, and ended up getting a C on my transcript, rather than an incomplete. I felt distant from NYU again, trapped in an unfinished, lonely apartment, and away from my family and friends. I was beginning to panic, and in my heart I knew I couldn't yet release my anorexia. I also realized that Dr. Klab didn't know me well enough, and wasn't invested enough in me to realize that I was slowly lapsing again. I realized that she wouldn't stop me. Even if I was looking for salvation, ready to break from my illness and unburden myself to somebody, Dr. Klab was not the person for me.

The error in staying with Dr. Klab lay in my mistaken belief that by intimidating me she could bully me into being "normal." She could "klub" my anorexia out. I hardly ever feel fearful of anyone, so this new sensation made me think that she could accomplish the seemingly impossible. As I grew weary of her gruff, detached ways, I realized I was simply getting bored. The tape I played for everyone regarding anorexia—the script in my head that really had nothing to do with me or my illness, which I used all over the place so I could avoid my real pain— was starting to be played in her office. I stopped saying much about my true self and instead spent sessions listing my symptoms, my general health on a day-to-day basis, and the work I was doing in school. None of it meant *anything,* and she wasn't catching on at all.

At Renfrew I'd learned all about lapses and relapses, how even those who want to shed their illness will occasionally have a lapse, and those who relapse will have a harder time of ever truly recovering. I had lapsed in Boston while my relationship with my mom was deteriorating. I wanted to be happy again, but I was now convinced, more so than ever, that the only way for me to be content was to stay in my anorexic shell and never grow out of it.

Anorexia was like a protective suit. I didn't see myself as a dying, sickly girl, but simply as Laura, the girl in a costume designed to protect her from the rest of the world. I would walk down the street and watch people turn quickly away, or stare at me in horror. My bones were visibly sticking out of me, and I could count my ribs as though they were plates on a rack. But I didn't see myself this horrific way. In my mind I was still the same girl, only now finally brave enough to outwardly display her pain and despair. My body was my way of venting my frustration. This time, I was relapsing.

That winter I didn't want to grow. I didn't want to know about the world and suffering anymore. I no longer wanted to hear stories of my friends or anecdotes about the outside world. I didn't want to get older in years, develop, or progress. I wanted to stay the same, frozen in a time-and-space bubble where I could finally rest and feel safe. I hadn't yet learned the lesson Gilbert died teaching me. He had struggled so hard to grow, shed his old skin and become a new, stronger being, that he'd died trying to get his old husk off his back. He tired himself out completely in this struggle of renewal, but was too weak to survive. Life is funny when you can learn something profound from a little lobster.

But I didn't understand any of this at the time, during the winter of 2002. I wasn't receiving any of the signs, and I was blocking everyone and everything from my life. After I got back from Renfrew my mom bought me a long, gray shearling coat that was thick and warm enough to protect me from the harsh New York winters. Being anorexic I was always cold, and so felt grateful for my new coat. I remember that winter as one of the coldest I've ever experienced—and I grew up in Canada and Chicago. I'm not sure if the temperature was lower than usual or if my body was simply unable to produce any heat, but I was constantly frozen and exhausted. Walking the few blocks from the subway station to Dr. Klab's office took every ounce of energy I had. I never took my coat off, so she was never able to see that I'd stopped eating once again. She never even asked me what my body looked like under my thick coat.

I had completely given in to my anorexia, and it didn't help that living in such a dirty apartment nauseated me every time I went home. I would have felt sick even if I'd wanted to eat. But we had no plates or silverware, and the fridge stood in the middle of the decrepit living room, filled with containers of old take-out food the workers left behind each day. Every day I walked into the apartment and cleaned up other people's old lunches out of fear of living with vermin, yet again. Even if I wanted to recover I would have felt too disgusted to eat.

In just two weeks I got even worse than I'd ever been before I went to Renfrew, but The Klub didn't notice or say a word about it. And so everywhere I went, even if I was indoors for hours, I wore my shearling coat and didn't take it off until I stepped into my apartment. I was hiding myself in every possible way and feeling more miserably alone and misunderstood than ever before.

When I wasn't with The Klub or doing my schoolwork, I took to wandering the streets alone. Fran and Josh were always at work, and I hardly saw either one of them. My parents were in Boston, and my mom was still quiet, going through her own depression. I had stopped talking to my friends and they'd stopped calling me as well. I was all alone. To worsen matters, for the first time since moving to New York I was living in midtown. I had always lived downtown, where I preferred the intimate, funky atmosphere and vibe. Each street downtown was like home to me, from the Financial District to Chinatown, Greenwich Village to the East Village, Little Italy, and most of all, Soho. I loved and knew each corner.

I was now in the "business" section of the city, where the only human contact came from the angry shouts of business-men on cell phones if I ever accidentally bumped into one of them while walking. Midtown seemed like a different world to me, one that I could never be a part of. I knew I'd never be a businessperson, and that even if I made a career for myself in genetics or scientific writing, I could never belong to this capi-talist clique. Besides despising my dirty apartment, I began to resent the very neighborhood I lived in. I hated everything around me. But for a while I still wandered. I needed to be out-side doing something, because the alternative meant giving up completely and lying down to die. I wasn't that desperate yet—but I would be soon.

By Christmas I still hadn't heard from two of my professors, but the professor from my Violence class finally granted me a meeting, though I had lost interest at that point. My main task was to create an experiment in which a hypothesis would be theoretically proven or disproved, and then write a final paper based on my results. I was exhausted, but I decided to do the work anyway, and chose to do my research on the following topic: "Catching Anorexia: A Case Study of an Individual's Self-deprecating Actions, Influenced and Modified by the Group." The question posed was whether a self-destructive act—such as self-starvation—might be contagious. Could an individual who does not normally possess the impulse for self-starvation begin to exhibit said symptom if placed within a group of people who display the behavior strongly?

When I handed the first draft of my paper to David, the teaching assistant, he looked at the title and gave me a puzzled, irritated look. He knew why I had missed the last portion of his class and probably put no value in my claims of anorexia as a real disease. I didn't hear from David again for weeks, until he emailed me one day to explain my premise was flawed and suggest I work on a different issue. I didn't follow his advice. Instead, I wrote a paper on anorexia that I felt was quite provocative and very properly researched. I turned in the finished product, but was never given a grade. According to David, he couldn't possibly evaluate my work since he hadn't agreed with the topic of the argument in the first place. I took an incomplete for that class, which after another semester, as per NYU policy, became a failing grade. I had failed a class that I'd attended ninety percent of the time, missing only those sessions towards the end when I had deteriorated so badly I simply couldn't muster the energy to get up. I had failed a class in which I'd completed all my work, and spent much time and emotional energy writing about something very thoroughly. The only course I passed that semester was my Irish class. In every other subject I was marked incomplete, and that grade eventually became an F. This was from the girl who had spent her entire high school career working frantically, pushing herself to the extreme, and getting the best grades.

I didn't bother to tell The Klub about all that had happened at school, or mention the incredible sense of failure I was now experiencing. Walking around midtown every day I felt so left out. At least these businesspeople were doing something with their lives. I didn't necessarily admire them, but they were supporting their families, fulfilling their goals, and helping to keep the world in motion. I began to feel more and more dissociated from the world around me, no longer even fitting into the small niche I had worked so hard to create for myself in New York. Even my school had rejected me. Unlike the thousands of people who could go to school each day, I couldn't even match the average person's ability to cope with daily life.

Left with no other alternative, I continued going to The Klub's office in my long, thick coat, where I rattled off anorexic clichés. To be fair to her, she was only working with what I gave her, but she didn't really attempt to figure out who I really was.

If even a PhD doctor who specialized in eating disorders and deals with anorexic girls each day couldn't help, what were my alternatives? I had been to so many therapists already. What was I going to do?

My twenty-first birthday arrived, and with it, Christmas. I spent both occasions in Boston with my parents, Fran, Josh, and Caramel, as well as my cousins, Teo and Alex, my aunt Lia, my uncle Andi, and my grandmother, Elena. Fran and I had grown up with Teo and Alex, they were like a brother and sister to us, but my anorexia had robbed me of contact with any member of my family—including my grandmother, who had always been especially important to me. Finally, we were all together, but not like we had been before. A dark cloud had descended on all of us, and people either tried to ignore the fact that I was sick, or else argued about "what to do" with me.

On my birthday, with all of us gathered around the dining room table, I received a beautiful dress from my mom. The only problem with it was the size. It was a size 2, and I had stopped buying clothes since all my size 0 garments had to be tailored to make them even smaller. Everything I wore was now more like a size −2. The realization that my mom thought I was still a size 2 sent me into such a panic that I broke into uncontrollable sobbing at my birthday table. I felt like I couldn't breathe, and I experienced the same sensation I had on the phone with my parents that night at Renfrew. With everything around me deteriorating, the only thing I'd had left was my nonexistent size. Now, with that one dress, that was being taken away as well.

Seeing me in such a state, my family began to nervously walk out of the room after giving me a quick hug or pat on the back. My mom, dad, Fran, and Josh remained standing to one side, clueless as to what they should say or do. They simply stood there, watching helplessly. But when I lifted my head, I saw through a misty veil of tears my grandmother, facing me across the table, crying the same way I'd been crying, as though the sadness of the world now rested on our two shoulders and there was nothing left to do but mourn where we were and what we had become.

I saw my grandmother, and I immediately froze. I couldn't believe, simply didn't understand, how somebody could be right there with me, in that same dark space. I saw my grandmother's face and knew she was now feeling everything I'd felt. At that moment she was experiencing my anorexia, loneliness, and pain, and for a second I realized I wasn't truly alone. Somebody had shone a light into the tiny place where I was living, and I was momentarily brought back by this woman who loved me so completely. Without thought she threw herself into the depths of my despair. It was, perhaps, one of the most lucid times of my life, but again, as with Gilbert's lesson, I needed much more time to fully comprehend it.

On my twenty-first birthday, when most people get drunk with their friends, I experienced a quiet moment. I was struck by my grandmother's face and by the love I'd always known existed but had never realized the true depths of. Even now when I feel isolated and unprotected I conjure up her image in my mind. Her beautiful, sad face, full of love and despair, that without hesitation says, "I am with you not out of obligation but because of that great, unknowable force called love." The fact that a woman as strong and unique as my grandmother could be so loyal and completely accepting of me engraved itself in my spirit, strengthening me in the depths of desperation and throughout my recovery.

My grandmother, Elena Boeriu, was born the daughter of a poor Romanian farmer. She was the only girl from the second set of children her parents had after her father returned home from working in the United States. She and her brother, the babies of the family, were very close. In the 1930s, Eastern European women were taught to marry early, give birth to as many children as possible, and tend to their husbands who worked all day in the fields. My grandmother had different plans.

My grandmother is, and always has been, a strange mixture of girlish blitheness and womanly asceticism. While those around her spent their lives taming nature, she was from a young age fascinated by its wild power. She earned her nickname, Zea Mais, or goddess of the corn, by tying her thick hair in two long braids and wandering every morning through her family's cornfield with a dreamy look in her eyes. When she was older she moved to a nearby city to work for several years as a journalist before finally following her dream and enrolling in medical school.

A female doctor, in my grandmother's world, was not only unheard of, it was simply unimaginable. But she was determined, and so she bid her parents goodbye, boarded a bus, and set off on her own.

I don't know much about my great-grandparents. I often think of them, but have trouble imagining what their lives must have been like. Exploring history is like traveling to a different planet and searching for clues. When I search for clues in my grandmother's past, knowing what I do about the culture and traditions of her time, I can't picture what her parents must have thought of her grandiose ambitions. A woman was not supposed to be a free-spirited child of the earth, a journalist, a doctor, independent, or any bit as poetic as my grandmother. A woman was born to prepare food, be a good wife, and continue the circle of motherhood. A woman was supposed to be content without asking questions, not head out in search of new answers. My grandmother knew the rules and she bravely chose not to abide by them.

Medical school was a cutthroat environment and Elena became famous not for her gender, but for her extensive knowledge and competitive spirit. She spent night after night studying in the library, pursuing her dreams, and fulfilling her true self. Every morning she walked into the classroom before all her male colleagues and always occupied the first seat in the front row, eager not to miss the slightest gesture or tone from her professors. At the end of the year the surprise final exam was deceptively simple. It consisted of just one question. The professor grabbed a bone off the cadaver table, flung it up, caught it with his other hand, and asked, "What was the bone I just threw into the air?" My grandmother was the only student who knew what bone the professor had tossed. The other students would have to prove themselves as worthy potential doctors in their second year.

There was one student in particular who greatly admired my grandmother and desperately enlisted her help. He was a tall, blue-eyed Russian boy who had moved to Romania with his father after they'd lost half their family, all of their possessions, and their extensive vineyard in Moldova. My grandmother took one look at him and knew she would never be able to say no to this man. He was the perfect male counterpart to her ferocious femininity—tall, lean, graceful, and brilliant. His name was Mikhail, and years later he would become her husband, my mother's father, and my grandfather.

A person can take one look at my sister and know Mikhail's DNA floats through our bodies. He passed away many years ago but still lives through us on this Earth, in this time. My anomaly of a sister, with her fierce blue eyes and porcelain skin, was only born because my grandmother realized that fulfilling her seemingly impossible dream of becoming a doctor didn't mean she had to abstain from getting married and having children. She could have a husband, but she would never serve him after he returned home from the field. They would exist as equals.

In their third year of medical school she became his friend and colleague. They were married upon graduating from university and resided as the only two doctors in Victoria, the small town in Romania where my parents grew up. My grandmother chose her own path, and nobody could figure out how she'd accomplished it.

With the holidays over I returned to New York but continued to wonder about my grandmother. I often asked myself what I had in common with such a strong, vivacious woman. I seemed like her spectral opposite. I wondered how disappointed she was in me. She would never tell me, perhaps not even admit it to herself, but I knew part of her wondered why I couldn't work harder to overcome my one great obstacle.

In the New Year I began seeing The Klub again. The only real reason I was still going to sessions was to maintain the guise that I cared about my problem and wanted to get better. But in fact, I was starting to care less and less each day. The cold weather had now become so unbearable I could literally feel my bones ache, and I knew they were pre-osteoporotic due to my lack of calcium. I felt beaten up by life.

One afternoon, while talking to The Klub about some trivial matter, I realized she was even quieter than usual. My gaze moved from the pueblo poster I was fixed on to Dr. Klab's peacefully sleeping face. Her head had rolled back and her mouth was slightly open. She was sound asleep! I couldn't believe what I was seeing. In shock I sat there for minutes on end, betting against myself to see how long she'd sleep. About four minutes later her head snapped forward and she woke up with a jerk. She didn't say a word, but casually resumed writing in her notepad as though she had been listening intently the entire time. I simply got up and walked away. When I got home I mailed her the last check I owed. I never called to tell her I was terminating our relationship; I simply stopped going. I was offended, amused, and shocked all at the same time. I never heard from her again, either. I think she knew why I had left. That was the last time I got "klubbed." But things were about to get much, much worse.

Chapter *Eight*

The Big Black Dog

God is in a whisper, and I laugh.

God is in a whisper and I shut my eyes closed so tightly I see white, white fuzz, and I'm grateful because I enjoy it. Where does God fit in a city that never sleeps? A city with no bedtime prayers, a city where noise is the only true fizz to lie back on?

God doesn't live in the city, sleepless or not.

God lives in a field with grass and plains, a city of whoosh and fish and skip.

Wouldn't you if you were God?

In the city that I live, the darkened city of my enclosed heart, the city that made my heart God tries to scream and is drowned.

God opens his mouth and he is engulfed.

God is engulfed!

God opens his mouth to scream and nothing comes out but a whisper, a laugh.

Nothing makes God more powerless than an enclave, a whisper.

Yes! Yes!

God is in a whisper!

God is in a sunset, God is in my pot of coffee, God is in my soy milk and tapioca pudding — all that is natural and soft and bedded.

Nothing terrifies God more than sleeplessness and white light — and fuzz, all around me fuzz.

Maybe God is in a nullified scream, a surrendered whisper. Maybe God is when I close my eyes and I'm dizzy on nicotine and stale air, it's the life that I've made to block out whispers in caves and all that is natural.

Maybe God is in a whisper, or maybe I've noticed him scream.

I had now managed to fully isolate myself. I had nothing to do all day but obsess about what had happened to me and convince myself that turning back to the anorexia was my only remaining solution. After all, it seemed like everything and everyone else had abandoned me. Therapy hadn't worked and I'd been to many different psychiatrists and therapists. My family and Josh didn't know how to talk to me anymore, or how to respond to what I was going through. How could they? It was like I was living on a different planet. My friends had stopped calling long ago, and I felt sure that if they knew why I was absent from their lives they would have made fun of me for it, at least among themselves. At Renfrew I hadn't been given the freedom or insight to begin unraveling my illness and its seductive power over me, and so I had to leave. Dr. Klab was no longer my psychiatrist, and I'm convinced she never gave me a second thought. NYU had been a beacon shining in the lower part of Manhattan, my old home and my old life, but it was no longer there for me. Every-where I turned doors were slammed in my face, and I was trapped in the dark, narrow hallway of my mind's illness.

I had convinced myself that I could put my life on pause and just exist in a safe, closed-off cross-section of time. But I couldn't stop the planetary motion or expect the people I loved to put their lives on pause because I was incapable of participating. Life was going on and it was passing me by. I knew this, but I thought the more I closed myself off and ignored what was happening, the more I could live with my anorexia, just the two of us, content in our own miserable sphere.

When I stopped seeing The Klub it was the beginning of

February 2003 and miserably cold outside. Every day seemed like a repetitive, endlessly monotonous moment. Every morning I woke up and opened the shades of my window overlooking 36th Street. I would look and just see gray and black. The gray sky, gray clouds, gray pavement, and steely gray buildings of Manhattan with the dark gray streets dotted in little black figures, people bundled up, all in the same dark winter clothes, walking hurriedly somewhere—anywhere. But where? Perhaps *they* didn't even know. Life seemed to be easily automatic for all of the people I observed from my prison windows.

Didn't they realize how ridiculous they looked, like scurrying, insignificant little creatures? What was life to them but an endless bustle to their miserable jobs, quick fast-food lunches, days spent gossiping about other people, and an impossible fantasy of a better life that would never be fulfilled? I was enraged for myself and for humanity. I felt like we had all been tricked into this game, this ploy known as life. I felt like I could see things no one else did, that the point was the pain, and the world would keep coming back to that, like a common thread woven throughout the fabric of history and into the future. The whole world seemed so hopelessly cruel, and to continue trying to succeed was like waging a tired, silly battle. I felt I could no longer be part of that pretense.

And what set me apart from all those other people? What made my misery noble and worthwhile? It was my anorexia. I figured that as long as I was starving to death I could feel something deeper than the mundane challenges of life. If my body was in constant, chronic pain, then maybe all the suffering going on around me would be more bearable, and I could deal with it in relation to my own waning health. I was literally holding on to nothing but the anorexia. I was living to die. Nothing else really mattered anymore because everything seemed so bleak, and dying from starvation seemed like a good way for me to express just what I thought of the world and its messes.

Unable to talk to anyone, I was now left with vast, open

spaces of time with nothing to do and no one to relate to. I couldn't turn to my family because I figured they all had their own problems, they wouldn't understand, or they would panic at the notion that I was giving up after all this time and suffering. I couldn't turn to Josh because he had a high-stress job on Wall Street, and I didn't want to add to his daily pressure. Also, I doubted that a man in his twenties could ever truly understand the thick desperation that I had sunk into. How could he? He had always been such a happy, optimistic person.

In the cold dreariness of that winter after my failed Christmas family vacation, my absence from school, and The Klub's obvious disinterest in my well-being, I decided to give up. I became a recluse within the walls of an apartment I didn't even have ownership of. I decided that the voice in my head that gave my anorexia its full strength, the voice that told me I was not worthy of a happy life, that whispered "Kill yourself, and at least accomplish one good thing," was the right voice, and the only one that truly knew me. I had been battling this anorexic voice so long, and it was always stronger than me. I felt exhausted. I decided to give in. Once again I complied fully with my anorexia, knowing that with every passing day I was sabotaging any chance that I had to make a real life for myself.

That winter I took to bed and hardly ever got out. Days went by and I stayed in the same curled-up position on my side. I was never fully awake or asleep. My only option was to breathe and be, breathe and be, like a meditation in keeping myself barely alive. With each second I knew that I was no longer going to eat, no longer going to do, no longer going to feel. I was like a breathing corpse. I lost track of time in bed, and each moment was the same unforgiving gray snapshot.

It's complicated to construct a valid explanation of how time unfolded during those cold months. Einstein taught us that time is relative, and we—as a society that loves clichés—have adopted his brilliant equation into our everyday lives. But to live in bed for months on end, incapacitated by one's own desperation and loss of hope, can make days unfold into hundreds of miserable lifetimes—lifetimes in hell. I spent lifetimes in hell, by Einstein's physics and my own accounts. Even now it's hard to go back and remember those days when I was dead, yet still burdened by a life that I no longer wanted. If I had won the lottery, been handed my dream job, offered friendship by David Bowie or Bob Dylan, begged by all the people who cared about me to get up, beseeched by the entire world and Jesus himself, I still would have wanted nothing more than to lie down and starve. Nothing mattered in the universe except my anorexia and me—two entities now inexorably entwined.

Josh told me the scariest time in his life was coming home to find me alone, with the lights off in all but one small space of the apartment, where I sat and quietly cried. He told me for a long time he came home late at night and saw the same pathetic sight. I was no longer the person he had known, the young girl he'd met who was so full of life, so happy and tenacious. I was a miserable wreck, a phantom haunting his apartment and his life. I believe him when he tells me this, but I don't remember most of those times. I don't remember days on end simply because I began, more and more, to live in my own mind. I was so detached from my body and everything around me that I recall only my thoughts like snapshots, like my eyes were taking rapid pictures of small, unimportant scenes. My days consisted of ruminations about being left alone to die, not eating, being taken over by my anorexia, followed by a quick picture of my bedroom wall in the winter afternoon, all degrees of gray. Those are my memories for nearly an eternity.

My life was going by without me. As the winter passed I got out of bed much less frequently, and quit life with a vengeance. I hardly spoke to anyone. I stopped bathing, drinking water except in tiny amounts, eating anything, reading, watching television, sleeping, smiling, laughing, crying, worrying, and caring. Nothing really mattered anymore because my humanity was slowly being stolen from me. I was giving up and giving in to a disease the media makes light of, people make fun of, and some girls and women romanticize. It was destroying me from the inside out. I hardly even went to the bathroom anymore. I would go twice a day to urinate but never looked at myself in the mirror or washed my hands or even flushed the toilet. I would just go and immediately return to my bed, my personal torture chamber.

One day, walking from my bedroom to the bathroom, I caught sight of a hunched person clinging to the walls for support, with long, unruly hair, and a skeleton for a body. For a moment it truly scared me because I thought there was someone else in the apartment—maybe even a ghost. When I realized it was me I went into a state of shock. I had become the corpse I had felt like all these months.

After that day I didn't look in the mirror or shower or do anything that wasn't absolutely necessary for a long time. Sometimes at night, with all the lights off in the apartment, I would take a quick shower without looking in the mirror. I was afraid to touch my body or to have any kind of unnecessary physical contact with my body. I simply wanted to evaporate. I didn't really know what was happening to me. I knew that things had never been this bad before. I thought for a while I was going insane or had some other mental disorder besides the anorexia. I called my mom and told her I was sick with something we hadn't yet figured out, and maybe the best thing was to keep me in a mental hospital so that everyone could forget about me and I could rot in peace. I told her these things, but I don't even remember what she said. I didn't think about what I was doing to her by hating myself so deeply in front of this person who had created me.

But I did know the truth, and it was disturbingly simple. I had given up. I had a disease that had beaten me up so badly that it had made me my own greatest enemy. Every day it was growing stronger while I was becoming weaker and filled with more self-hatred and shame. At the time I wasn't scared about how deep I had sunk because I was sure I would never have to dig myself out of my bottomless grave. I didn't know myself any-more. I didn't understand that I had once been happy, because I was convinced that happiness didn't really exist. I didn't believe that I had anything worth salvaging. Redemption was impossi-ble and I had proof in the form of my weak, cold, little body and confused, stubborn mind.

Each day and night evoked the same feelings in me. Between the bouts of self-hatred and the knowledge that my body was get-ting weaker, I experienced periods of dreaded acceptance. I knew my fate was to be miserable, live unhappily, and die, and I breathed these thoughts in with a mixture of sadness and surrender.

Winston Churchill was a depressive, and he struggled with a mental disorder his entire life. He referred to his illness as "the big black dog—the familiar beast that quietly pads in during the evening and settles down at your feet." When I read this about Churchill—a figure so many people admire, including my aunt Lia and Josh's dad—I understood immediately what he was referring to. These feelings of despair and dread are foreign to mentally stable individuals, but are frighteningly familiar to a person who is psychologically unwell and struggling.

My big black dog was my anorexia, and the depression and despair I got used to after a while. The scariest aspect of the big black dog was its seeming innocuousness. A big black dog is both threatening and familiar. It overtakes you eventually by quietly settling into bed next to you instead of engulfing you in one painless bite. If the big black dog is the only creature that won't go away, then you choose its companionship over the alterna-tive—torrential solitude. The big black dog is something you can never force to leave or truly get rid of. You can only train it and become its master, or merely survive its stifling presence.

Every day I felt the big black dog slowly climb up on my bed and rest its heavy body on my chest until all I could take were shallow breaths. I grew accustomed to this feeling of suf-focation and felt like any action I took to stop it would just prove my frailty.

One afternoon, however, I decided on a whim to take a walk and feel the outside world again. I hadn't felt the air or even stuck my head out of my living room window in almost two months. Without showering or putting on makeup I pulled on a pair of sweatpants and a navy wool sweater over the red plaid pajamas I had been wearing for weeks. I laboriously laced up my sneakers, put on my shearling coat and a red hat and gloves, and bitterly remembered my college friends playfully referring to me as the "fancy girl." Nothing about me seemed elegant anymore.

I suddenly, eagerly wanted to be outside walking, breathing new air, and just being around other people to ease my sense of isolation. In my heavy gray coat, walking on the cold pavement, I soon became one of the masses of dark pedestrians crossing the street with their heads down, going somewhere mysterious in an exaggerated rush. I could also feel my other self—the one who had been living alone in bed and staring out the window facing 36th Street—looking down at me and wondering why I even bothered to join Manhattan's ambling army. But for twenty minutes, simply by walking, I was again a small part of the human race, a small part of *something*.

For me this journey outdoors was a great trek and a frightening adventure. I was doing something most people do and take for granted every day: leave their house. I felt unprepared, scared, nervous, and self-conscious, as though everyone around me knew that I had become an outsider to society, my family, and myself. In my failing struggle against the big black dog I had slowly forgotten that I was a force unto myself. At the moment, the only way I could fight my illness was to continue walking down the street, staring at the cold, hard, dark gray pavement. I couldn't bear to catch a glimpse of myself in the reflection of any store windows.

My progress was painfully slow. The cold cut through me and I imagined myself in the spectrum of human limitation— I was a sick person, I was a new person, an infant, I was an old woman who knew she was dying and could barely carry herself

anymore. Either way the wind knew my weakness and mercilessly battered me, uncaring about the small mission I was
hoping to accomplish.

I remember this voyage as though it lasted years, and yet I
remember thinking how natural it felt to be walking outside
again. Suddenly I couldn't remember what my apartment looked
like, where the furniture was placed, or the characteristic smell of
each room that made it unique. I also didn't know whether I
wanted to go back to my cage. It was a cage I had built by giving
in to my anorexia and by letting my anorexic thoughts, voices,
actions, and inactions pummel me carelessly and easily. I had
become a victim of myself and I didn't want to go back to the
small space that reminded me so much of my own primitiveness
and cowardice. The more was taken from me, the more I had
adapted to my new life, like a zoo animal that had once roamed
freely but was now captive and afraid. I had accepted that and
had forgotten that other possibilities existed for me.

After what seemed like a great trek, the wind finally forced
me into the shelter of a furniture store. I didn't see the name of
the place I had just entered, or what street I was on, because I
simply assumed that I was very far downtown and miles from
home. As soon as I walked in three sales women asked me what
it was *exactly* that I wanted. It wasn't so difficult to see that I
wasn't welcome in their store. I was, after all, wearing pajamas
under my opened shearling coat. Maybe I even looked homeless. I hope I didn't smell homeless. As casually as possible, I
informed them all that I was just browsing, and then as proof
began inspecting their faux English country sofas, chairs, and
room dividers painted with hunting dogs, horses, and men
wielding shotguns. Yeah, sure, *I* wasn't welcome *here*. If only
these people could see who I truly was, what I was truly like,
they wouldn't be treating me this way. But I was no longer the
person I had been. I had become a sick person, a shut-in, a
hopeless girl, and someone who was certain life was over.

I left the fake British furniture store and on my way out

looked at the name to make certain I would never accidentally enter it again. When I saw the words Ethan Allen printed on the green awning I became disoriented and confused. I was only four blocks from my apartment. I was at the Ethan Allen on 32nd Street, the one I had walked by all the time but had never gone into. I wasn't downtown and I hadn't walked miles, but had instead gone on a trek that should have lasted eight minutes round-trip. I couldn't believe how weak I felt after walking just four blocks. I was the girl who had taken expeditions with her adventurous dad, hiking through the Carpathian Mountains in Eastern Europe, camping out in the Everglades and Ozarks, and going on deep-sea scuba diving trips in the West Indies and throughout the Florida Keys. I couldn't believe how I had changed so drastically in one short lifetime. Was there no limit to my own destruction? Was there nothing more sacred to me than my devastating anorexia? Did I have such lack of character and personality that I could become somebody totally different in only a few short years? I feared myself.

When I got back to my apartment the doorman let me in with a sympathetic but slightly alarmed look on his face. I had no idea what the people in my building thought of me. They saw Josh all the time on his way to work, running errands, coming home late at night, going out with friends, but they rarely, if ever, saw me. Perhaps they didn't even know I was still living there.

That day, the Ethan Allen Day, scared me. I couldn't bear the thought of spending many future years trapped in this kind of life, in an apartment that doubled as a prison. I couldn't pretend to enjoy reading all day, trying to escape soap operas and talk shows on television. I didn't want to be this way. Yet the problem remained: if I wanted to start living again, I would have to start eating again. Harder still, I would have to find a way to ignore or fight my anorexia. If I kept giving in to the anorexic voice I had only this life of sickness, loneliness, and isolation to look forward to. I felt too tired to carry on with my empty existence and too tired to think of recovery.

Time continued to pass in much the same way, and soon nothing seemed important to me anymore. The only company I had was the big black dog. Since reading Churchill's analogy and understanding it so fundamentally I now thought of my depression, isolation, and starvation as a calm creature, patient and powerful, sucking the life out of me in no particular hurry.

I began to think of NYU again, and wondered if my medical leave of absence had any time restrictions that I was never informed about. I figured, perhaps naively, that since I had been accepted into NYU, and since people often take year-long breaks from college, I could go back to school anytime I was ready. After all, between the thousands of students entering and leaving NYU each year, why would they care about one random sick girl trying to get her life back together?

I missed being at school, in an environment where philosopher kings rule and intelligence is the highest commodity. I missed feeling the spiky vibe of the city. But more than anything, I missed being a living person. In a way, I was already deceased. My soul had sunk into a place I once had had no idea could even exist within me. And the world, with all those who cared about me, was acting as though it was in mourning. Hope was more myth than force; it was a word that I heard often but never gave credence to.

There was still a part of my mind that had a plan about how I could, perhaps years down the line, pull myself up again. My one remaining connection to the outside world, NYU, was weakening but still in existence. This is not to say I didn't have people who loved me and for whom I wanted to get better, or things in life that I had once been passionate about and yearned to feel passion for again. But I was convinced, after seeing so many "professionals," that returning to school would help get me in motion again and give me the necessary momentum to conquer my anorexia.

The idea of returning to NYU was like a solid brick in the

building of my life where everything else had deteriorated and toppled. It was with this last whisper of peace and reassurance that I comforted myself after I woke up in the middle of the night in a cold, sweaty panic. I knew fear then. Yes, I was living a nightmare, but I could see a faint path leading to the ivy towers of NYU.

So the weeks went on and felt like one long, nightmarish day of impossible doom, misery, and cold. How could winter last so interminably in a person's life? I begged God, or whoever was listening, each day for a bit of snow, something to whitewash the streets so that from my apartment window I could see clean majesty and purity, and fool myself into thinking that every-thing—including my own slate—could suddenly be wiped clean. Then I could start anew. But I didn't really believe in such possibilities. I didn't really think I would ever feel any different or change my outlook.

I was trapped, pinned down by the heavy black beast whose foul breath made me grimace but, nonetheless, still kept me warm. I begged God to make the sun shine for just a few hours so I could bask in it and feel comforting, golden warmth. I wanted these simple things, but neither snow nor sun came. When I thought of all the people in the world dying from dis-ease, starving because they had no food, and in constant misery, I wondered why I should be any different. Why should I get help when so many others had none? So many others had no hope and no chance of ever seeing anything but gray, even on the sunny plains of Africa.

By that time I was leaving my apartment only to go to the Starbucks down the street. Coffee was the only edible I could publicly partake in. When my thoughts became overwhelming I attempted to escape them by focusing on my Starbucks out-ings, even if they lasted only a few minutes. Josh and I began to frequent Starbucks as the one last thing we could do together, besides watching television in the apartment. Normal social activity, like going out with friends or getting a drink together, now seemed impossible. Our lives had shifted to a different, abnormal place that very few people really understood. Only people who have been through an illness themselves or truly followed a loved one into the depths of disease, like Josh did with me, can comprehend this place. I was warmed by his presence, but I always wished he wouldn't follow.

As the winter began to fade and spring approached, I began to walk again. At first I walked very slowly and lasted for only a few blocks, like the time I'd gone to Ethan Allen. Soon I began to move past Starbucks, feeling adventurous and relieved that I was outside and away from the apartment that had held me captive for so long. I began to arrange my days according to those walks. I wasn't walking for the exercise or to lose weight, but simply to air out my mind and experience things that were physically real and outside of the shaky world built by my illness. For the first time in many months I started to feel like I was accomplishing something again.

In reality I wasn't doing anything I hadn't first done as an infant—learning to take my first steps. I was a young woman, but may as well have been only a few years old. Everything I had known and taken for granted in my other life, my pre-anorexic existence, had been lost to me. Of course I remembered my previous social, hard-working, determined self. I remembered all of my old friends, my family and Josh—people that I could no longer join.

I began walking into my new life because the only relief I could get from my self-punishing thoughts and actions was constant movement. I wanted to move so as to escape the dark walls of my apartment. I craved a respite from the feelings of unrest and hopelessness that engulfed me each time I dwelled on the staggering path my life was on. I was walking to feel like I was a human being capable of leaving tracks in the mud of this earth, rather than a spirit living far above it, staring down from a lonely window. The spring passed quickly, as though it lasted one day. I was doing so much living in the world of my mind that I experienced days differently, and my physical calendar became useless. Specific dates and events no longer held any meaning. It now only mattered that I could leave my apartment, pull myself out of my own mind, and start thinking of more than what I'd lost and what my illness had done to me.

Anorexia is a tricky disease to deal with because so much of it takes place in the secret corners of our minds. These are areas no one wants to publicly reveal. This place becomes so powerful for an anorexic that the frail physical aspect most people associate with the disease is really just the tip of an iceberg that reaches far down into a dark, cold sea. In order to understand what anorexia is, why it exists within a person at all, and how to master it, the impossible must happen: the anorexic must uncover this dark place, sort through it, and willingly overcome it. Then life must go on, but not life as before, when the anorexic was alone and shielded from everyone and everything. A new life must take shape and it must triumph over the old one. This new life must be crafted carefully. Ironically, a new life is what the anorexic fears most and also secretly most wishes for.

That summer I started thinking I wanted a new life too. But I didn't have the courage, hope, or faith in the workings of the world and God to really believe anything like that was possible. I began to have theoretical conversations with the people closest to me—my mom, Dad, Josh, and Fran—about starting my life again. Specifically, how would I eat if I wanted to? What would I eat? Where would I get the help I needed? What if when I began to eat I panicked and wasn't happy? What if I was even more miserable as a "normal" person than I'd been as an anorexic? Obviously no one had the answers, but I wasn't really asking anyone but myself.

The truth was that I had the answers within me. I was just afraid of giving myself responsibility. I was afraid because the next step after asking was either definitive action or obvious inaction, and neither seemed acceptable. Months ago I had been happy not doing, content living in a bubble—but that bubble eventually became so horrific I had to get out, if only to walk and gain distance from the walls that symbolized my suffering and quiet grief. What I feared even more than the big black dog was becoming its master. Was I powerful enough to master a disease that was stronger than any force or person I had ever met? If indeed I was strong enough, why had I been so obviously beaten down by it? These complexities engulfed me every day and night, but at least I had begun to visualize a change.

That summer, Josh and I went for walks almost every night. He had stopped working as a financial consultant and was working with my dad on his business. This allowed Josh more time at home, ensuring that I was not always alone. Sometimes we walked to Starbucks and sat down, but usually we walked to the East Village so that we could taste the bohemia we both sorely missed since moving to Murray Hill. We were mutually surprised every time we left the apartment together and I had managed to shower, wash my hair, and care about my clothes again. It was invigorating to be part of the world on ground level, mixing with other people instead of always watching and observing them from above.

Our nighttime walks were mostly quiet. We were both afraid to talk or imagine the future. Would it be together? Would I ever get better? How long could Josh be with an anorexic girl without having to move on with his life? With each step we took together towards the East Village our minds worked separately to figure things out and plan for the future as much as we dared. With each step I began to feel a new sense of relief that I was no longer so alone. With each step, my mind reeled with thoughts of what to do next. I was terrified and hopeful at the same time. I was on the brink of something, but I didn't know what.

By the end of summer, hundreds of walks later, I decided to start making plans for myself again. I was feeling more empowered than I'd felt all that winter. I figured I could start deciding some things on my own. I felt as though the anorexia's grip had loosened a little. I had been talking more and I was in tune with the city and its spirit again. All these things added up to a tiny edge I hadn't possessed before.

At this point, however, school was set to recommence and I hadn't made contact with NYU for nearly a year. I had received no letters, phone calls, or signs that I had ever attended that school, or even set foot on its campus. All I knew was that I was still on a medical leave of absence, getting myself back together before I could get my degree and move on with my life. At the same time I was nervous about the lack of communication I'd had with NYU. While actively attending class I'd received mail consistently—letters announcing open houses, flyers regarding basketball games, dinners with deans, and other pamphlets that as a student you don't really care about, but expect to be informed of anyway. I would go home to Boston and find a stack of the same kind of mail on my desk in my room. But now I had no mail. I decided to call the school and make sure I still had my medical leave status.

On one of my afternoon walks in Midtown I decided to call Christina, the woman who had granted me my medical leave, and who had seemed so proud of herself for knowing the term "electrolyte." I called the counseling department at NYU and was automatically transferred to Christina's answering machine. I left her a message describing who I was, in case she had forgotten, and stated I was just checking in to make sure all was well with my paperwork. I also told her I needed a signed document from NYU for my insurance, confirming that I was on a medical leave of absence.

A few days later I got a call back from Christina. She told me I was still on my medical leave and should take my time getting better. However, for the insurance form, I would need to talk to Dean Short. Why the person who had granted me the medical leave in the first place couldn't just sign a paper authorizing her decision was beyond me, but I decided it was wise to remain polite. I said goodbye to Christina and left Dean Short a similar message on his voicemail.

Dean Short remains, to this day, somewhat of a mystery. Throughout college I was referred to him regarding all academic issues, but rarely met with him in person. I spoke with him on the phone a number of times and spoke many times to his assistant, who reminded me of a scared rabbit. He consistently remained elusive, unavailable, and Wizard of Oz–like. I called Dean Short, but days went by without hearing back from him, until one uneventful afternoon. After missing a call and innocently checking my messages, I received a shock. In his usual, unnervingly neutral voice Dean Short calmly told me that he could not sign any forms or help in any possible way, since I was, in fact, "out of matriculation." That was it.

"I'm sorry, Miss Moisin," his message said, "you are currently out of matriculation at New York University. If you have any questions, you can reach me at . . ."

If I had any questions? If I had questions? I couldn't believe my one safety net, my one anchor and distant hope for the future, for escaping my miserable state of sickly darkness, was now gone. Gone, and in such an anticlimactic way.

The end of anything is so disappointing. It is never the fireworks and tears we come to wish for and expect. It is never Hollywood, as most of us are duped into believing. It is usually quiet and unassuming, and comes at you when you just happened to miss answering your cell phone. "I'm sorry, Miss Moisin . . ."

I called Dean Short. Eventually, I was able to speak directly to the Wizard himself. His voice, so sickeningly reserved, made me angry with him for being so dispassionate, and even angrier with myself for being so riled up. The conversation went something like this:

"Dean Short, my name is Laura Moisin, and you left me a message on my cell phone the other day telling me that I am currently out of matriculation at NYU. I am actually on medical leave of absence for anorexia, so how could I be kicked out of school?"

"Well, Miss Moisin," replied the Dean, "your medical leave

has expired and you have, in fact, used up all of the time that is given to a person for medical leave. If you are not better by the end of two semesters, then perhaps you had better take care of your problems and not be at NYU."

"Yes, Dean Short, but I just spoke with Christina, and she told me I could take as much time as I needed and that I was still on medical leave. The only reason I called you at all was because I needed your signature for my insurance form."

"Well, I am sorry, but I don't know what Christina said to you. It's hard for me to believe she would say something like that, but if in fact she did, I will ask her about it." (Said in a very unconvincing way.)

"Well, Dean Short, I never even got any letters or calls from anybody about no longer being a student at NYU."

"Miss Moisin, do you know how many students go to NYU? What are we supposed to do, keep track of *all* our students' comings and goings?"

My mind immediately flashed back to the stacks of junk mail that NYU liked to send all of its students. But my reply was, "So all this time, as I'm trying to get better, I was kicked out of school without even knowing it?"

"Well, perhaps you can try going to a community college. After all, your last semester grades were extremely poor, and they drove down your entire GPA. You were doing well, and then I don't know what happened, but that doesn't look good on your permanent transcript. Maybe you're just not cut out for such a competitive, challenging school as NYU."

"Yes, I failed most of my classes last semester because I was very, very ill and was not able to complete any of them. I went to an inpatient hospital. The school has records of all this."

"Well, Miss Moisin, I really have to go, but good luck," was his snooty reply.

I knew that any minute he would hang the phone up on me, possibly mid-sentence. After all, I didn't matter anymore. I didn't belong at NYU. I wasn't one of the students he *had* to, albeit resignedly, deal with. It was like I no longer existed for him. But I felt compelled to say just one more thing before he hung up on me, one thing I felt pressing down on my chest, so I blurted out, "Dean Short, do you have daughters?"

I could almost hear his shock on the other end, and with a decided sigh he answered, "Yes, I do."

"Well, I hope none of them ever has to deal with anorexia and eating disorders. Because you may not take it seriously now or think it's a real illness that would prevent me from going to school or doing work, but it's a battle. And if you and your daughters never have to know anything about that, you're much better off and a lot luckier than I am."

There was a pause for just a moment, the slightest pause in time, in conversation, in my world, and then the only response I got was, "Good luck, Miss Moisin," before he hung up the phone.

I hung up the phone and knew that those few moments had completely changed my life. I was now officially cast out from the institution that had been my reason for moving to New York in the first place. I looked out my window and interpreted my view differently from before. The small part of me that still had a claim on the city had disappeared. I was no longer a student. I was no longer in the safe haven of the system. The downtown buildings that had once beckoned me to class, dreaded exams, or dorm-room parties were now just ghosts in my painful memories. I had been forcibly detached from all of that now—officially. Where would I go from here?

For a moment I allowed myself to soak in the hatred I felt for Dean Short. I despised him so intensely that the force of my ill will towards a man and a father I didn't even really know frightened me. I felt so powerless in comparison to the amount of control he somehow had over my life. I kept thinking that he could have given me a break. He could have at least been nicer to me, or more sympathetic. He could have asked his twitchy rabbit secretary to send me a letter after one semester informing me that my time on medical leave was running short. He could have told me that since Christina never informed me of the time limit, since she had cleared me, he would clarify with her and get back to me. I didn't really stand a chance when put at the mercy of the Wizard of Oz, the dean I would think about so often in the future.

I hated Dean Short, and then I became envious of him and his family. I was jealous that they'd never been through anything like I was now experiencing. If they had, surely he would have been more sympathetic, more understanding. I know I would have been. I would have tried to change university policy to help people.

Now I simply feel sorry for Dean Short. Enough time has passed that I am over that day, past the phone conversation that crushed me and made me feel more worthless than I had let myself feel in weeks. Now I feel sorry for a man who couldn't find compassion for a desperate, sick girl clinging to something small for help. I feel sorry for him, because so many other people go out of their way to help others. They even look for it, but when that chance fell on his lap he didn't seize it. I feel sorry for a man who, though many years older than me, knew so little about what life really means. I feel sorry for him, and when I am feeling optimistic, I hope my assumptions about him are untrue. I hope I just caught him on a bad day.

For days I told no one about that conversation, about what had happened to me, about the proof of what I really was—a bona fide failure. I no longer had the technicality of my "medical leave" status to fall back on. I was so disappointed with myself and with what had become of my life that I was ashamed to tell my parents about the loser their daughter was turning out to be.

That weekend my dad had a business meeting in New Jersey and he stayed in New York a couple of nights. On his last night in the city, Josh, Fran, my dad, and I all sat in my apartment talking, before the three of them went out to dinner. I sat mostly in silence, listening to their conversation, watching everyone chat about idle things, knowing that the one fixture keeping my life hinged to some semblance of normalcy had been severed. I was alone with my terrible knowledge.

I was used to being alone with my shameful and horrible feelings. I was accustomed to being up all night, thinking that starvation was the only way out for me and that without it I would never be happy. I often believed that it would be best to die from anorexia and escape a world that had become so unbearable and a mind that tortured me so unrelentingly. Yet being kicked out of school was somehow different. Up till now, my parents could take solace in the idea that I was still in school. Up till now, I had had a plan for my future. Now, I had no plan, no future.

As we all sat in the living room, chatting about daily annoyances and happenings, I exposed my crushing secret. I burst into tears and allowed myself to be held by the older sister I hadn't really hugged or been affectionate with in years, because of my unwillingness to be touched. I told my gasping audience all about the new development in the terribly sad saga that was, in fact, my own life. Thoughts that I didn't know I could share with people escaped my lips and became public property. Tears came streaming down my face, but they were real! This was so unlike the numb, deadened inklings of emotion I had been living with so long in my anorexic stupor. I cried for a long time and hadn't been so refreshed in months.

I cried for myself, and the death of a vision I'd had for a Laura who was now fading away into the not so distant past. This was a Laura I could still see, still imagine, but simply not reach. I cried for my parents, because they had a daughter who was nothing but sick. I cried for my sister who had a little sibling she couldn't hang out with or talk to, because my life revolved around one thing, and it wasn't her. I cried for Josh, for allowing himself to hang on to a relationship that had no happiness in sight, no bright future. I cried for all the anorexic girls I had ever known and that I knew existed, for the magnitude of pain that such a fragile person can withstand.

Crying was one of the best things that ever happened to me.

The truth—that nebulous thing we are always trying to grasp—sometimes seems rather simple and rather stupid. The truth for me was obvious: I had to disconnect from my old life and start anew. I was now crying for all that I had to leave behind. All of the pressures I had put on myself as a young woman had to be released, along with the rather narrow visions of what I had hoped to become. It was all going to be different from what I had planned or imagined. I wasn't a college kid anymore. I was fearsomely, violently on my own. I belonged to no establishment, to no one, and was beginning to doubt I belonged to the anorexia as well.

What good had my anorexia done me if I was getting kicked out of school? It didn't make that much sense anymore. The thrill just wasn't the same; it just wasn't *working* the way it had before. As soon as I had opened my mind a little, observed the world around me and peeked out of my starving bubble for just a moment, my anorexic shield was weakened.

It took getting kicked out of NYU for that to happen. It took getting my NYU umbilical cord ripped painfully away for that to be accomplished. It wasn't that I was suddenly better, or that I wanted to get rid of my anorexia at that precise moment, but things did looked altered. My anorexia, I realized, had not protected me the way I thought it would against the pain and uncertainty of life. My anorexia wasn't powerful enough to buffer me from such catastrophes, and life eventually got through.

The night I burst into tears in front of my family, Josh and I decided to drive back to Boston with my dad. I needed to see my mom, escape the city for a while, and return to a home base filled with some good memories, unlike my New York apartment that had only seen the worst of me. In Manhattan, I was a depressed, sick, misunderstood girl; but in my Boston room I could perhaps just be Laura. I could begin to remember all the memories my life had created, the good and bad, and recall the full life I had once had.

The next morning we dropped Fran off at work, all of us

sitting silently, except my dad who was characteristically swearing at the cars ahead of him and gesturing wildly at the drivers he deemed unruly. Fran and I were in the back, both peaceful in our own contemplations. I was so used to dropping my sister off as she embarked on a new adventure, and feeling left behind. I had felt this way when we had moved from Chicago to our new home in Boston while Fran spent the rest of the summer with her friends. I'd felt this separation when we had dropped her off at the airport on her way to study in Paris, and I slowly walked out of the terminal, away from my sister with all her heavy bags and her big blue eyes. It seemed like this had become routine—my dropping her off but never accomplishing anything myself, never *getting* anywhere. Why couldn't I have stories of great adventures rather than being asked what my latest EKG results had been?

My sister got out of the car and I watched her carry on with her day and her life, while I remained stuck. As we drove out of the city I thought of this in silent sadness and passive acceptance, and slowly, the seat that Fran had occupied was taken over by the big black dog. The feelings of loneliness and quiet despair began to wash over me again. How was I to ever get better? How was I to go on with my life? What would I do? It would take a miracle, I thought, to ever be happy again, to ever really be at peace and rest. How was I to overcome the control the big black dog had over me?

But we drove on, Josh and my dad talking business, while I looked out the window at the autumn scene unfolding before me. It was autumn, again and again, and I hadn't noticed it in New York. Out there, out of the city, things seemed more peaceful and serene. For a few precious moments I took in the bold reds and oranges mingled with the green leaves that, now, for the first time all year, looked exotic among the rest. For a few seconds I ignored the big black dog. I ignored the image of my sister walking away, Dean Short, NYU, and the word *failure* pounding through my chest and heart, cutting into my mind. I ignored it all and just took in the simple majesty that seemed to have been waiting for me all along.

If I had never taken this simple respite I would have missed that gorgeous autumnal scene. I wondered what else I had missed, and what other scenes I would miss if I continued on the way I was. If I were as brilliant as Einstein I would create my own theory of relativity. It would be the relativity of color. It would speak of how, in the same span of months, a sick girl could go from dying in the solitude of a gray of winter to living a life of color in a thin border of trees along a small stretch of road somewhere between New York and Boston. It would explain big black dogs in our minds, rather than big black holes in our universe, and it would prove the existence of second chances brought to our awareness in a sudden burst of sunlight flashing for a moment through the sweet thicket of maple trees.

I knew that I could have another chance. I didn't know how to grab it, but I would somehow figure that out. I knew that my anorexia had let me down, I just didn't yet know why. I would simply have to accept it and use this new knowledge to my own advantage—to *Laura's* advantage, not Kid Rex's advantage. And really, though I hate to admit it, I had to thank Dean Short for disposing of me so easily and with such utter lack of care. He exposed the impotence of my anorexia. My big black dog could not, in fact, protect me from the world or keep such things from happening. It could only bully me and consume me alive. It could not make up for what I had lost, or fill my life up the way I really wanted my life to be realized. It really could, and did, only turn on me. Ultimately, leaving NYU may have been the best thing that ever happened to me. Because now, driving smoothly down that autumn highway, I knew I too was on a very different stretch of road.

Chapter *Nine*

Tightrope Walker

I begged on my hands and knees. And I was once so proud! I begged on the carpet I bought for us and secretly, curiously wondered if tear stains would mar the raw, yellow silk of our hand woven Tibetan rug . . . the one you carried to the trunk of the car laughing and chatting about paint samples, plushness and floor patterns.

I lost any identifying whatevers. I have no characteristic whats-its. And when I looked in your blank eyes the last time I knew I would see you— the you who was still accountable to me (sort of). I realized I hadn't been there in years. I was stolen, taken to the underworld, in a place even Dante wouldn't dare tread.

And so where does one go looking? Where does one find a place to begin, a place to find whatever they feel entitled to? What walk-about, pilgrimage, voyage, crusade, journey, Amazon expedition do I commence on to find just one . . . one speck, dot, lining, spot . . . crumb? Where do I go if not in your globe?

B ob Dylan's voice frequently echoed through my mind those days, "Why wait any longer for the world to begin when you can have your cake and eat it too?" As much as I wanted to dismiss that question it remained with me because I was puzzled about why I had allowed my life to halt. I was at LaGuardia airport listening to my iPod and trying to gain some insight from Dylan. But all I could come up with were questions, never answers.

My problem was that anorexia wasn't really a solution anymore. Leaving NYU was the most painfully liberating event that had ever happened to me. That winter, I was still recovering from the shock of it all. It forced me to see that my anorexia wouldn't protect me from any pain or damage; I had once been so sure it would. It had felt at times like having an invisible shield around me that guarded me from the debris of life. But when things really blew up, I'd been hit anyway.

What happens when someone invests that much time, energy, faith, flesh, bone, and spirit in a shield that proves to be fallible? What then? Why couldn't I have my cake and eat it too? I wondered if Dylan knew the answer to the question possessing me. Maybe if I ever ran into him on the streets of Manhattan I could ask. But maybe he didn't know either. Maybe no one did.

I was sitting in the same seat I always did before embarking on the shuttle flight to Boston. It was Christmastime, a few days before my twenty-second birthday. Yet it may as well have been my second year on earth, based on all the simple things I didn't know and answers to questions I still couldn't perceive. My boat had been rocked. Now I was no longer a student, no longer waiting to return to school. I wasn't "doing" anything, and I found that predicament agonizing.

In order to calm my nerves I began going through all my LaGuardia rituals—listening to music, buying gum and diet Coke, observing fellow passengers, and nodding in recognition at the employees who, after over four years of flying between Boston and New York, had become so familiar. Eventually, I got up and stood in front of gate 20, waited to board the plane, and began to pray silently. My prayer was always the same, every time I flew. I focused on the air, speed, and space, hoping that being physically detached from a world I found so perplexing would erase my past and somehow give me a fresh start. As I handed my ticket to the agent and wished him a merry Christmas for the fifth time in my life, I also wished that I could somehow be reborn.

"Let me start over," I whispered a little too loudly as I stepped onto the plane. "Excuse me?" the cheerful flight attendant said.

"Oh, I'm sorry, I wasn't talking to you," I replied.

"Okay honey. Well, merry Christmas; and do you need help finding your seat?" I shook my head and kept walking down the plane's narrow aisle, my heavy suitcase periodically bumping into the seats, and wondered why I couldn't just be fresh and untarnished again. I had made such a mess of things. Would I ever be normal and happy?

I didn't know how things could change for me, but I knew it would take something drastic for any type of transformation to occur. I had been a premed biology major when I began at NYU, and despite the fact that I hadn't acquired a proper degree, I always considered myself a scientist. Any self-respecting scientist would have known that the methods I was employing in this particular experiment, the one entitled "My Life," were failing dramatically. It was time for me to procure a new set of rules, no matter how difficult they might be.

I had once read that some of Bob Dylan's most famous, rambling songs were written while under the influence of cocaine,

opium, and marijuana. As soon as his fans deduced the drug
connection they began to expect such behavior from their idol.
But rather than embrace it he distanced himself from the drug
culture, cleaned himself up, and began to write in a different
way—at least until he was no longer predictable. In a way, that
was how I felt. My life for the past few years had been psyche-
delic, not due to drugs but lack of food. And everybody had
gotten used to it and almost come to expect that behavior from
me. Now I wanted to rebel, not through my anorexia, but by
railing against it. I wanted to do the unexpected. It was time for
me to shake things up, like Dylan had.

The only thing I knew I could do to get my life back again
was to start eating. As was usual in my life, the simplest solution
was also the most difficult for me to grasp. My holy grail was
something people do with ease, what an infant does naturally
when first emerging from the womb . . . and I couldn't do it. I
hadn't eaten real food since leaving Boston after Renfrew. I
thought my behavior might somehow be normal, though.
Everywhere I went people were talking about the "zone," calo-
rie-restricted, and Atkins diets. I figured everyone else was
doing the exact same thing as me. It was difficult for me to refer
to myself as an anorexic: I didn't think I was thin enough, isolated enough, on a restrictive enough diet to fit into that group.

But now all of the doubts that had been building in my mind
were welling up and nagging me like little voices that wouldn't
go away. It was the truth that I needed change, and it was annoying me. Why wait any longer for your world to begin? It was
time to eat. How could I eat without wanting to punish myself
afterwards? And what would I eat? How would I figure out
what I would eat and when? Again, I didn't have the answers,
but the same pesky sensation told me that I couldn't do it in
theory. My only solution was to act, to go ahead and attempt to
consume food again.

At some of my worst times and lowest weights I read books
written by recovered anorexics and I always felt frustrated by a

common disparity in them. The authors would all describe what it was like to be sick, unhappy, and anorexic, and then cheerily proclaim that being healthy and recovered was so much more "fulfilling" and "rewarding." Not once did I really understand how they evolved from one end of the spectrum to the other.

That kind of radical transformation warranted some kind of explanation. How, specifically, did they get better? That was such a mystery to me that I thought perhaps the ability to recover simply wasn't in my genetic makeup. In most books I read, the anorexic progressed linearly, from being on her deathbed to eating, getting married, having kids, dining at fine restaurants, and then appearing on *Oprah*. I wanted to get my life back so that I could really start experiencing all of the fullness, complexity and nuance that I had been discarding in the pursuit of my single-minded obsession. I thought maybe I could recover into a new version of myself—a person with a possible future.

After the drive through the leaves with my dad and Josh that autumn I began allowing myself to contemplate food in a less theoretical manner. The idea of food being something that I could partake in was a revolution of blatancy. Once I began thinking about how and what to eat, rather than how to avoid food at all times, my anorexia began losing power. Every time the thought of being "normal" again frightened me I focused on no longer being at NYU, and how much that had wounded me. My identity as an intelligent person and a good student rivaled that of my anorexia. I had developed a permanent lump in my throat that I had to audibly swallow every time I even thought about school.

I slowly began to visualize myself, as best as I could, eating again and starting to get healthy. I began concentrating intensely on a single image: sitting down at the rustic kitchen table in Boston, or the round, glass table in my New York apartment, with a plate of food before me. At first that was as far as I could go. But I visualized every single detail, from the color of the tablecloth to the decorations on the walls around me. Then, slowly, I began to imagine the food itself. It could be anything—a small salad, a piece of fruit, one cup of cottage cheese with two crackers—anything, just as long as the food wasn't overly intimidating. I would picture myself eating, deliberately and meticulously, but calmly. I struggled to remain calm, even in my imaginings. I would see myself finish the meal, wipe my mouth, place the dishes in the sink, and continue on with my day as though nothing outlandish had happened.

After a while, those daydreams became so mundane that I felt I could actually try to make them a reality. I no longer had a "professional" working with me, but I figured I knew myself well enough to take things slowly so as not to panic after every meal, like I'd done at Renfrew. My goal was to make steady, consistent progress.

I set mid-January as my deadline—by then, I would start the actual eating. Every day I meditated, visualized, and prayed for a new beginning. This time I wanted a change that could last me the rest of my life. I prayed I would be strong enough to eat again and, more importantly, brave enough to live again without hiding.

In Boston I began to make meal plans for myself as I'd once done with my nutritionist Adelaide. Only this time I was hatching a legitimate campaign instead of simply fantasizing about food I never felt I could consume. The meal schedules were grueling. Every night before bed I wrote out what I would eat the next day, including the specific times at which I would consume my three meals. Usually, things went horribly wrong. I would sit down at the appointed hour, take a bite of my food, and realize I wasn't comfortable with what I'd chosen. That would often lead to my skipping the meal altogether, and the entire day's plan would be thrown off track.

Another problem I encountered was how hard it was to break from my old eating habits. I had to abandon the ritual of picking at my food in order to retrain myself on all food-related matters. I invented a few simple but unbreakable rules, which I still follow today. They include eating the entire portion off my plate, instead of nibbling at crumbs and deceiving myself into thinking that I'd consumed that meal. I also use silverware with each meal and sit down at a table where I can take my time and be mindful of what I'm doing. Once I'd finished a meal I had to remind myself, thousands of times afterwards, that I had done a brave thing and not a shameful one.

Oddly enough, one perk about recovering from anorexia is that it is so difficult. Anorexics are people striving to prove themselves by setting extremely challenging tasks and putting themselves through rigorous, punishing ordeals. Pain becomes a lifestyle. If recovery wasn't so wrenching, I doubt any anorexic would be interested in trying it. It was specifically because each day was so grueling that I knew I was succeeding at something. That intense sensation of emotional exertion and physical discomfort was so familiar, only this time, it came from eating.

Eating replaced anorexia as my full-time job. Every day was scary. I needed all my energy to concentrate on it one moment at a time. If someone had at that point inquired as to what I did for a living, I wouldn't have hesitated before proudly declaring, "I'm waging the war of a lifetime!" And waging war, though frightening and dangerous, at the very least makes you feel alive. While in the trenches of this battle I realized I wasn't just eating. I was also reevaluating every part of me that the anorexia had once controlled; I was attempting to reverse the damage and start again.

Rather than run on the treadmill for hours of daily punishing cardio, I abandoned the gym altogether. I put away my exercise clothes and started taking more long walks. Walks, since the one I'd taken to Ethan Allen during my darkest days, had come to symbolize new hope. Getting ready in the morning became a small victory, especially after the period when I'd lived in bed in my pajamas without showering. Some of the things I'd lost became available to me again. Every time I got up in the morning, ate breakfast, showered, got dressed, and went out for a walk, I felt like I'd been given an amazing gift and had accomplished something unusual. I no longer had anything to rebel against when it came to eating, because I was in control of choosing when and what I ate.

At Renfrew, strangers had been deciding things for me, just as the anorexia had controlled me. I'd been completely unable to determine what I would do or put into my body next. That lack of empowerment at Renfrew eventually, ironically, contributed to my mental and physical deterioration. Now I was making conscious choices, and though, at first, they may not have been part of what a nutritionist would consider a wholesome, complete diet, I was at least choosing to eat.

I returned to New York at the end of January and the city walks I now took were different from ever before. I began to see things very differently. I started to feel relaxed in New York for the first time in my life. All the fast-paced businessmen in Midtown became nothing more than a constant rush of water. It was like standing calmly under a waterfall and just letting my body quietly feel the movement. Uptown, I was amused by the rich old women who shoved their puffy little dogs into large leather purses. I still hate Times Square, but I loved, most of all, spending time downtown. The downtown streets still felt like home after all that had transpired.

I walked down 4th Street and listened to Bob Dylan's "Positively 4th Street" at the same time. I returned to all the places where I'd lived and looked at them in wonderment, barely believing I'd once inhabited such a cool space. Those places will forever bear my mark, as will the streets, because I know I have left just a whisper of myself behind, a small imprint of who I was at the time. And I know that that person, though troubled, was not irrevocably flawed.

Walking became my meditation in motion; and it was something I could do with my mom, who I had once done everything with, and then nothing at all. I'd violently shut her out of my life with bars she could see through but never penetrate. I didn't realize any of this until I started eating and walking again. But now every time I went home to Boston I asked my mom if she wanted to go for a walk. In that invitation existed another—the request to come back into my life. Slowly we began to know each other again. As we passed other walkers, including friends, mothers and daughters, even loners, I started to wonder about the rhythm of life. It had a beat, one mirrored in the act of walking. A daily walk might seem boring. It might after some time become routine in pace and setting, but if one can't uncover the small truths in simple acts, like walking, it will be impossible to discover the greater realities of life. Or worse, the quest will never even begin.

My body surprised me in many ways as I began to eat again. I was shocked at first to learn that my body could even *process* food. After years of not eating I almost couldn't believe my body knew what to do with a meal. There were times I felt so full after only several bites that I could barely breathe. There were many moments of nausea, and I often had to lie down and breathe deeply, even after a light meal. I never got sick, and I also didn't suddenly gain weight like I'd been sure I would. I had dreaded, yet also expected, an immediate weight gain after my first meal. My body needed the food and it was adjusting to everything new that I was giving it.

One of the most dramatic symptoms I experienced after I began eating was night sweats. As my metabolism started again, like an engine, I began to wake up in the middle of the night drenched in sweat, dehydrated, shaking, and cold. I eventually got so used to this that I would place an extra pair of pajamas by my bed at night and change my sheets every morning. During the day I got hot flashes and I joked with my mom that I'd reached menopause before her. In a way, I actually enjoyed my night sweats, because they were the tangible manifestation of my reawakening body. I also began to feel warmer, more energetic, and more capable of concentration.

After some time, I began to slowly gain weight, but it wasn't as terrifying or uncomfortable as I was convinced it would be. It happened so gradually and over such a long period of time that I was able to adjust to the changes. But there were also times of despair. I had one pair of jeans I'd used to monitor my weight, rather than stepping on a scale. When I had bought them, about a year before Renfrew, they were tight. If I was going through an extreme week of starvation I would wake up in the morning, put on my jeans, and depending on how they fit, figure out how many hours I needed to spend in the gym that day. At Renfrew my jeans were loose. Now, every morning, they were progressively becoming tighter. I knew that before long they wouldn't fit at all. Truthfully, those jeans had no business fitting a 5'8" girl in the first place. But on days of panic I would try on my now-tight jeans and collapse onto my floor in a fit of angry tears. I did this so many times that the feeling of dread became commonplace. Eventually I tired myself out, took off my jeans, and went on with my day.

I also often felt an extreme sense of loss, as though I was grieving. I knew that I was mourning my dying anorexia. I knew what those jeans represented: they were the symbol of my disease. Now I needed to put them away, bury them and never look back. I could no longer behave like the anorexic girl I'd been for years. I was starting over as a whole new Laura. And as scary as that was, I also knew that it was my only hope.

One of the benefits of having a daily meal plan was that I inevitably grew accustomed to my usual foods and so the predictable ensuing guilt began to weaken. Separating food from emotion by becoming almost bored with consistently eating my meals was empowering. I no longer felt at the mercy of my own fear. This was more significant than all of the academic accolades I had ever received. With each passing day my emotions about food were replaced by the knowledge that I was capable of eating and carrying on with my day.

No longer feeling terrified of the meals that had become standard made me begin expanding my options and trying new, intimidating foods, like 1% cottage cheese, a couple of cashews, or an extra piece of fruit. I wanted to challenge myself, but progressed slowly, so that if I had a negative experience I wouldn't stop eating altogether. I knew that if I tried something I didn't feel right about, or simply didn't like, I would merely remove it from my plate, revise the plan, and by the next meal be back on track again. In the past, trying something new would have made me scurry back under the dark wings of my anorexia. I would have punished myself for days, instead of just acknowledging it and moving on.

Even though I was making good progress it felt strange to be working for myself, rather than self-sabotaging. It was still difficult for me to adopt a healthy lifestyle instead of a self-punishing one. I've always had a certain masochistic streak to my personality—this has made maintaining a proactive attitude towards weight gain while attempting to pursue a healthy lifestyle extremely challenging. This was especially true on the few occasions that I allowed myself to pause for a moment and truly dissect the meaning of my actions. Every time I reviewed my newly ingrained habits and compared myself to the girl I'd been only months ago, I questioned which version I preferred.

My family was encouraging me to continue my progress, buoying me with praise and love, but every time they told me how well I was doing it only scared me more. Every time someone said they were proud of me or that I was looking better, I felt certain my anorexia would come back in full rage. In a way, I still wanted the disease to engulf me with its tornado force. Part of me wanted it to take over completely so that my mind could erase the pain of struggling to eat again and the knowledge of the hurt I'd caused my family. I didn't want to remember the relationship I'd once had and lost with my mom, or feel frightening hope at the thought of the new life I was trying to carve out for myself. In a way I wanted my anorexia to rub out the footsteps I'd taken through downtown New York City streets, and erase all my life's happy memories, because they were frail and could so easily be tainted. I longed for anorexic amnesia. Living with anorexia meant I could live easily and alone in my misery; these two states of existence are synonymous.

I didn't give in to my persuasively destructive urges. I simply could not let myself do that again. I knew if I lapsed just one more time it would be final. I had enough energy for one more try, and if I let go and fell off the tightrope on which I was so precariously balanced there would be no net and no one to catch me. This is not to say I didn't have people in my life who wanted to save me. It's only that none of them knew how.

The balance between the temptation to starve and the desire to live again became a daily, nearly unbearable, battle. I simply could not focus on anything else. Any real conversations I had at that time took place in my own mind as I argued with myself. What would I do now? I had taken myself far, made a lot of progress over the past few months, but I also realized I had reached the limits of my own power. I had two main problems I couldn't solve on my own.

I was first and foremost afraid of falling off the thin rope on which I was unsteadily teetering. I needed backup. I needed to know that if the desire to starve myself suddenly became too overwhelming, I could talk to someone who would know what to say. But where would I find such a person? I had been to so many misfit professionals, most of whom made me darkly cynical of ever finding any real help.

Far greater than the fear of slipping back into my anorexic habits were all of the questions I urgently needed answered. Why had I become anorexic in the first place? What had caused it? Why had it been triggered? Who was I? Who was I capable of becoming? In this regard I was no different from everyone else who was searching for those same answers. But every solution is different; there is no single, universal truth.

I realized it was time for me to find my own, personal truth. I needed to answer my "why," but I couldn't do it on my own. I wanted to think that was because I knew myself too well, but in reality, it was probably because I no longer knew myself at all. I was so exhausted, but I still had so much work to do. I didn't know where I would go, but I had one final option and had to find out, for myself, where it would take me.

There was only one person left for me to call—he was someone my mom had been pestering me to call for at least a year. Now I suddenly knew that it was time.

Chapter *Ten*

Levenkron's Net

Columns of my tunnel collapse. Pillars in my mind are gray.
Stone; gray matter; gray brain; gray rock, pile upon pile; gray being; gray lump; gray eyes.
Poets are for Renaissance days, diplomat artists, multi-purpose whispers.
Poets are for Renaissance days, and I am neither the designer of my own space nor the contributor of which words decide to haunt me (particularly my own).
I have been to a world so deep, a time so cut, so fresh that it can only be stitched with one jagged motion at a time — like a fibrous wound, gray scar, gray sky, gray scratch, gray groove.
I have been to a space so fortuitous it could only have been built with one granite boulder at a time.
My mind is a nomad and it can't yet shake these birds of time. My mind is still a nomad and it wanders through caves where gray was born — caves where rock was born, where fossils were fresh — and caves where the two first met.
My mind is a nomad with a home, a pillar of whooshing flight and whirring fizz.
A settlement so strong you can sit and sit and sit like a mother rock.
Wear me down . . . tear me down . . . but then I remember the velvet curtain of my own Renaissance craft.

It seemed as though my mom was always reading books about anorexia, but especially books written by recovered anorexics. I didn't understand her compulsion. The last thing I wanted to talk or think about was this disease plaguing me day and night without pause. I couldn't imagine buying and reading books on the very subject I was trying to avoid. For nearly two years she called and told me about the newest book she'd read. After a while I lost track of the extensive list of books she beseeched me to at least consider reading. I never remembered their names, but the formulaic premise always seemed so tired.

In one of the books a girl was only able to recover after the death of her boyfriend. In another one a girl recovered because her mother died. In yet another one a girl recovered because her sister died. Why were people only recovering after the death of a loved one? It seemed implausible and overly dramatic. Wasn't *anyone* getting better without first going through a major tragedy? I hadn't read any of those books, but I certainly felt annoyed by the questioning that always ensued after my mom described them. They ranged from "Do you think you'll have to have a traumatic experience before you can recover?" to "Don't wait for something bad to happen before you recover!" But at that point none of it really mattered to me.

No matter who wanted me to recover or how I was supposed to go about doing it, I still didn't know what my lasting solution would be, or if one even existed. Anorexia still had a tight grip on me, even after all of those genuine attempts at recovery. But the experiences of others, those plots, never left me. The more I tried to push out the detailed accounts that my mom constantly chronicled, the more they stayed with me as I began to better understand the magnitude of anorexia's hold.

I remembered one of those phone calls from a couple of years back because of my mom's insistence that there was one book that was totally different, and that stood out from all the rest. It wasn't written by a recovered anorexic, but by a therapist. It wasn't overly dramatic or dull. It simply expressed every stage that we had been going through, as a family dealing with anorexia. The part that distinctly compelled her was in the description and explanation of the relationship between anorexic girls and the people in their lives. This writer, whoever *he* was, knew something more about the mysterious lives of anorexics.

The book was called *The Anatomy of Anorexia,* and it was written by a man named Steven Levenkron. I had never heard of him, and though I'd heard the excitement in my mom's voice while talking about him, I remained unyielding. So what? So some guy figured he knew a lot about this disease. To me it wasn't a disease—it was my life, my *entire* life. I don't care what other people think they know, I reasoned. You don't know it until you live it. But my mom would not relent. We just *had* to get in touch with him. This became her mantra.

A week before I went to Renfrew I was in Boston preparing for my trip. While going through my extensive list of things to buy and pack one morning, I walked into the kitchen and my dad suddenly informed me he had found the number to Levenkron's office, that Levenkron lived and worked in New York, and that he was calling him "right now." Before I could utter any discouragement about his idea, I was handed the large portable phone with a force that my dad hadn't exhibited in months. Obviously, he was keen to have me talk to someone who might be able to help.

I didn't want to talk with Steven Levenkron, or anyone else. I didn't know who this man was, what he was about, or why he would take me as a patient if he was supposedly so famous and well established. I was busy preparing for my stay at Renfrew, which I assumed would be like a stay at a women's minimum-security prison. I needed to get ready and I couldn't be chatting with some New York therapist about future appointments or help. I was in turmoil *now*. Also, I had already decided that Suse Klab would be my psychiatrist upon my return to the city. My parents had agreed to those arrangements, but they were both convinced that I needed to be in touch with this man.

Despite these thoughts, I took pity on my dad's hopeful, eager face and decided it would be rude to run out of the room as I had intended only a few moments ago. I was holding a phone that was now busy ringing some office in Manhattan, though to me, it may as well have been an office on the moon. After several rings a pleasant-sounding woman answered.

"Hello?" she said.

I had no response. I had forgotten the name of the man I was supposed to be talking to. Was it Robert Zimmerman? No, that was Bob Dylan's birth name. And what was I even asking for? I couldn't make an appointment because of my dreaded upcoming rendezvous at Renfrew. What was I doing talking with this woman? After a long, silent pause during which all of these thoughts raced through my mind, the pleasant voice asked, "Do you want to make an appointment with my husband, Steven Levenkron?"

For lack of any better solution I angrily—and lamely—blurted out to the agreeable voice that my dad had forced me on the phone, that I didn't know who Steven Levenkron was, and that even if I did know, I still wouldn't want to see him. Instead of the irritated retort I'd been expecting the nice voice became even kinder, telling me that if and when I ever did want to meet her husband I could just call back.

I felt very satisfied with myself after I hung up the phone and walked into the living room where both my parents were seated, eagerly waiting for me.

"I'll show them," I thought. "I'll show anyone who claims

that they can help me and anyone who pushes me into something before I'm ready not to mess with me."

I was feeling very tough until I saw the happily expectant look on my parents' faces. Then suddenly I felt sorry for them, very sorry that they had created such false expectations for themselves. They were hoping maybe I could get help from someone after Renfrew. Maybe their daughter could get better and finally find some solace. I knew that I would be seeing Suse Klab after my Renfrew stay, but my mom had a feeling about this Steven Levenkron, and she kept reminding me about it.

"He knows," she would say. "He just knows."

That was what scared me. I didn't want anyone to be able to look into me. I didn't want anyone who "knew." If my mom was right—and I knew she probably was—then Steven Levenkron was the last person I wanted to see.

Nearly two years after that brisk conversation with Steven Levenkron's wife, Abby, I found myself eating again, and trying to recover from anorexia alone. But I knew that no matter how much I wanted my life back, or how hard I was willing to work at it, I simply could not do it on my own. Even if I could, it would take me the better part of a lifetime to figure out all the intricacies of my anorexia. I had also never forgotten the book that changed my mom's perspective on anorexia, or her excitement about the person who wrote it. I certainly hadn't forgotten how rude I had been to Abby, but I hoped that she had. I had come to a point, finally, where I was ready to willingly make that call for myself and meet with Levenkron in order to hear what he had to say. I wanted him to be able to help me navigate through my recovery, and I wanted to have someone there who I knew was capable of catching me if (and when) I fell.

"Don't invent the wheel if you don't have to," my parents always told me. "Don't rock the boat" was another gem my mom always offered me, and one that particularly irritated me. That's exactly what I had been trying to do, but I was now putting so much hope in this person who I felt sure would disappoint me. Despite all of that, I decided to address my mom's intuitions and determine if this therapist would be of any value to me. Maybe I could learn something about myself through his insight.

On May 5th I called the same number that my dad had dialed for me nearly two years before. But this time a man answered. The voice was calm (maybe too calm, I thought), steady, and slow, compared to my own nervous, wavering tone. I could hear how ridiculous and scared I sounded, and knew that could only mean one thing: I finally cared. Two years ago, my voice had been tough, aloof, and nonchalant. Back then I'd really had no desire to recover or seek help. Now I had some hope invested in my recovery and a curiosity about getting my life back.

Slightly relieved that I didn't have to make the appointment with his wife, who might remember the rude girl I once was, I made plans to have a consultation with Steven a few days later.

I didn't really know that much about Levenkron, and I hadn't read any of his books for two specific reasons. First, I didn't want to be intimidated by his fame and feel like I needed to impress him or act falsely. Second, I didn't want to know the details of his other treatments, in case I became one of his patients. I didn't want to compare myself to anyone else.

My plan of remaining uninformed failed. A couple of nights before my first appointment with Levenkron I was watching the *E! True Hollywood Story of 101 Most Shocking Moments in Hollywood*. Without knowing what to expect, I ended up watching moment number seventy-something, the death of singer Karen Carpenter. Steven Levenkron had been Karen's therapist before she died, and I saw a picture of the two of them together in his office talking face to face.

For the next few days I tried to analyze every single aspect of the picture I had seen. I closed my eyes each night and was met with the same black-and-white image of therapist and patient looking at one another and conversing as though they had no sense a photographer was anywhere near. I couldn't place myself in Karen's position, but I also couldn't imagine going through yet another round of therapy. I didn't know how or if I could make it a real part of my life. The pressure was mounting.

The morning of my consultation with Steven Levenkron—who I now knew something about—I woke up to a gray, rainy, dreary spring morning. I had barely slept the night before in nervous anticipation of what the appointment would reveal about my future. I felt like no matter what happened, the day would be a momentous one. For one thing, I was now in a different place on my road to recovery. Just the thought of possibly finding a therapist I could finally be compatible with, one who would know how to deal with me, was a surreal concept.

I was also afraid I wouldn't be the type of patient that Steven was looking for. I had been eating for almost a year and had put on a little weight. I was still thin, but I knew I was no longer skeletal. This worried me. Would the famous anorexia man treat someone who wasn't in danger of falling over if they skipped one more meal, as I had been that first day I called his office? Would he take one look at me and say, "Sorry, get back to me when you've lost a few pounds?" I knew I was paranoid about not being thin enough to fit into Levenkron's group. On the other hand, I couldn't truly trust my own self-image. I could no longer look in the mirror and see what my body really looked like. I had lost that ability years ago.

To ensure I wasn't scrutinized too closely by Levenkron, or anyone else I might encounter in this new universe, I wore the little black Burberry trench coat I had bought before going into Renfrew and considered one of my "skinny" coats; I thought I could go incognito. But I was foolish and naive. After all, wasn't the point of getting help to stop the mind-numbing anorexia games I had been playing for so long? Wasn't part of the new deal to be vulnerable, expose all of my problems and concerns, so that someone else could help sort through them with me? After all I had been through, I was still hiding from myself. I still hadn't realized that no matter what I looked like, no matter what I wore or how I portrayed myself, the only way I could ever be rid of my anorexia was to finally, boldly face myself, once and for all. I had been hiding from myself for so long I could no longer recognize the person behind the black Burberry trench coat. I knew that if Levenkron accepted me I'd be in for a long, difficult journey, but at least I would be *in*.

After carefully constructing my "therapy outfit" I left my apartment with Levenkron's office address scribbled on a piece of paper, and Josh at my side. It was a drab, humid day, and I was nervous and uncomfortable with what I was about to do.

Levenkron's office was more than forty blocks from my apartment and getting a cab was difficult even in the afternoon. Any New Yorker knows that on a rainy day, open cabs are as scarce as roomy, rent-controlled apartments. The clock ticked on, I still couldn't find a cab, and I became so nervous about Levenkron refusing to meet with me because of my lateness that I started to yell at Josh and flail my limbs at any passing car that looked like it could give me a ride. I felt like I was going to the most important job interview of my life and that any bad move could spell much more trouble than a career mistake—it could mean death. Getting a cab had now literally become a life-or-death situation. If I wasn't accepted as one of Levenkron's patients, I reasoned, maybe it would be a sign that I should just finally give up. Everything seemed like a sign those days, and any small snafu at that moment would have pushed me back over the edge. I knew that I would remain true to my one-time deal with myself: If I couldn't get better after trying my *hardest* this one, last time, then I would go back to the full-blown anorexia.

We finally got a cab about fifteen minutes before my appointment and miraculously there was no traffic on 3rd Avenue. We made it to Levenkron's office with enough time to marvel at the beautiful Madison Avenue buildings surrounding his own stone town house. After we were buzzed in to the spacious waiting room Josh sat down on a beige leather couch while I remained standing, wading in a puddle of nervousness, apprehension, and fear. I must have waited for ten minutes, during which I lived an eternity of thoughts and emotions.

There, in the waiting room, resting my eyes on the various safari photographs that lined the walls, I began to go over all the things that had happened to me in the past few years. I recalled the turmoil and misery I had lived through, as well as the oppressive blackness that had rested its sad weight on my frail shoulders. I remembered all of it, began to live through it all again, until suddenly the office door swung open and I met Steven Levenkron for the first time.

Steven Levenkron is a composed man with a very calm, low voice. It has taken me over a year of therapy to trust this calmness. I was always waiting for whatever lurked behind that serene exterior to unveil itself and send me running. Now I know that there is fierceness to him, but instead of it ever being aimed at me it is instead my shield.

On that first day I could do little more than study him. He looked different from the black-and-white television image I had seen. Now he was alive. His icy blue eyes, white hair, and beard made me think immediately of a tough mountain goat. If goats are stubborn and demanding, then so is Steven, but in a good-natured, loving way. By the time he led me into his office, after he had shaken hands with Josh and flashed me a quick, almost offhand smile, I was already emotionally raw. I had worked myself up so much on the street and in the safari waiting room that as soon as I sat down and he said, "So, you're concerned about anorexia," I just burst into tears.

I sobbed for the next fifty minutes, with a few long pauses of quieter, shoulder-wracking crying, so that I could actually hear a few things he said. I know I spoke, but I have no idea what the words were. I know he spoke, but I don't know what it was about. I went through a fistful of tissues and when I got tired of reaching over for a new one I began reusing the tissues that had been crushed and crumbled in my ever-moving palm. I didn't care; I just needed to finally unload. And so I did, thinking that

I hadn't passed the test, that I hadn't gotten the job, and that it finally felt good to cry like that in front of someone who *knew*. But it especially felt good to cry for myself. I hadn't grieved for myself in so long. At the end of our session Steven asked me if I could start seeing him two days a week, and I nodded yes in silent shock that he would ever invite this overly emotional girl into his private office again.

That afternoon when I got home I fell into bed and slept more soundly than I had in months, maybe years. I knew it was the start of something for me, a new, hopefully better path. Maybe now I had someone to fall back on if I found myself on the verge of collapse or self-destructive illness again.

A few months later I found out that my first appointment had, in fact, been like a job interview. Steven had tried to figure out whether we could work compatibly together. I'm glad I was able to express my emotions, because if I had been acting overly professional or fake the way I often did with therapists, I'm sure he would have been hesitant and doubtful. That day Steven and I both understood that we could relate to one another, guaranteeing that our therapy and progress would be real.

Our first few appointments were straightforward and easy, because we were simply getting to know one another. But after this introductory phase, things became quite rocky. I began to resent Steven for being famous and feeling so confident in himself and his ability to help me. I resented myself for having to constantly seek help and therapy. I had never thought of myself as a "therapy-type" of person. I had always been so self-sufficient. What had gone wrong? How had it all changed? I knew how complicated my thoughts were, so how could this guy even be so sure he could help me? For one straight month—though I never directly brought it up to Steven and only expressed my feelings by snapping at him randomly—I thought I would quit therapy. Every time I left his office and took my usual path down Madison Avenue, my thoughts a jumbled, troubled mass of emotion, I was certain that this was the last time I would ever see Steven Levenkron, the Mountain Goat Therapist, again.

I got into the habit of calling my mom promptly after emerging from each appointment, telling her about my frustrations and sharing thoughts of what I would do next. My relationship with my mom had changed dramatically since the days of Renfrew and Adelaide. We had become better at communicating with each other and were both willing to flip our worlds upside down if it meant we could reach each other again on the other side. I could talk to her now with honesty and less apprehension. I could tell her precisely what had frustrated, aggrieved, or scared me about my sessions with Steven, without panic that she'd blame me, judge me, or become so frightened by the prospect of my quitting recovery altogether that we'd fall back into our old slump. That never happened because every day we were learning how to better navigate our new, improved relationship. She was becoming my confidante again.

Every day, for the first few weeks, I left Levenkron's office, angrily yanked my cell phone out of my bag, called home and waited for one of my parents to answer and ask in a tense but decidedly "under control" voice, how things had gone and what had happened. I knew my mom had alerted the whole family about the dangers of my quitting therapy and that everyone was hoping I wouldn't act too rashly. Everyone was pulling for me once again, and I felt it. No matter how much I persisted in doubting Levenkron, my mom—the one who'd found him in the first place—gently kept reminding me that I had no other place to go. She always reiterated that he knew what he was doing, and that I should just give myself some time to work through my frustration.

Her words have always been very important to me and I tried to hold on to them as precious little jolts of renewal. I was being proactive in my own life, something I hadn't done in years. My dad and sister also always tentatively, gently asked, "So, how's Steven?" or "How are your appointments going?" There was always a note of fear in their voices when they asked me these questions. I knew that everyone's nervousness stemmed from the proof that I could self-destruct, that I could very well go to that dark, unreachable place again. Would I go back to starving, or would I finally accept help? Would I start to work for myself even harder than I had been working against myself? My family was afraid, and those simple, silent questions were so full of meaning, emotion, and fear of a future they'd glimpsed and knew could be full of suffering and destruction.

In the end I stuck it out with Steven for three main reasons. The first was that I hadn't yet realized that I wasn't simply "going to therapy," but forming a true, complicated relationship with a person who had the ability to demystify for me the workings of my own brain, my own personality. I was also confident that Steven wouldn't be scared or put off by all the grief that I could, and eventually did, give him. I knew he wouldn't act like The Klub, who had been incapable of dealing with my emotions and had reacted by simply falling asleep. I knew Steven was very caring, but also sharp and tough when he needed to be. Although it was only later that I experienced his persistence firsthand, I saw it in him from the beginning and felt safe—this resoluteness was born of caring and concern. I knew I needed to be with a therapist who wouldn't be frightened by the events that came up in my life, or the emotions that emerged during my recovery. I had to know that he could handle it.

The second reason for my loyalty to Steven was that I knew I had no one else to turn to and that without help I would only get worse and return to my full-blown anorexia. But now, that prospect was scary instead of reassuring. I knew what anorexia had meant for me and what it would mean for the rest of my life. I knew that it had nothing but misery and cold fear to offer, and now that I had just one shred of hope I felt like maybe, *maybe* my life could be momentous. I clung to that prospect because my very existence depended on it.

The crack in the façade of my anorexia had widened to reveal a living hell, something Dante forgot to mention in his

Inferno. I was scared to go back to that life, but I knew about the magnetic pull anorexia had on me. I would have to actively struggle against it with somebody there to coach me.

The third reason I decided to stay with Steven was my growing curiosity. He made me interested in myself again. Here was a man who didn't provide all the anorexic clichés that every other therapist, psychiatrist, and social worker had slapped me with, most of which didn't even make sense or ring personally true. Here was a man who had a refreshing twist, who learned about me as an individual and proceeded to treat me like a person instead of a disease. In fact, he wasn't the least bit impressed by my anorexic history. Anorexia was a nuisance to him, and he treated it that way.

The primary obsession of my life for so many years was squashed like a bug in the hands of Steven Levenkron. I liked that, and I thought I could finally get some answers about me, Laura, not about the anorexic person I'd become. I felt that if I could figure out where all my overwhelming fear had come from and why my despair and grief had so overtaken me, I could finally move on. I could essentially reprogram myself and not need the anorexia anymore. Only then could I find the real happiness born not of the pretense that defined my anorexic state, but born of a confident, real understanding of my true, unhampered self. I knew that this was a modern-day quest for the most worthy prize I could think of—the reclaiming of my spirit.

As soon as I began therapy, things began to change, as though I was making up for all of my previous stillness and solitude. In mid-June, just as I'd decided I would continue to see Levenkron and invest myself in this new process and relationship, I got hit by a car while walking down Madison Avenue.

On the corner of Madison Avenue, surrounded by fancy designer shops, well-dressed ladies, and men in suits, I was bumped by a bulky Lexus SUV turning left onto 66th Street. I had the pedestrian right-of-way and was crossing slowly when I noticed the beige SUV move, but I still didn't comprehend what

was happening until it accelerated into me. My body was propelled down the street, and for a moment my world went black.
When I lifted my head I realized that I'd been tossed halfway
down the street. I had a coffee and shopping date with Josh that
day and had put on a new outfit I really loved. Now I was lying
in the middle of the street with my shoes yards apart from each
other, my bag wide open, my wallet, cell phone, makeup, and
iPod all littering different parts of the street, and the denim jacket
I had been wearing somehow torn from my body.

My first reaction was denial. I figured I could collect my
belongings, brush myself off, and still meet up with Josh on
time. I couldn't call him because I had no idea where my cell
phone was, even though I had been talking to my mom at the
moment of impact.

The moment I stood and attempted to walk back up the
street I could hear the people who had gathered around me
begin to protest. The old male driver in the SUV was staring at
me ashen-faced, and I couldn't figure out why everyone was
causing so much commotion until I finally looked down and
saw what surely had to be a broken ankle and a broken or dis-
located knee. My right leg had swollen so badly it looked like it
belonged to an elephant.

The next few hours passed quickly as someone called an
ambulance and a construction worker found my phone. When
I pieced the battery back to the body I was shocked to see it still
miraculously worked. I immediately called Steven.

I knew he was close and would be able to reach me quickly,
but I also called him first because I was certain he would know
what to do and how to help me. He was in the middle of
another session but ran out the door when I'd explained what
had happened. Just as I was being wheeled into the ambulance
I saw him dash down the street in his beige cowboy hat. Just as
the ambulance door was about to close he jumped in and sat
down beside the paramedic.

I called Josh and asked him to meet me at the hospital, but

hesitated before calling my mom back. I didn't know how to explain what had happened without making her panic. I had been on the phone with her when the car hit. How much more could this woman take? It seemed like life had been a nonstop series of hits these past few years, culminating in an actual strike from a car. I hoped she wasn't thinking the worst but knew she had probably heard the thump of steel smack into her daughter. I knew she had probably felt it. My mom hadn't been at home while we'd been talking, so I called my dad instead and told him what had happened. I figured he could gently break the news to her without causing too much panic.

When I got to the hospital I was put in a wheelchair outside the ER. That's when I started to black out—in the waiting area, then in the elevator on my way to the emergency room, and in the cot while waiting for an ER doctor. I blacked out every few minutes and I was convinced that I had some kind of brain damage. Josh arrived just as I was being rolled into the elevator, and he waited with me while I was taken into my new room for tests.

A few hours later, I was released from the hospital with a severely sprained ankle, badly bruised knee, and a concussion. As I hobbled onto the street on my new crutches I passed people who, I realized, would probably never leave the hospital. These were the unconscious, the sick, the fearful, the hopeless and wounded. And all of them, like me, were scared. It gave me vivid recollections of leaving Renfrew and knowing that my room-mate Sara would never be given that same opportunity.

I realized that if I hadn't been drinking milk, taking calcium and eating again to reverse my bone loss I probably would have snapped in two. I knew my bones had become stronger and my body and mind had evolved along with them. I had been given one more second chance.

While recovering from the car accident I began to think of how easily I could have died. I started to remember flying through the air, landing on the hard cement, and lying motionless for a few moments. I began to imagine the old Laura dying, while the new Laura emerged. Perhaps she was slightly injured, but she was also stronger and more ambitious. I began to visualize leaving my old self behind, the one that had endured so much personal turmoil, physical pain, and psychological confusion. I would become a fresh, untainted version of my old self.

Another good thing happened as a result of my getting hit by the Lexus SUV. I realized the first person I had called, on impulse, was Steven. I never would have considered calling The Klub or any one of the other doctors for help if something like that had happened back then. I wouldn't have called The Klub even if my life depended on it, but I had instantly phoned Steven, who had reacted immediately. He'd arrived on the scene in seconds and mentioned how positive it was that I had called him. I could trust and depend on him, but these were scary thoughts for someone who considered herself autonomous and solitary. I'd realized early on that in order to get help from Steven I would have to trust him, and I was obviously beginning to do just that. And so that accident was another new beginning for me, in many ways. There was no way I wanted to waste a fresh start.

I'd started seeing Steven to understand what had triggered my anorexia in the first place, but began learning so much more from him. I slowly realized that my anorexia had been fed by all the negative, unhappy thoughts I'd had about myself. The more I'd let this misery take over, the more I had become the physical incarnation of pathetic sadness. I'd once thought anorexia was powerful, both as a weapon and a shield. Now I just felt sorry when thinking of myself as an anorexic. Now I saw my anorexic self as someone who had been guided by four main emotions.

The first was fear. I had been afraid of living my life without guarantees, and terrified of being surprised by events I wouldn't know how to handle.

The second was a need for control. I'd felt like I needed to keep a tight rein on my actions, and I was excessive with the self-punishment anytime I lost control and ate. This was ironic because I unwittingly gave all my control to the anorexia, thereby losing entirely what I had been so intent on keeping.

The third driving emotion behind my anorexia was mistrust. I was skeptical of myself on every matter. I felt I could no longer make the right decisions, act appropriately, look the right way, or be the right person. I stopped trusting my family, everyone who loved me and everyone I loved. I became suspicious and felt that by attempting to take away my anorexia they wanted to rob me of happiness. In reality, they were giving up their lives to look after me.

Finally, when the anorexia took total control, I was overcome by a drowning, suffocating hopelessness. I stopped feeling like my life could ever again be joyful. I stopped dreaming and creating a future for myself, except the one that involved a skinnier and skinnier Laura. But how would that end? Would I simply disappear into thin air like a tiny wisp of smoke?

These four emotions were the principles that guided my thoughts, actions, and overall outlook on life while I was a full-blown anorexic. I realize now how little power I actually had while starving myself. I'd thought I was mighty, but had become instead a cowering, fearful, vulnerable little girl.

Steven helped me see myself as two people—the person overcoming anorexia and the anorexic person. Only one could survive, and I now knew who I wanted it to be. I no longer wanted those harmful, soul-crushing convictions to guide me through my life. My life belonged to me and nothing and no one else. As such, I had to value and respect it, not destroy it from the inside out.

I didn't blame myself for the anorexia. I had been broadsided by it. I now knew better and thus couldn't let it control me anymore. Beginning to unravel myself from the anorexia in my mind was a new stage, and it was as difficult as separating conjoined twins. I wanted a free, new version of myself and I knew that I would really work for it, with Steven's help.

Chapter Eleven

Kid Rex

I told him that I was entering a new, rebellious phase.
And in his green eyes
I saw tumult, appreciation, recognition — fear?

I told him that I would always love him, but that I have to move on, to continue.
And in his blue eyes
I saw sadness, regret, resentment — relief?

I told him I would love him forever.

I did love him, fully, but he chose another path.

I told him that I liked him, knew him, would be his wife, and he stayed and kissed my hand and got down humbly, wordlessly on one knee.

I told her that I accepted her, liked her, looked forward to getting to know her, and in her large brown eyes I saw a new kind of fire
about to burst aflame.

I had stopped referring to myself as Kid Rex only a month before my first appointment with Steven Levenkron. It's not that I no longer saw myself that way, but I was trying to recover and therefore couldn't consciously address my alter ego anymore. I had decided to give it a rest, and take a break from the shame and self-mockery that I'd been shrouded in for so long. I decided to release Kid Rex, and prevent her from methodically killing Laura. But I felt sure that no matter what, Kid Rex would always be there, lurking somewhere inside me.

One of the problems with having to displace my alter ego and allow the real person to resurface is that I had to accept living in a world full of other people. I had to resocialize myself. Despite all of the intoxicating power anorexia had over me, I'd always suspected the day might come when I'd have to replace its rules with new, real-life solutions. I always feared that I might someday be forced to reverse the anorexic spell. The day every anorexic dreads is when she finally admits that anorexia is a dead end. Then what? Either you decide you're willing to drive yourself over a cliff and give up on life completely, or you choose to see what other possibilities may exist.

Anorexia can be so charming! It's the drug that provides escape—the vacation everyone always promises to go on but never takes. The trouble is, as an anorexic, you're on a permanent vacation that's gone awry, and you therefore miss every other aspect of your life. Anorexia had once felt romantic, but it now had to be traded for the grit of sober life and solid food. I had even liked Kid Rex. She was a tough, unaffected, nonchalant bad-ass . . . or so I'd thought.

Once I finally realized that Kid Rex was a weak, scared little girl hiding behind a mighty illusion, I discovered something else. It was a fundamental realization that Steven pointed out as he rolled his chair closer to where I sat on the green leather sofa.

"You're surrounded by strong women!" he cried, as if the epiphany had just dawned on him from nowhere. And that was it. With that one sentence I knew Kid Rex could never return, even if I used a séance to bring her back. I had been molded by strong women all my life, thus the core of my being was tougher than I'd realized.

"And feminists," I added, pointing to him. We shared a laugh peppered with irony, and then both fell silent. Yes, Steven is a self-proclaimed feminist, and not afraid to say it. And he, like Fran, my mom, and I, understands the real meaning of that term. The days of bra burning and male bashing are over, and really, they were never part of the true movement. To be a feminist means recognizing the beauty of being a woman and realizing that women who work together are a formidable force. For an anorexic, reclaiming her personal power as a woman is a big step towards shunning the illness and leaving behind her Kid Rex persona for good.

Yet, I wondered, sitting in Steven's office that afternoon in my second year of therapy, why, with all the strong female role models and innovators in my family, had I chosen anorexia in the first place? The truth was I never consciously chose anorexia, and I failed to see the true weakness behind it. I'd thought I was emulating the women I knew and acting strong. By freeing myself from all basic physical necessities, which I viewed as burdens, I'd thought I was achieving a new level of power. In fact I managed to accomplish the exact opposite, by denying my femininity and weakening my body.

To become an anorexic is to shed your womanliness. Feminine beauty becomes a curse. You lose your breasts and natural curves, your menstrual cycles, your estrogen and other hormones. You become genderless. I, as an anorexic, revolted against women and became the perfect example of frightening androgyny, even though I had grown up in a family of warriors, rule-breakers, and breathtaking examples of female beauty. My grandmother, mother, aunt, cousin, and sister are all such empowering examples of brave women that it would have seemed unlikely that I, the youngest in the group, would try to rid myself of that identity.

But now, fighting so hard for my femininity—something I'd been taught to honor and should never have lost in the first place—I was grateful to have so many examples from which to draw inspiration. For the first time in my life, I began to truly evaluate the women around me.

I left Steven's office propelled by the energy of new realizations. Aside from the astounding fact that I'd never used the support of these women to my advantage, I found the life-altering impact his words were having upon me remarkable. With all of the power Kid Rex had seized, it was incredible that after a little more than one year of therapy I could so readily accept some of Steven's ideas, and use his anorexic lingua franca as though it had always been my own. His thoughts had sunk into my subconscious and now I was accepting them as readily as I had previously embraced my anorexic rhetoric. I began carrying his voice with me when I was out in the world, and that afternoon I realized what was really going on. Steven Levenkron had become my mentor. With his help, I was reprogramming my brain and learning how to embrace my womanhood again. But to fully accomplish this feat I would first have to carefully examine the women in my life.

That afternoon, as I did after each session regardless of the weather or the way my session went, I left my appointment and began to walk home. This was the time to clear my mind of self-destructive thoughts and allow myself some space for new ideas. But that afternoon was different. That day I filled my head instead of clearing it, and I started by thinking about all of the women in my life. This is something I still do often. Just by noticing the words, actions, ambitions, and personalities of the women in my family, I have become a more complete person.

There are some people, like my grandmother, I can always rely on. They are buttresses in my life, erected by the architect who designed this existence so that I may have something to lean on when I am weak. And then there are people, like my aunt Lia, who are reliably outrageous and full of adventure. In my opinion, a person needs both quiet strength and wicked humor to be complete.

Lia and I are similar in many ways. On the outside we look tough and fearless, but that bravado masks an inner softness and foolish spontaneity. Our swimming-with-sharks-in-the-middle-of-the-night mentality seems like lots of fun, but could be construed as a slight mental deficiency by those around us. If I didn't share this defect with my aunt, my life would have been considerably more boring.

Lia is my go-to girl when I know everyone else will consider my proposal crazy, dangerous, or strange. When I feel like acting with abandon, I go to Lia. She is the only person I know who would wake up in the middle of the night while camping in the woods in northern Canada, just to watch the stars and drink vodka. She is the only person I know who moved to Algeria as a young dentist to start a new life and get out of Communist Romania. She is the only person who could make a horrific story—like how she destroyed a nest of Algerian cockroaches in her kitchen by dousing them in boiling water—sound funny. If I ever go to Thailand, I will choose to share a room with Lia, because I know sleeping in a bed beside her she will ignore the plopping noises of tarantulas falling from the ceiling and say laughingly, "Never, under any circumstance, turn on the lights!" She had the courage to tell me I needed a root canal, knowing full well that my irrational fear of dentists might trigger an explosive reaction. She is the only person who looks forward, year after year, to going on a family ski trip even though she still can't ski, and the only person who asks to be seated at an outdoor dinner table in the middle of winter.

One of my most carefree memories—and in those years I wasn't able to collect too many—involves Lia, the open sky, and me. During a family trip to Europe we stopped for one night in Como, on the Italian-Swiss border. This was before George Clooney had his villa on the lake and the whole world knew about our special spot. I was thirteen when we visited, and I thought Como had a beautiful, dual personality. During the day it is a lively, charming town with houses that surround a tranquil lake. When the moon rises, however, the town bows to Lake Como, and the lake becomes master of all its surroundings. It controls the minds of every resident and looks knowingly into the depths of women and men. Staring at Lake Como, even the most practical scientist might come to believe that it could house the Loch Ness Monster, sunken ships, pirate treasure, and people's dreams. Then day breaks again every morning and the magic recedes with the fog, sinks to the bottom of the water's steely surface, only to rise once more with the night. With one blink, the intellectuals snap back to their practical senses and Lake Como becomes nothing more than it ever was—a lovely pool of water on the Italian-Swiss border.

The night we were in Como we stayed at an old manor on the lake. After a long day of walking through the sloped town we were all tired and ready to sit down for a fancy, proper dinner. The dining room was stately and massive. It seemed unfit for twentieth-century guests, or anyone not born into royalty. Every surface was draped in luscious burgundy-and-sapphire velvets with matching drapes, waiters' vests, and napkins. The heavy oak table at which we sat was large enough to comfortably accommodate another twenty people. The menu was inspired, and I couldn't help but giggle, not because the Comonese had invented marvelous new ways to prepare escargot, but because they confirmed all my preconceived notions of living in old world formality by doing so.

That night we feasted on each other's company more than

on the tiny delectable dishes served. And although we had no business being where we were, with our contemporary North American clothing, obnoxious laughter, and purple wine-stained teeth, we were lulled into comfort by our view of the lake from the dining room's full-paneled windows. The lake was beckoning, and soon Lia and I couldn't resist the temptation.

"Let's go out for a swim!" I nearly shouted at my aunt, after the last drop of cappuccino had been consumed.

"Of course, we must!" she yelled back. Rising from the table we impolitely excused ourselves and hustled back to our hotel rooms before anyone could swallow their tiramisu and give us a long lecture about why bathing in a dark, mysterious lake in the middle of the night may not be such a good idea.

I put on my purple Speedo bathing suit while Lia dressed in her matching violet suit with black racer stripes along the sides, and began to envision the types of creatures we might possibly encounter in the lake that night. There could be leeches, water spiders, poisonous plants and fishes, alligators, all manner of strange and wonderful beasts that only made me want to jump in sooner.

I met Lia outside her door and we made our way down to the lake, so determined we barely spoke a word. We didn't quite know how to access the back of the hotel so we wove our way through the fancy dining rooms in the rear. The first room we stormed was even grander and more sophisticated than the one in which we'd just dined.

We pulled open the enormous wooden doors with their huge brass handles and let them slam shut behind us, only to discover a group of elegantly dressed Italians. Middle-aged men and women decked out in tuxes and ball gowns stopped dancing long enough to stare at the two crazy people, dressed in nothing but purple bathing suits, clutching white bathroom towels that "by no means, signore," were supposed to leave the hotel.

Neither humbled nor sobered by their puzzled looks, we quickened our pace and crossed brazenly through the ballroom, entering yet another dining hall. Three rooms later we burst in on the rest of our family, who were lingering over dessert and *digestivos*. They all stopped and simply stared in a fatigued, resigned way. Of course Laura and Lia were doing something spontaneous and crazy. They would have been shocked if we weren't in a hurry to get into the water. If I were a knight in the Middle Ages I would have battled monsters and fought evil wizards beyond the palace gate to reach the magical lagoon.

Lia and I finally arrived at the water's edge. We had woven through winding passages and navigated secret doorways to reach our prize. Mist rose off the water and blanketed the chilled night air. It looked like the lake was smoking a huge cigar. The surface was *nero, nero*—blacker than black—dark, thick, and oily as squid ink, and along the bank lay three half-submerged, mossy green steps that descended to the bottom. I shivered in anticipation. There's nothing I like and fear more than dark water. To this day I am obsessed with the desire to go night diving, and though no one will agree to join me, my dad has assured me that "when the time is right" we'll go together.

Lake Como had offered us an invitation, so, without further hesitation, we both jumped in, feet first. At first the water was frigid, but that provided us with added incentive to swim around and get warm. The lake engulfed us. For a while no one existed in the world but my aunt and me, two adventurers hungry for life, eager to explore anything that came our way. The water carried us gently and allowed us to paddle around in her velvety depths. And through the fog, as though from an apparition, five white swans emerged and glided towards us. They were not afraid. In the water they were much larger than we were, two heads bobbing on the surface of their abode. Their bright whiteness against the dark stillness of the lagoon made me believe, for just one moment, that color had faded from the earth. Nothing could have been more beautiful or perfect than the contrast I beheld before me. The swans seemed to study us, then looked at each other and swam away, but remained close enough to us to reach with a few doggy paddles.

Time didn't matter for a while, because it got lost in the deep mist that embraced us. For a while we just existed, at peace with the lake, its swan guardians, and the night sky that seemed enormous. In tranquility, distance and size cease to have much meaning.

And then our family called us back. They were on shore and couldn't find us, and for all they knew we were now sitting in the bowels of an aquatic monster, struggling to escape, like Jonah. Shocked back into reality, Lia and I swam towards the light, giggling hysterically.

"How cold is the water?" our family demanded. "Is it full of leeches?" "How deep does the bottom go?"

Wracked by peals of laughter, we couldn't answer, and suddenly our group fell silent as the swans slid up behind us, beckoning the two thrill-seekers back into the lake. But we didn't belong in the water, and magic cannot last forever. Lia and I finally stepped out onto dry land and dripped our way back to our rooms, past the fancy dining halls and ballrooms, through the heavy wooden doors, ignoring once again the horrified expressions on the frozen people dressed in black and white.

My relationship with my aunt has always been easy. But with my mom, it's been a more elaborate journey.

It wasn't until my family moved to Boston and I entered high school that my mom and I truly began to understand each other. It was only about eight years ago when it dawned on me that my mom, Michaela, had become my best friend. Our relationship is still new by most standards, but it works so seamlessly it feels as old as time. The first vacation my mom and I took together, just the two of us, was during my sophomore year at Newton Country Day School. I was still too young to travel with my friends, but luckily for me my mom understood it was spring break and I needed a release from the intense demands of school. That year, Fran went to Cancun with her college friends, and my mom took me to Providenciales, a small island in the British West Indies that our family had been traveling to each Christmas since I was ten.

We knew the island well. We knew where we wanted to stay and what we wanted to do. We were also curious, if not a bit intimidated, by the prospect of spending an entire week together and sharing a hotel room.

As it so happened, we discovered on that trip that we had the same interests. We both liked being in the ocean, but not lying in the sun. We liked coconut shrimp at lunchtime, and going to the realtor's to look for beachfront property on which we dreamed of someday building a sprawling palace that my mom would design. We liked driving around the island with the windows down, blasting Bob Marley. I still tease my mom about her misinterpretation of the lyrics to "Jammin." She thought Bob was saying "pajaming," instead of "jammin'," and using that word as an innovative way of referring to sex. She found this mildly offensive, yet it didn't stop her from belting out, each time the song came on, "pajamin', pajamin', pajamin' . . . I hope you like pajaming too!"

We spent time together shopping at the island's few boutiques, and in a matter of days we'd gotten to know all the sales clerks. And oddly enough, we discovered that we both liked gambling, and guiltily wound down our evenings with a few hours in the hotel casino.

Every afternoon my mom and I ate lunch on the hotel's patio overlooking the ocean. She would then take her daily afternoon siesta, and I would make my way through the piles of biology and chemistry homework I'd brought along. In the late afternoon I would meet her in our room, and we would resume our nightly routine.

When I got back to school in April I turned in two long papers: one on evolution, the other an explanation of molecular structures. Both my biology and chemistry teachers returned my work with similar emphatic comments. "Laura, this is an amazing amount of research . . . wow!" I kept those papers permanently filed on my bookshelf, not because I was particularly proud of the work I'd done but because I finally understood why I was doing so well in the first place. After so many years, I had gotten to know my mom as a woman and a mother. I discovered that I admired and liked her so much, that all I wanted to do in the world was make her proud of me.

Every afternoon in Provo, while she napped and I wrote, I was inspired by her dedication and the amount of suffering, studying, grit, and persistence (I now realized) it had taken for her to become the incredibly accomplished woman she is. My mom has two bachelor's degrees in architecture, a master's degree in interior design, and is an exceptionally talented painter and printer. Her artwork is now her full-time passion, and this inspires me to work harder to cultivate my own passions.

The last night my mom and I spent together in Provo we decided to eat at a new restaurant we hadn't yet tried. It was called Coco Bistro, located in the heart of a palm tree grove, owned and run by a nice French couple. Drinks were served in split coconuts, and as we sipped them we marveled at the extraordinary amount of coconuts that could exist in this particular grove. "How could there be so many coconuts?" we asked our waiter, but he just shrugged and brought out succulent Moroccan lamb dishes in clay pots.

We ate under a tent made of stars, and I felt so safe, sitting across from the woman who had provided me with my first home, my first incubated tent. At that moment, ten years after she had left me, I finally understood why my mom had gone to study in Rome. It was at the University of Toronto that she had first begun to understand all her previous years of schooling had been a lie. The Communists in Romania had rewritten history to serve their own purposes and advance their propaganda. They had tried to erase religion, individual rights, civil liberties, and even Christmas (the ultimate holiday and celebration in my family).

In Toronto, when the magnitude of those deceptions had finally become completely clear, my mother was overwhelmed.

She'd been forced to catch up quickly, to try to discern truth from lies and reality from fiction. After all, she reasoned, what could she teach her own kids about freedom and authenticity if she did not fully understand those concepts herself? She'd understood her task. My mother would have to travel and open herself up to the world, so as to take it in and pass it on to us. I finally understood that she went to Rome for Fran and me! Upon her return, my mother was a changed person. She had accomplished her mission and embarked on a whole new life that she had created for herself. She had become illuminated as certain cruelties and falsehoods of her past were expelled. She had also managed to break into her male-dominated profession and carve a name for herself as a talented architect. My mom, in a complicated yet very real way, followed my grandmother's mighty legacy without even realizing it.

Whenever I miss my mom I try to "tent" myself. I get very odd looks from people who walk into my apartment and find a small camping tent set up in the middle of the living room, complete with fluffy pillows, assorted reading materials, an iPod, and piles of blankets. I have Josh assemble my tent whenever I feel like I need to regroup. At the worst point of my anorexia the only moving I did was from my bed to the tent and back. Ever since I was little, when I missed my mom, I would put a blanket over my head, create some breathing space by sticking one leg in the air, and inhale evenly while looking at the finite roof I had created.

My mom is my living tent. Being around her gives me a simultaneous sense of security and freedom. I know that I am safe within the confines of her being, and am therefore free to move around my own existence without ever straying too far from home.

During Christmas 2004 I spent a few weeks in Boston taking stock of what that year had meant in the grand scheme of my life. Fran and Josh traveled back and forth from New York while my mom and I spent several consecutive days together, visiting all our favorite city spots. I needed time to read through the first draft of my book undisturbed, so every day we traveled to our much loved Italian coffee shop on Newbury Street, sat down with cappuccinos, and always said the same thing. "How can this coffee be so good, and taste so much like the kind we get in Italy?!"

Then my mom would leave and I'd be alone for hours at a small table, engulfed by piles of paper and scribbled notes. For hours I would work, and then, after what seemed like moments, my mom would be there again, waiting to pick me up. We would always walk and talk before driving home, sometimes about important things, other times only about trivial, ridiculous matters, but always as one confidante to another. Then we would get in the car, blast the heat, roll the windows down, put in our favorite song and belt out, "pajamin', pajamin', pajamin', I hope you like pajaming too . . . I wanna pajam' it, I wanna pajam' it with you! . . ."

I now understand who my mom is, and that knowledge overwhelms and motivates me. I'm glad that at crucial points in our lives we decided to give each other a chance. And I'm relieved that every time I'm around her, regardless of the place or season, it feels like sitting under a canopy of stars in the center of an incredible coconut tree grove. Yet I'm still wondering one thing, several years and countless lessons later: How can there be so many coconuts?

Thinking about my mom immediately brings to mind my sister, Francesca, as well. I was born on December 22nd, but I was brought home from the hospital on Christmas Eve. Although it was illegal to celebrate Christmas in Romania at the time, my parents always figured out a way to put up and decorate a small tree in the living room of our Bucharest apartment. In Europe, Christmas is celebrated the night of the 24th, and when my sister woke up from her nap to open her gifts she found a basket with her new little sister under the tree. My parents doomed me from the beginning by literally gifting me to

Fran. From that moment on I was her possession, her toy, her pet, her sister, and her daughter. When my mom left for Rome, Fran, though only a little kid herself, took on the burden of raising me. My sister has a different parenting style than my mom—she's more possessive, bossy, and protective. When I tell her that I don't actually belong to her she just looks at me and laughs. To that retort I have no defense.

I was in Starbucks the other day and almost started to cry just at the moment that it was my turn to order a cappuccino. With a long line of businessmen behind me I knew I mustn't hesitate to order, but I was too busy listening to "You Are My Sunshine" playing on the radio. I was picturing my older sister as a little toddler. Even then she acted like a full-grown, mature adult, and she'd sung that song to me in our Calgary daycare center. I was suddenly transported out of Manhattan, to a different time in my life when Fran and I were babies and had just moved to Canada with our parents. After escaping from Romania we lived with Lia, Andi, Teo, and Alex in Toronto for a while, until my dad acquired an engineering position in Calgary and moved us to yet another foreign city.

Calgary is a very cold place with brutal winters, and I can't help but think that my love of winter, Christmas, snow, and pine trees has something to do with the first things I saw, heard, and smelled in Calgary. My mom and Fran, regardless of these experiences, can still barely stand the long, cold months. During our first winter in Calgary, we hardly ventured outside, making full use instead of the indoor bridges that connect the buildings like a giant spider web. Fran and I experienced much bitterness that year, both from the harsh weather conditions and the Polish immigrants who ran the daycare center that we attended. My dad, Michael, had to work and our mom attended English class so she could obtain a degree recognized in North America, get a job, and help provide for her family.

Our building was directly adjacent to the neighborhood bordello. With very little money, we'd had no choice but to rent a unit in Calgary's red-light district. The prostitutes got to know us, and one in particular fell in love with my sister, vowing that her first child would be named Francesca, regardless of its sex. When it was warm, my mom, Fran, and I always spent a few minutes outside, chatting with this friendly woman. But when it got unbearably cold, we would skip the red-light conversation and go straight to dreaded daycare. Every morning Fran and I feared what the afternoon would bring.

The center where we were forced to spend our days was located in the building next to our apartment. It accommodated a diverse group of roughly thirty kids, most of them children of fellow immigrants. I was two years old at the time and can't recall much, but what I do remember stands out in vivid detail. For example, after participating in a series of inane morning activities, we were forced to take a nap at noontime. I was a hyperactive child, so I found this quite difficult, but Fran, always the consummate mother, would settle me down, tuck in my blanket and fluff my pillow, and go to sleep holding my hand. "I'll never let go of your hand," she always said. No matter what happened or where we found ourselves, she explained, we would be in the same sleep world together, connected by our finger conduit. Yet without fail, every time I awoke, my sister was gone, but not of her own volition.

For some reason our Polish caretakers bore against us a vendetta. Maybe it was because we spoke no English, while the other kids could at least communicate. The mean Polish ladies took pleasure in their torture. Whenever Fran needed to use the bathroom she would hop from foot to foot, unable to vocally phrase her request. They understood perfectly well what it was she needed, but refused to let her go until she asked in English. I luckily had no such problem and felt comfortable relieving myself whenever the need arose, but Fran would just look at me, obviously embarrassed by my lack of control, and chose the more difficult alternative. I guess she learned to hold it in until we got home, or maybe at an early age she weaned herself off liquids, but my sister was always brave and uncomplaining. As long as Fran was in charge and fearless, I was calm. I thought surprisingly little of the pain she must have been experiencing.

That's why I panicked on the afternoon that I woke up to my sister's screaming voice. The first day we were separated while taking our naps I heard five-year-old Fran screaming, yelling, crying, demanding in her crazy mixture of Romanian and Pidgin English to know what had become of her baby sister. My heart started pounding when I heard those shouts. I'd never seen Fran lose it like that before. Our sleep room was small but covered in a vast sea of tiny heads resting on the floor. To Fran's groggy eyes I could have been any one of them, or none at all. For all she knew the wicked ladies had kidnapped me, and I was now gone for good. Three women tried to control her but she kicked them off and started hunting for me madly. I finally calmed down enough to call out to her and we were reunited, but the trauma would take its toll on us during every naptime.

For weeks, Fran and I fell asleep next to each other, grasping hands ever so tightly, but to no avail. The trouble with sleep is that it relaxes your muscles, regardless of your will. As soon as our fingers were lax and our guard down, we were immediately separated. To this day I still have no idea why they kept pulling us apart. Maybe it was a strict Eastern European mentality of proper conduct. Maybe these callous women, who'd had their own dreams and aspirations, were tired of caring for children and took pleasure in torturing them instead. Or maybe they were just crazy. Either way, I found Fran getting increasingly agitated upon waking from her naps. She would always make her way immediately across the room to find me, but the trek was beginning to take its toll. I watched her silently and noticed she was finding it harder to fall asleep. Naps had become the enemy; they weakened her ability to keep a close eye on her charge. I, on the other hand, found comfort in pulling the blue wool blanket over my head and joyously picking my nose.

Salvation arrived in the most unexpected way. A young Canadian woman started working at the daycare and took an immediate liking to Fran. She probably had enough sense and tenderness to understand my sister's grief, and Fran became her personal project. She would walk Fran to a separate corner away from me, put her down and sing "You Are My Sunshine." By this time my sister was able to speak some English, while I could still only say her name in the foreign tongue. It usually came out sounding something like "Fran-chwo-ska," but I thought that was good enough, and for a while I refused to learn any more. Fran, on the other hand, probably grasped the general meaning of the entire song, but I think it was the melody that eventually soothed her. Soon it became her tune and she always wanted to hear it. She sang it for anybody willing to listen, and if no one was around, she sang it to herself. That melody became her comfort, just as her little hand on top of mine had been mine.

The truth is that Fran's fierce devotion to me hasn't changed at all. She would still grab my hand if I were sleeping next to her. Perhaps the fact that I was her gift, one she found on Christmas underneath the tree, has something to do with her ferociously possessive claim. But I think the simplest and best reason for her dedication is love. I know she loves me so much she would put herself in any dangerous or harmful situation, just so I could be spared the slightest modicum of discomfort. If it were up to Fran I would float through life, resting easily atop her shoulders while she carried me around, as per my instructions. This kind of commitment has turned me into something of a brat. Having a sister like that has made me feel special, yet also jealous of any boyfriend she's ever dated. But I realize now that every time I woke alone and scared across the room and heard my sister, pretending to be tough, sing "You Are My Sunshine," she was really singing about me.

Remembering those days living in Calgary always makes me think about the move my parents, Fran, and I made only a year later to Toronto. We were greeted at the airport by my cousins

Teo and Alex, Lia, my uncle Andi, and the grandmother I didn't yet know—Elena. From the moment I met my grandmother, at the age of two, some core part of me resonated with her. She had a shy smile, a brisk walk, and a strong embrace. She was just recovering from the death of her husband, the grandfather I never met, and had moved to Toronto around the same time we did.

My grandmother went through a period in her mid-sixties when she had to reinvent herself, yet again. She was now an immigrant living in Canada and no longer the self-sufficient, greatly admired doctor she had been in her previous life in Romania. It must have felt like that life had been savagely stolen from her, and yet I never once heard her complain. Instead, she combined her single-minded determination and her great humility and grace to learn English from me—her toddler granddaughter. Elena (or Mami as we've always called her) and I made a deal that I would speak only English to her and she would speak only Romanian to me. The plan worked in my favor and I quickly learned while she continued to struggle to grasp the tricky English dialect.

A couple of years ago Mami broke her arm after a nasty fall in her sacred place, her garden. The autumn after her accident she went to Boston to visit my parents, and I flew home from New York to be with her. For the first time in my life I witnessed vulnerability in my grandmother. During the week I was there, my parents, Mami, and I went for long walks. The three of us would walk slightly ahead while she trailed behind, propelling herself by swinging her arms, while her heavy cast weighed down the entire length of her right arm, wrist, and hand. Still, she willed herself to move as quickly as possible.

On the day of our last walk I slowed down to be next to Mami and savor a calm moment brightened by the jewel colored leaves that had fallen, like pronounced haloes around the tree trunks. For a few long minutes neither of us spoke until she asked me if I remembered a particular conversation we had had as she walked me to school a few weeks before my fifth birthday. In fact I did remember that time. Mami had asked me what I wanted for my birthday, and I told her that I would be happy to have anything, "even a leaf from the ground," if it was from her. I remember the way Mami's face brightened when I told her that, because I meant it. I was not, at the age of five, feigning disinterest in material possessions. Instead I was able to express, in that one glimpse, a deep-seated love, a mutual admiration, and a rare and wondrous fountain of friendship that I had found in my relationship with my grandmother.

One year after she broke her arm, Mami was in the hospital again, diagnosed with stage IV lymphoma. She had been there for two weeks before Fran, my parents, and I went to visit her. The four of us met at Pearson Airport in Toronto and immediately drove to the hospital. The trip was quiet and filled with anxiety about the Mami we would find in the hospital's geriatric ward. After wandering the disorienting hallways of St. Joseph's hospital we found her room and walked in. Mami was sleeping, curled up in a fetal position and reminding me so much of a small child. Lia was sitting in a chair next to her while Teo was organizing the room that Mami was sharing with another elderly lady.

I couldn't believe how small Mami had become. She had always been a short woman, but the power of her presence had made her appear monumental. Now she was sick, weak, and tired. I didn't know how . . . how she had become so small, how she was going to die, how to understand the depth of the grief I was suddenly harpooned by, how I would ever live without her, how I would ever stop crying, how any of this had happened, how any of us were expected to bear the pain of it. I was at a loss and felt like, no matter how long I lived or what kind of discovery process I would work through along the way, I would ultimately never begin to understand life.

When Mami woke up, I forced a smile and quickly wiped my tear-stained cheeks. My watery outburst had triggered a chain reaction, and I found my mom, dad, Lia, Fran, and Teo all wandering around the room, pretending to be doing something while they too dabbed their faces. None of us wanted Mami to wake up to a room full of people grieving her while she was still with us. I went to her, sat on the edge of her bed, held her hand, kissed her and hugged her.

I wanted more.

I wanted to take her all in, to inhale her.

I wanted something—anything—a leaf, an answer, her life back.

For the few days we were in Toronto we spent as much time in the hospital with Mami as we could. The day we left, I held Mami's hand and told her that I loved her. She looked at me, smiled calmly, and asked me if I remembered when I asked her for a leaf for my birthday. I nodded quietly and smiled because I realized that the leaf was our relationship—simple, beautiful and honest. I hugged her goodbye, left her to sit in her hospital bed, and turned around as I walked out of her room. The last glimpse of Mami that I saw was her foot, poking out from under the forest green blanket that Lia had brought from home. I loved that foot because I knew it so well. I would have recognized it immediately, anywhere—it was purely Mami.

In my mind, my and Mami's leaf is orange. It's the color of the pumpkins that she grew in her garden at the end of each summer. The leaf is orange with hints of brown around the edge—it is dying. And in its death it is beautiful, magnificent, and cherished above all else.

Mami spent a couple more weeks in the hospital before being allowed to go home on bed rest. That entire time, every moment of the day, Teo took care of her. It didn't matter to Teo that she had a business deadline. She had been working exhaustedly, launching her jewelry business and website that she single-handedly created and built. Now, nothing mattered to her but Mami's comfort and well-being. Every time I talked to Teo about spending so much time in the hospital, and having so many of Mami's physical needs to care for, she just gracefully smiled at me and said, "It's okay, Deer, I'm happy to do it. Mami needs me."

The day after our return from Toronto I had an appointment with Steven. After we were finished, I took my usual walk through the Upper East Side. I realized then that I had never been so close to freedom from anorexia. Somehow I was no longer alone in spirit. I am now surrounded by the women in my life who lift me up. They are brave enough to live each day with self-honor, and from them I am continuously learning.

The Madison Avenue sidewalk is not big enough for the big black dog, Kid Rex, and me. The sidewalks in my life are not big enough for all three either. They can comfortably accommodate just one. And with words still buzzing in my ear, of strong women, loving mothers, brave grandmothers, protective sisters, and carefree spirits, I know I have no choice but to walk through life with Laura. I choose myself.

Chapter Twelve

Venice Again, For The First Time

If you can find my body more beautiful than sad, like Venice, then there's also hope for me. A floating body island sinking, drowning in its own lack of mirrors . . . in a land built on deep, reflective glass. Who were you once, Venice, to parade your streets and hold your people gilded as if in a Virginal light? Who were you, Venice, to weigh yourself down with such chunky, block stone when really your floating is made of muck, and at best reed and clay? You are made of hardened pretenders and gold-painted edibles. Stay afloat! Well, you were just like me, a love-child of Venice, who played with numbered days as if they were surely jokes, as if somehow darkening hours could pull themselves up at the last, airy minute and stay dusk on the Rialto. And now, my Venice, you may as well be a slave of Disneyland. In other words, give up your ornamental pride! Parade yourself no more! If you could look at me and not see Venice I would once again feel as jovial as the fifteenth century night. If you could look at me and not see a decayed half-life who wasted her fairy days in some dark, sinking place, I could leave Venice behind. I could say, "Don't look back," because it sounds poetic. I could stay afloat!

I like to think that I am not a judgmental person, but I can't help cringing when I hear people say that Venice is nothing more than a tourist trap, or some sort of Italian theme park. It pains me even more when they go further with their disdain and label Venice "a dead city." If I ever had a pet peeve, something I found irritating and simultaneously preposterous, that is it.

I admit that Venice has its downfalls. I admit that sometimes the canals seem dirty, the narrow streets smell like rotting trash, the locals are rude and snippy, and the fish are not as fresh as their ocean cousins. But so what? I also know that Venice is full of wonders. The largest spider I ever saw (including the tarantula who shared an outhouse with me in Baja) was Venetian.

It has become a generally known fact that Venice is sinking. But to this I say again, so what? If the natives are bad-mannered, maybe it's to be expected. Who wouldn't get sick of clueless tourists after a while? Who wouldn't occasionally get lazy and fish in the nearest and wonderfully convenient canal for dinner? To all of this, I say: who isn't sinking?

When a person tells me they hate Venice, I question the person, not the place. I wonder how it's possible that so many years of history don't speak to certain people. I wonder how unromantic one must be to not feel moved by Venice's creeping ghosts and haunted walkways, or secret whispers that can be heard with the rolling fog that permeates the bridges and cobblestone passages.

But most of all, when people tell me they hate Venice it frightens me. Venice is the home of nomads who seek peace, protection, and strength. It is my home. And instead of finding refuge in an impenetrable medieval fortress or barricaded steel-framed prison, I attain it in a floating city that is deceptively delicate and capriciously unreachable. Venice proved its coquettish unavailability to many groups of people over many centuries. The most advanced armies tried to conquer Venice but were outwitted by her confusingly moody and dangerous lagoon. Time has tried to wear on Venice and gravity has tried to pull her down, but there she still floats full of a grace made more intense by her experience, many misfortunes, and gloriously damp architecture. The dark days, brazenly cold winters, frozen canals, endless whipping rain, and exaggeratedly outlandish floods she has endured have all shaped her. Venice has earned each lustrous new day; she deserves them all. She is a survivor.

I think Venice and I are kindred spirits. Despite her baroque splendor, Venice has witnessed sinister eras and is now in the struggle of her life. She is searching for a new identity, a modern way to be prosperous. Venice must remake herself. And the eyes that judge Venice harshly also judge me as I, too, now try to move on, find a new identity and a place where I can face my dark alleys rather than hide from them.

Being from a European family made Fran and me take European travel for granted. From the time we were kids my parents constantly took us on trips around the world, but especially to Europe. We went to France, Germany, Spain, Greece, Romania, Hungary, Ireland, Austria, Switzerland, Liechtenstein, and many more places. But we all agreed that Italy was our favorite. It became official—the Moisins unwaveringly preferred Italy. It was never strange to us that while our friends went to Florida with their families we went back to explore yet another part of the continent from which we had originated. Although we always looked forward to those trips we also eventually took them for granted. Fran and I figured we would go on them forever. To us it was easy. The four of us would pick a country, and then a few months later we would be in Europe again, visiting, driving, eating, drinking, laughing, and feeling at home, regardless of the specific location. We had become so accustomed to that pattern that we no longer truly appreciated what we had been given, as so often happens in life.

The last time we went to Italy with our parents, Teo, Alex, Lia and Andi, Fran and I were less than thrilled. The plan was to visit both northern and southern Italy with a stop in Capri, which we had not yet explored. The trip was set for the end of July, and when we made the plans, that future time seemed so far away. But as our trip approached, Fran and I became increasingly nervous. I was about to start my sophomore year at NYU, and Fran was moving to New York. We both kept saying we had too much going on and that the timing was wrong, but in reality we simply didn't want to leave our boyfriends. I hadn't seen much of Josh since he had finished his last year of college at JMU in Virginia, and Fran was moving away from her boyfriend, Rick. We both rolled our eyes at girls who changed their lives because of boyfriends, but we also couldn't repress our true feelings. We came up with numerous excuses to cancel our Italy expedition—after all, we had taken so many in recent years. Eventually, we decided to go for only one week. That way we could still visit Italy, but also have enough time at home with our boyfriends.

When I look back on my reluctance to go to Italy that summer I simply cannot fathom what I was thinking. I was taking so much for granted. Our parents had booked us a luxury Italian trip, including reservations at some of the nicest hotels in one of the world's most beautiful countries, and I wasn't interested in going. I took for granted the fact that my entire family would be together for weeks, with nothing more to worry about than which flavor of gelato to enjoy after lunch. I took for granted that we would be in Tuscany on my mom's birthday, a celebration I have always cherished as an opportunity to honor the birth of my best friend. And I took for granted that my dad had booked us in Venice for three nights and four days, a long stay in the watery city that no one else in my family particularly looked forward to.

Yes, even I betrayed Venice at one point in my life. I stopped seeing her as a beautiful survivor, the city that is simultaneously gold and gray, heavy and light, and so magical that, walking through the narrow alleyways, you believe, if even for a moment, that the lions of San Marco can really fly. Even I wasn't thrilled about a trip to Venice, and I was being handed a free ride to the city I've always been obsessed with, by parents who wanted nothing more than the pleasure of my company. What more could I have asked for? I took everything for granted.

That late summer in Italy, I felt trapped, as though I had been forced against my will into a large, beautiful enclosure. All I wanted was to be back in Boston, hanging out with my friends and Josh. All I could think about was home, and the fun my college friends were surely having without me. I couldn't help but feel provoked by my parents, and I blamed them for dragging me all the way to Italy. During our first week, Fran and I sat down each day to breakfast and cappuccinos and discussed how my dad could make new travel arrangements for our early departure, and why my parents shouldn't feel abandoned by their bratty daughters. I couldn't hear the way I sounded, but I didn't really grasp that we would be in Italy for only a few short weeks. But after the first week passed, we began our trip to Venice.

Though I had tried to be an inconvenience to my parents and make them pay for what they had done to me, I couldn't help but feel lighter as we stepped off the vaporetto and walked to our Venetian hotel. I had forgotten the spell that Venice always casts on me. It represents a great architectural feat, a perseverance of the human spirit born of necessity and steely determination. Venice enthralled me beyond all words or logic. I simply felt at home in her arms; and suddenly, I no longer wanted to be back in Boston or New York. I wanted only to be rocked at night by the slow, licking waves that met land at hundreds of tiny shores created by Venice's cheese-hole canals. Venice chilled me out—it was like powerful hypnotherapy. I was finally at peace again, and for the remainder of the trip I enjoyed myself.

Venice Again, For | The First Time

I danced silly German jigs with Fran in a Tuscan vineyard. I waltzed with my mom and the porcelain marionette cat she received for her birthday. I ate gelato with my cousin Teo while discussing the relevance of art in society. And I walked arm in arm with my cousin Alex, both of us pretending to act appropriately, while secretly we told each other dirty jokes.

This trip with my family feels like it was made of snapshots—rare, precious moments, frozen in time, which I will remember forever. When I take myself back to those memories they are so vivid I feel like I am reliving each one, in a time parallel to my present life, and it gives me some relief to know that the old, carefree Laura still exists somewhere. I probably also view that trip as though it was shot through a camera lens because it was the last time I really felt comfortable having my picture taken or seeing photographs of myself. Those photos of Italy were the last I cherished before I stopped eating and started feeling painfully awkward and self-conscious about my body. I had felt that way before, and I had already been on random spurts of fasting, but after that trip to Italy, the anorexia began to pummel me with a vengeance, inside and out.

For a long time afterwards, I remembered how pleasantly free and exhilarated I had felt in Italy. What had started as a forced vacation had, in the course of a few brief weeks, transformed into such a state of carefree happiness that I no longer even wanted to go back home. In Venice I felt like I was already on native soil. Those intense feelings of belonging and recognition made me start thinking about reincarnation. If I believed I had lived many lives before, I swear almost half of them were spent in Venice. Time and time again, after returning to New York, I thought of myself walking through the maze of narrow side streets, stumbling upon a brightly lit, pink-flowered garden in someone's backyard, and smiling coyly at gondoliers while realizing that inner peace often comes from the appreciation of simplicity.

I couldn't have known that when we left Italy that summer it would be a long time before we returned to Europe on a family vacation. I had no idea how jagged the road ahead of me would be. And as I began to starve myself and fall deeper into an anorexic coma, I couldn't believe I had ever been as happy as I was during those four days in Venice. It was like someone else had lived those moments and the only proof I had that it was real were photographs taken of me in the golden city.

After that, I no longer allowed anyone to take my picture. I simply did not want a depiction of my body to exist. I was afraid of many things when it came to picture taking. I thought I would look at the photos, realize that I was fat, and become even more rigorous about my diet and exercise rituals. Yet I was also frightened people would comment on my gaunt face, wasted body, and sad expression. Most of all, I was terrified I'd see the emptiness inside and lose all remaining recognition of myself. I felt so empty I didn't want to see the physical proof of it on my body, in my face, or on the faces of people next to me in the photographs. I felt like if I saw a picture and no longer recognized myself I would let go completely of everything that had once meant something to me. I would forgo all the things that had once made me human and exchange them instead with a meaningless disease. I was afraid I would forget about love, my family, the carefree girl I'd been . . . I'd forget about Venice.

For many years I couldn't go to Venice. For many years I couldn't go anywhere. A thirty-minute airplane ride from New York to Boston would dehydrate me, set off a chain reaction of electrolyte imbalance, and make me ill. Getting off the plane I would walk for what felt like miles to meet my parents outside the gate. The first thing they always did after hugging me and inspecting me with concern was to ask how I felt, if I was dehydrated or weak, and whether I felt like my electrolytes were off. The answer was always yes, but we had all become accustomed to my being sick and weak. During that time, our trip to Italy seemed unreal to me. Had I really been there? Could a place like Venice really exist in a world so full of problems? If it did, we were both drowning—Venice fought against it with grace, but I was doing so pathetically.

"Vacation" also seemed like a bizarre concept. Could people actually go somewhere and feel relaxed? Could they find a way to escape their problems and stress, if only briefly? It made no sense. I took my problems with me everywhere I went, like a slow, sick turtle no longer able to carry its burdensome shell.

I sometimes thought of Venice as I lay in my room at night. With all the lights off and my body under blankets, away from prodding eyes, I dreamt of a city I had once breathed in. I still sometimes could not believe such a place was built by human hands, and was not the work of a mythological artist-creature. I tried to recount all of the details of that place, which eventually blurred into a single watery image of a shimmering place, somewhere. This place seemed so far away, Venice might as well have been Venus, a planet I could reach with my heart but never visit physically.

After a while my family and I got used to never going away together, so we made up our own version of vacation. Wherever we were, as long as Fran, my parents, and I were together we would huddle together for a moment and shout, "family vacation, family vacation!" Then we would all kiss each other, laugh, and hug, before our short-lived vacation and small moment of happiness was over. We cherished those simple seconds. In some ways they had more impact than a full two weeks spent roaming aimlessly through the Italian countryside.

If years ago while on a real trip I could have seen our little family circle, joined together by bitter hardship and innocent love, I would have felt alarmed about the future. I would have wondered what had become of us. I would have been heartbroken, though in reality, something very positive developed through the course of my anorexia and our suffering. Instead of going our separate ways and moving further away from each other, we began to appreciate every minuscule, peaceful moment we had together, away from doctors, psychiatrists, Renfrews, and even electrolytes. We were nourished by those rare and carefree seconds spent together.

For years, the only family vacations we took passed that way, in seconds instead of weeks, and, for that time, we were together, alive, and full of hope for a better future. We weren't bold enough to demand this future, but we desired it intensely. And in my mind, the vision of my beloved golden gray city, my metallic Venice, was an omnipresent symbol of liberation.

It wasn't until I had been seeing Steven for nearly six months that I could even fathom going on a real vacation again. It's not that I spoke so much to Steven about going on a trip, rather that, as my self-confidence grew, my dependence on my anorexia began to wane and occasionally even bore me. I was tired of being plagued by the same thoughts night after night with only a few hours of rest. The primary emotion I felt when I thought about exercising compulsively and consciously starving myself was fatigue. I was so sick of the feelings and thoughts that had once nearly driven me to my death. Mine would have been a needless death and one that only a handful of people closest to me would have truly mourned. Everyone else would have felt sorry for the family of the anorexic girl who killed herself, but my family would have never recovered.

One day I received a phone call from my dad asking me, in a misleadingly casual voice, if I might be interested in taking a real family vacation to Italy in September. I had always believed that if I did recover from my anorexia I would feel a deep boom in some deep, hidden cavern of my chest and know somehow the anorexic poison had trickled from my mind, released its toxins from my bloodstream, and loosened its grip on my strained heart. But instead, something subtle happened, and I knew things had changed when I heard my own voice reply meekly, as though from a place other than inside me, "Yes, I think I can go. Let me think about it."

Usually, as most people knew, the words "let me think about it" are a polite attempt to say no. Yet this time was different for me. I really did want to think about going to Italy, think about all of its implications, about what it would mean in my life, and how I would handle being on a real vacation again. There was a lot of fear connected to my tentative decision to take a real vacation. It meant I was no longer in the throes of the disease I loved and hated, dismissed and cherished all at once. It meant proclaiming to my family, "I'm not so sick anymore! I can go away now, not to a rehab center, but on a real vacation!" It meant I would have to figure out my daily meal plans, as I did in New York, then make sure I could find what I needed in Italy. But most of all, it meant I was slowly becoming stronger, less the vulnerable girl and more the independent woman who would get her life back in order. The challenge was alarming. And yet, somehow a part of me was able to slip away from the rest of my neurotic, anorexic self and calmly say, "Yes, I should do this."

Almost a week after I told my dad I would think about it, I asked everyone about their thoughts regarding the trip. I grilled Fran, my mom, Josh, my dad, Steven, and myself. I was still not used to eating in front of anyone. One of my main rules as an anorexic was to eat by myself, no exceptions. And although I was eating again, I wasn't near the point of being able to consume a typical Italian meal that consisted of pasta, bread, cheeses, wine, and dessert. I was still planning out my week in advance, making sure my fridge was well organized and each meal would be available at the time I had predetermined. In every meal there existed still a strict semblance of control. I had to feel like I was in charge of my own food decisions and that nobody was watching me eat or handling my food. Just the thought of a relaxed restaurant atmosphere made me uneasy.

I also knew that I would have to join my family at dinner nearly every night. Dinner in Italy consists of much more than food. It includes an entire night of walking, window shopping, chatting, laughing, and recounting the events of the day. Missing dinner in Europe would be like spending half the day in a hotel room. I knew I needed a plan, and luckily for me I had been to Italy often enough to be familiar with the major markets in every city. I went through a typical Italian day in my mind and decided to go grocery shopping in Boston, bring a bag of food to Italy, and eat breakfast and lunch in the privacy of my hotel room. During dinner I could order something small, like a fruit plate, and then eat more of what I had brought with me when we got back at night. Anything I didn't bring from home I could buy fresh at the market and eat in my room. That way I could still eat most of my meals alone, but also start eating in front of others during dinner.

Eating around other people was a step I knew I would eventually have to take. I couldn't dine in private for the rest of my life, hiding from my family and friends. I had first begun to eat in private because I was ashamed of failing to starve myself and giving in to hunger pains. I knew I could no longer encourage those guilty and self-punishing emotions. I was not trying to starve anymore, but rather reconnect with life and food.

With a well-devised plan I called my dad a few days later and unceremoniously said, "Yeah, why not? Let's go to Italy." But my aloof voice was a mask for true feelings of panic, apprehension, and blissful anticipation.

And then, after a few short months, I somehow found myself on a plane going, of all places, to Italy, leaving behind, of all things, my anorexia. As the plane lifted bumpily off the ground I felt really, physically separate from all that my anorexia had meant to me, and all that had kept me down in one small dark place, away from the happiness and freedom I had once known. Now a new kind of freedom, a nervous and surreal liberty, was upon me. This sensation of detachment from my anorexic umbilical cord was novel, and I couldn't believe I was flying away from the misery I had not only become used to, but quite good at bearing. I couldn't believe I was finally learning to give myself a break. And of all things, it actually felt invigorating! At that moment, even if I hadn't been on an airplane, I could have flown myself to Italy on the new wings of my own faith.

My excitement grew when we landed. The four of us got off the plane and looked at each other incredulously—family vacation indeed! I followed my food plan easily and smoothly from Rome to Florence. I was under as much control as I wanted to be without starving myself or overly obsessing. I shopped at Roman markets that were worthy of stories my nutritionist Adelaide would tell, and ate a portion of my dinner in public at a restaurant with my family. At times I got curious looks from waiters when I ordered a fruit bowl along with the other plates of hot pastas and meats. More often, though, my mom got dirty looks from Italians who believed she was allowing her daughter to fast while the others around us feasted. People simply could not know what a true accomplishment we were all celebrating. The days passed quickly and with surprising ease until it was finally time to go to Venice.

My dad told us we would drive from Florence to Venice's Marco Polo airport, return our rental car, and take a water taxi through the lagoon to the golden city. We had never been to Marco Polo airport and were very curious about how this strip of technological advancement would look, attached to such a stately old city. I imagined it might be similar to an old duchess wearing black leather. I also thought about how, despite our scientific achievements and breakthroughs in the field of engineering, human beings will never build another Venice. We have lost the touch of faith and magic it once took to construct a city on the water, surrounded by a shallow and perilous lagoon.

I rolled my black suitcase in procession behind my sister and in front of my mom, all of us racing through the airport parking lot to keep up with my dad who is always twenty steps ahead, whether running to catch a flight or taking a late-night summer stroll. And all the while, wheeling our little bags stuffed with Roman booty in the form of shoes, purses, clothes, and jewelry, we voiced our doubts of ever finding the water's edge. All we could see from our narrow pedestrian walkway were freshly painted white walls on our left and car-filled streets on our right. How could a water taxi possibly exist in the midst of all this solid land? I began to doubt the existence of my elusive city.

Every few minutes my father stopped and in his stilted Italian asked busy, animated locals, *"Dov'è aqua?"*, "Where's the water?" Using as few words as possible, they all mumbled something and pointed forward—just keep going, you'll find it. Over and over again we witnessed this ritual between my dad and the Venetians, a group of people who live somewhere between the terra firma of mother Italy and the ghost of her daughter, Venice.

As we kept walking, I was struck by the symbolism of this long journey. We didn't really believe that we would soon find water. How could it be possible, when all there was to our right, left, in front, and behind were walls, streets, cars, buses, and busy people dressed in suits and pilot's uniforms? How could Venice really be so close? We couldn't see it, we couldn't sense it, and so it simply could not be that close at hand. Yet we had no choice but to believe. We could either keep walking or simply stop and turn back out of plain, unabashed fear of never reaching our destination. Then what would the remainder of our journey be but defeat, a waste of a highly anticipated adventure? We could not give up, so we kept walking together. I walked on my road towards faith, away from fear, doubt, and the desecration of life that defines anorexia. Many long minutes later, right off the edge of the airport walkway as everyone had promised, was a small humble dock, parallel to the main Marco Polo runway. It was complete with water taxis and Venice's own version of taxi drivers casually sunning themselves.

Our ride to Venice through the complicated waterways of her lagoon turned us instantly into tourists. It was like we'd never been there, or even on a boat, before. My dad settled himself between Fran and me in the bow of the taxi-boat, one arm around each of us, flashing his most winning smile when Fran and I laughed at his famous showiness. My mom, hiding in the Rococo interior, snapped picture after picture of the same scene, with only slight variations in our facial expressions and hair depending on how fast the boat was moving. Soon we got tired of posing for the camera and I began to examine each small island we drove past, trying to determine which one was the cemetery, and which was the island from which most of Venice's working class commuted on a daily basis. Though my identifications were almost certainly incorrect we were all willing to accept my statements as truth. We were eager to swallow everything Venice had to convey.

We had three days in Venice, which we spent in appreciation, awe, and total contentment. Fran and I went mask shopping for Josh, glass-ring shopping for ourselves, and somehow managed to coerce our dad into entering one of the numerous Venetian Prada stores, where we made him look at a purple-and-green blouse. He commented on its unique beauty until he saw the 2000 Euro price tag and forced us out the ornate front door. A line of goofily grinning Italian men watched us go and made our dad move even faster.

On our second day we stopped for lunch at a well-hidden café where only locals dared to tread. Over cappuccinos and snacks the four of us sat, joking about nothing and everything. We laughed harder than we had in years, and it felt foreign to laugh instead of cry into our perfectly brewed coffee and thick froth. The laughter was exaggerated, almost harsh. It took up every neuron, used every corner of our brains, so we didn't stop and realize that we hadn't laughed that way together in years. Sitting in the basement-like Venetian hideout, surrounded by rough fishermen and middle-aged, dark-haired waitresses, I felt another new Laura emerge. She was wearing a bright, turquoise velvet skirt that contrasted with the dark, rough teak of the bench that it rested on. She was older in wisdom, if not so much in years. She had experienced physical pain and emotional torment and could still, somehow, let herself laugh, even if that laughter was not quite as light or innocent as it had once been. But in fact, I liked this new girl. She was stronger, no longer shirking life but rather struggling to embrace it. And most of all I liked that, through a vast, incredible network of support and determination, she had gotten herself back to her favorite place, surrounded by her favorite friends.

On our last night in Venice, as we all sat casually enjoying a slow dinner in a restaurant that had been around since 1909, I found a spider walking around my plate of grapes. I let out a small shriek of panic, mostly because I hadn't expected to see a spider in my food and not so much because of the spider itself. I leapt from my seat, yelled to my dad to find and kill the spider, and finally settled back down amid our room of unfazed Italian diners. Apparently in Italy that sort of outburst is expected and appreciated better than it is in the United States.

Later that night, as my mom and I sat on her hotel bed, I told her about my fear that finding an arachnid in my grapes—a food I particularly enjoy—would make me nervous about eating fruit again in the future. Yet while discussing this topic with her I realized something profound. The fact that I could talk about my eating fears instead of keeping them locked inside meant I would not stop eating fruit, nor would I stop enjoying grapes. If I had been planning a new way of slowly cutting out all the foods I had worked so hard to reincorporate into my life, I would not have discussed my fears with my mom or anyone else. I would have been unable to consciously admit them even to myself. Things had changed for me, and no spider, regardless of its size or location, could ever turn them back.

It was only on the morning of our departure that I truly realized the enormous impact Venice had made on me those three days in September. At 6 a.m., as we finished our breakfast and cappuccinos and walked back to our hotel rooms, I stopped suddenly in the middle of the narrow street facing Campo San Moise. The sky was gray like I always remembered, and there were few people out that early—so unlike the bustling streets in midtown Manhattan. I held an Italian newspaper under my arm in an attempt to absorb as much of the language and culture as I possibly could.

I was no longer a fixture of my dark New York apartment.

Venice was a different kind of gray, a silver-purple gray, a blue-periwinkle-navy gray, a gray with gold in it, a gray mixed with spring green, the promise of eternally new life, a gray that possessed a mystical quality like the silver of a twinkling night sky. It felt like living inside an extraordinarily precious antique. This gray was one the big black dog could never recognize. It was one the girl who lived alone, spent days and nights in the darkness of her bed and mind, could never understand. This gray was one I couldn't have appreciated while under my anorexic spell—*that* would have been infinitely more difficult than making sense of the Italian newspaper I carried under my arm that morning.

And so, walking through the gray mist, I felt ready to leave Venice and continue with my life. Venice had given of herself, and I had greedily taken in as much as I could hold and understand.

Once again we found ourselves wheeling black suitcases to the dock, where our previously commissioned taxi driver was to pick us up and take us across the canal, past endless unknown islands. We were going back to the physical world of Marco Polo Airport where planes flew and followed the laws of explainable physics, and where the metaphysical, ever-changing rules that governed my mysterious lagoons ceased to apply.

This time we were sure we'd reach the water. We knew where it was because we had scouted this voyage out and were now seasoned pilgrims. This time I got on the boat and sat in the bow with Fran, but wasn't the excited, obnoxious tourist I had been. I was now a reverent explorer. I no longer doubted the existence of miracles. I knew they did exist, even small ones most people fail to consider. My family, a previously tormented group that had found peace and joy on a simple vacation, was a miracle.

The little motorboat started and the wind picked up. Fran insisted I put my orange pashmina over my head, like a Polish granny, and chastised me for wearing only a thin denim jacket on such a windy Venetian morning. My mom could rest easily, I thought, because Fran acts more like the hands-on, take-control mother than anyone else I know.

Venice at that moment seemed fresh and untarnished by the millions of feet, hands, and eyes that had over the years taken a piece of her away with them. It was like I was seeing her for the first time. With a grumble, the boat picked up speed and I looked back once more, hoping I wouldn't be turned into a pillar of salt, but knowing that if I was I would still be happy. I could leak slowly back into the salty lagoon and make her infinitesimally more salty.

And then suddenly Venice was gone. This is how elusive she is to me. I had been there only moments ago, had just planted my feet firmly on her cobblestone paths, and yet she was already nothing more than a faint outline, hazy and unreal, defined by fluid buildings and bridges that no longer looked so solid. There was nothing left between us but the new gray I had learned to embrace. I faced forward once again, no longer needing to look back. I knew that I'd left Venice behind, but I was simultaneously reassured of her existence—mainly because, now, Venice lived in me.

I looked at Fran, into her surprising aqua eyes that somehow matched our surroundings, and we smiled at each other knowingly, nobly, as though we were one hundred years old and had lived through every war, every time of peace, every day and era known to history. Three days? I think not.

A few weeks later, Fran had prints of all the pictures we had taken in Italy. For the first time in years I looked at them and faced myself. The picture I eagerly pocketed was one a German tourist had taken of us on our final night, the evening I nearly got my daily protein supplement from a rogue grape spider. The four of us had posed on the water's edge outside of San Marco, while our cameraman told my dad in a choppy German accent, "You should be kissing the ground, surrounded by such beautiful women." And that's exactly how my dad looks in the photograph, a silly grin on his face like a guilty wolf who's just swallowed three innocent lambs. Fran, my mom, and I, dressed in our fancy, last-night-in-Venice clothes, look like we have wind fans in front of us and fashion photographers telling us how to pose. The picture is amusingly glamorous, and somehow not at all accurately symbolic of our lives, or of this very real, humbling trip. I place the photo as a marker in whatever book I happen to be reading, rather than freeze it in a fancy frame and hang it on my white walls.

But there is another picture. It is one I developed within my own mind. It shows me, and I am sitting in the bow of a small boat next to my blue-eyed, overly protective sister, with my parents watching us from inside the cabin's dark interior. It is a picture of a lagoon so shallow I can see the silt-filled bottom whenever this boat slows. But I know the low, seemingly passable lagoon is deceptive. It is, in fact, not so easy to cross, yet its loving citizens have learned to master it and can now live with it in harmony. This picture I took with my own eyes is of a city that is slowly fading yet will never truly be gone because it lives within me. And I will never let it go. It has given me a second chance, and a new outlook on how complicated and exquisite gray can be, how beautiful a life can be, if only you fight hard enough to live it.

Acknowledgments

I would like to thank my publisher and all of the people who have worked tirelessly to make this book possible, including Jack David, Crissy Boylan, and Gil Adamson. A special thanks to Jen Hale for appreciating my message and representing me so well.

To Steven Levenkron for teaching me how to understand myself.

To my aunt and uncle, Lia and Andi, and my cousins Teo and Alex for loving me unconditionally.

To Josh for his love, fierce devotion, and enlightening friendship.

To Brett for giving me the courage to love again, fully. You are the amazing part of my next, unwritten chapter.

To Michael V (Buffa) for becoming my brother, friend, personal photographer, and baking devotee.

To my dad, Michael, for persistently teaching me what it is to have faith, trust, hope, and courage. He is my *pietra*.

To my mom and best friend, Michaela, for following me into the depths of despair and coming back out with me. She is the Beatrice to my Dante.

To my grandmother, Elena: the quiet warrior. My world is a better place because of what she taught me through her gently whispered words and fearless actions.

And I would especially like to thank Fran, my brilliant and beautiful sister, twin, other half and first editor. If this book has any value as a written work it is because of her input and guidance along every step and through the years it took us to complete. She has always given me her utmost protection and perpetual felicity, and I kindly ask her to never get out of my head.